Co

Portuguese
Phrasebook and Dictionary

Portuguese Phrasebook and Dictionary

Other languages in the
Collins Phrasebook and Dictionary series:
French, German, Greek, Italian, Japanese,
Mandarin, Polish, Spanish, Turkish.

HarperCollins Publishers
Westerhill Road, Bishopbriggs,
Glasgow G64 2QT

www.collinslanguage.com

First published 2004
This edition published 2008

Reprint 10 9 8 7 6 5 4 3 2 1 0

ISBN 978-0-00-785254-3

Typeset by Davidson Pre-Press Graphics Ltd,
Glasgow

Printed in Malaysia for Imago

Contents

Your *Collins Portuguese Phrasebook and Dictionary* is a handy, quick-reference guide that will help make the most of your stay abroad. Its clear layout will save valuable time when you need that crucial word or phrase. Download free all the essential words and phrases you need to get by from www.collinslanguage.com/talk60. These hour long audio files are ideal for practising listening comprehension and pronunciation. The main sections in this book are:

Everyday Portugal - photoguide
Packed full of photos, this section allows you to see all the practical visual information that will help with using cash machines, driving on motorways, reading signs, etc.

Phrases
Practical topics are arranged thematically with an opening section, Key talk containing vital phrases that should stand you in good stead in most situations. Phrases are short, useful and each one has a pronunciation guide so that there is no problem saying them.

Eating out
This section contains phrases for ordering food and drink (and special requirements) plus a photoguide showing different places to eat, menus and practical information to help choose the best options. The menu reader allows you to work out what to choose.

Grammar
There is a short Grammar section explaining how the language works.

Dictionary
And finally, the practical 5000-word English-Portuguese and Portuguese-English Dictionary means that you won't be stuck for words.

So, just flick through the pages to find the information you need and listen to the free audio download to improve your pronunciation.

Useful websites

Accommodation

www.maisturismo.pt
www.pousadas.com (Luxury properties to rent, often former convents, etc)
www.pousadasjuventude.pt (Youth hostels)
www.roteiro-campista.pt (Guide to campsites of Portugal)
www.turihab.pt (Rural properties to rent)

Culture and Activities

www.ipmuseus.pt (Museums)

Currency Converters

www.x-rates.com

Driving

www.acp.pt (Portuguese Automobile Club)
www.drivingabroad.co.uk

Facts

www.cia.gov/library/publications/the-world-factbook

Food and wine

www.gastronomias.com (In Portuguese only)

Foreign Office Advice

www.fco.gov.uk/travel
www.dfat.gov.au (Australia)
www.voyage.gc.ca (Canada)

Health Advice

www.dh.gov.uk/travellers
www.thetraveldoctor.com
www.smartraveller.gov.au (Australia)
www.phac-aspc.gc.ca (Canada)

Internet cafes

www.cybercafes.com

Passport Office

www.ukpa.gov.uk
www.passports.gov.au (Australia)
www.pptc.gc.ca (Canada)

Pets

www.defra.gov.uk/animalh/quarantine

Tourism

www.algarvenet.com
www.player.pt (Info for disabled travellers)
www.portugal-info.net (info exp for USA travellers)
www.portugal.org (Welcome to Portugal)
www.portugal-live.net
www.portugalvirtual.pt
www.visitportugal.com (Portuguese Tourist Office)

Transport

www.ana-aeroportos.pt (Portuguese airports)
www.cp.pt (Portuguese Railways)
www.europeanrailguide.com
www.metrolisboa.pt (Lisbon Metro)

Weather

www.bbc.co.uk/weather

To make the pronunciation guide used in this book as clear as possible we've broken the words into syllables using hyphens. The syllable to be stressed is shown in **bold type**. Here is a brief explanation of the pronunciation and the sound it represents.

Portuguese	sounds like	example	pronunciation
g**a**to	**a** as in p**a**t	a	**ga**-too
um**a**	**uh** as in moth**er**	uh	**oo**-muh
esta	**e** as in p**e**t	e	**esh**-tuh
ir	**ee** as in p**ee**k	ee	eer
olá	**o** as in p**o**t	o	o-**la**
p**o**r	**oo** as in p**oo**l	oo	poor
m**ai**s	**i** as in p**i**ne	aee	maeesh
oito	**oi** as in p**oi**nt	oy	**oy**-too
c**o**mo	**aw** as in p**aw**n	aw	**kaw**-moo
p**au**	**ou** as in p**ou**nd	aoo	paoo

Nasal vowels Vowels with a tilde ˜ or followed by **m** or **n** in the same syllable should be pronounced nasally as in French e.g. **não**, **manhã**. We have used 'ñ' to represent this sound: **tem** (tayñ), **muito** (**mweeñ**-too), **com** (kawñ), **um** (ooñ), **manhã** (man-**yañ**).

Other letters

Portuguese	transcription	sounds like	pronunciation
ç	s	'**s**' in **s**it	**almoço** (al-**maw**-soo)
nh	n-y	'**ni**' in o**ni**on	**vinho** (**veen**-yoo)
lh	l-y	'**lli**' in mi**lli**on	**filho** (**feel**-yoo)
ch	sh	'**sh**' in **sh**irt	**chá** (sha)
h	*(always silent)*		
g, j	zh	'**s**' in plea**s**ure	**gelado** (zhuh-**la**-doo)
s *(after vowel or at end of word)*	sh	'**sh**' in **sh**irt	**esta** (**esh**-tuh)
rr, r *(at start of word)*	rr	rolled	**rolo** (**rraw**-loo)

Everyday photoguide

Everyday Portugal

Open Small shops tend to close between 12.30 and 2.30pm, but stay open later till about 6 or 7pm, Mon–Fri. Most close on Sat. afternoon and all day Sun. Large shopping centres stay open late every day.

Entrance Look out for **entrada livre** meaning 'free entry'.

Exit **Saída** is also used for exit on motorways.

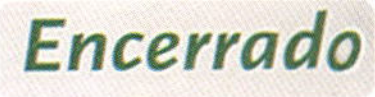

Closed

Opening Hours

The word **proibido/a** means something is forbidden.

Emergency Exit

Pay Here The word **caixa** actually means till or cash box.

Push

Pull Can be confusing as **puxe** is pronounced poosh!

Danger

Symbol for the **euro**. Portugal is in the euro zone.

Prices are generally written with a comma. This is 1 euro and 80 cents per kilo.

Banks are open from 8.30am–3pm Monday to Friday. They may stay open later in tourist areas.

Currency The euro is the currency of Portugal. It breaks down into 100 euro cents. Notes: 5, 10, 20, 50, 100, 200, 500. Coins: 1 and 2 euros, 1, 2, 5, 10, 20 and 50 cents. Portuguese people call **cents** '**cêntimos**' (sen-tee-**moosh**). Euros is pronounced **eoo**-roosh. Euro notes are the same throughout Europe. The backs of coins carry different designs from each of the member countries.

Banks' names usually include the word **banco** or **caixa**. The main ones are **Banco Espírito Santo**, **BPI**, **BCP** and **Caixa Geral de Depósitos**.

If you need a cash machine (ATM), look for the **Multibanco** sign. You can choose English instructions for transactions. You can also buy some train tickets from **Multibancos**.

24 Hours Some cash dispensers are accessed by swiping your card in the door.

Cash machines operate as at home.
Anular = cancel
Corrigir = error
Continuar = proceed

Service is usually included in a restaurant bill so tipping is discretionary.

Receipt

Notas = banknotes

Moedas = coins

Tariffs The word for price is **preço**.

No Smoking
Smoking is now banned in all public places although this is not always strictly adhered to. Whether to allow smoking in restaurants and bars is still the choice of the proprietor.

You can usually buy postcards and stamps at a **tabacaria** 'tobacconist'.

Police The emergency no. is 112. It is operated in Portuguese, French and English and will connect you to all the emergency services.

Tourist Information

Tourist offices can help with accommodation, and all local details.

You Are Here

Lisboa Card

The **Lisboa** card is available from the tourist office and gives you free entry to many of the city's museums. It also incorporates a handy map. Concessions apply for children and there are cheaper tickets for most places for the over 65's if you show some ID or a passport.

A **pensão** is a cheaper form of guesthouse.

R and **Residencial** indicate guesthouse, i.e. breakfast only, not meals.

Town maps are available free from all tourist offices. Museums, castles and art galleries usually charge a small admission fee. Most places are closed on Mondays.

quartos livres

Rooms Available

The word for 'rooms' is **quartos**. The word for 'vacancies' is **vagas**.

Aluga-se

To Rent

Ordinary postboxes are red (as in the UK), blue is for priority mail **correio azul** - air mail.

água potável

Drinking Water

The word for water is **água** (**ag**-wah).

Sanitários

(superloos) are beginning to appear in towns and cities. They carry easy-to-follow instructions in English.

Toilets are generally shown with a pictogram. **Senhoras** = ladies, **Homens** = gents. **Casa de banho**, **sanitários**, **lavabos**, **retretes** - are all words for toilet. Public toilets in Portugal are difficult to track down; try to use those at public attractions where you may find an attendant issuing loo paper. You are meant to tip them out of courtesy. There might not always be loo paper so take tissues with you.

quente

Hot

occupado

Engaged

livre

Vacant

frio

Cold

avariado

Broken Down

não funciona

Out Of Order

Timetables

Departures/Arrivals Board

Timetables, especially in tourist areas will often have English translations alongside the Portuguese.

Yellow Line Bus Timetable

Paragem
= stop number

Designação
= name of stop

Timetable

Monday - Friday (notice how **-feira** is omitted)

Sábado = Saturday

2ªf	Mon
3ªf	Tues
4ªf	Wed
5ªf	Thur
6ªf	Fri
Sáb	Sat
Dom	Sun

Abbreviations for days of the week

hoje = today

amanhã = tomorrow

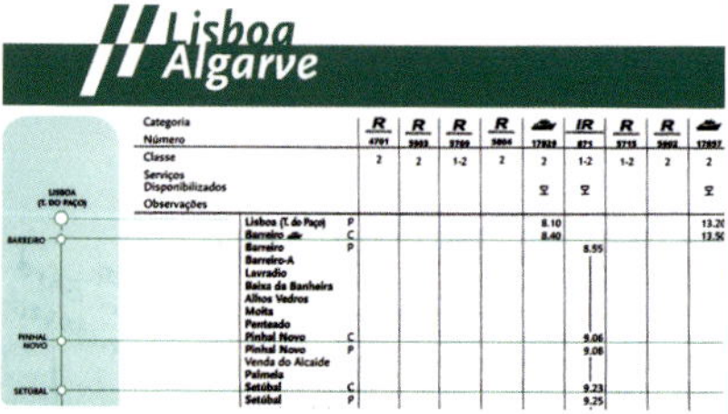

Train timetables like this can be obtained from regional or national railway stations. All timetables use the 24-hour clock.

Tickets

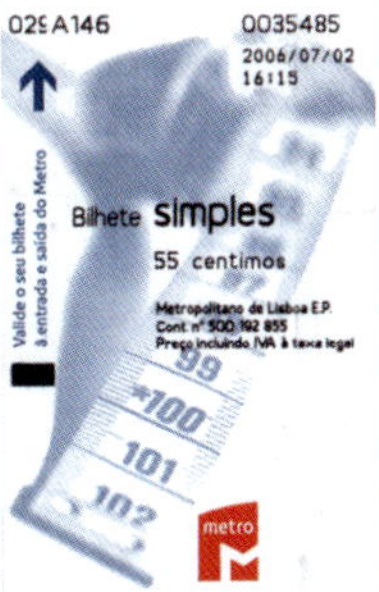

Metro Ticket
A single (**simples**) ticket for the Lisbon Underground. Another word for single is **ida**. **Ida e volta** is a return ticket. One day (**diario**), 7-day (**7 dias**) and 10 journey (**10 viagens**) tickets are also available.

Train Ticket This is a day return with booked seats. **Carr** = coach. **Lug** = seat.

Automatic ticket machines are more common now in larger towns and cities. You can also buy some train tickets from **Multibancos** (ATM).

Local Train Ticket
Ineiro e volta is a full price adult return.

Arrivals

Departures

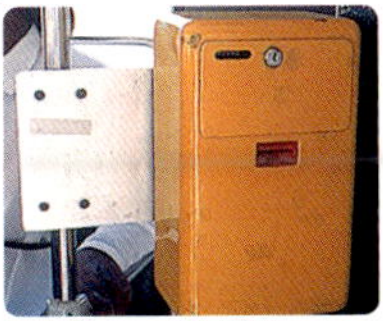

You have to validate any ticket you buy for public transport in a validating machine. These are found at the entrance of buses, train platforms and metro stations. Simply insert your ticket in the slot for punching.

Getting around

Largo Square

Rua Road or street

Travessa Side street

Local signs are white, hotels are usually blue and places of interest brown. **Câmara Municipal** is the town hall, **Bombeiros** is the fire station.

Museum

Town Centre Note the pictogram used on signs for centre.

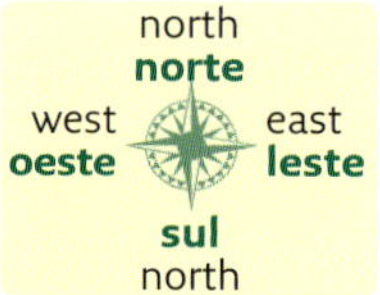

Most town centres have street maps. To find where you are look for the symbol below. **Você está aqui** means 'you are here'.

R/C is an abbreviation for **rés-do-chão** (ground floor)

Piso = floor

o is an abbreviation for 1st, 2nd

The number 28 tram (above) does a great circular route of Lisbon.

Trams Both old and new style trams operate in Lisbon. On the new trams you press a button to open the doors.

Metro Maps with details of stops for connections, parking and shopping are available from Metro stations and tourist information offices.

Bus Stop There are route maps at most bus stops. You must validate your bus and tram tickets when you get on board.

Metro Lines These are colour coded and each has a pictogram.

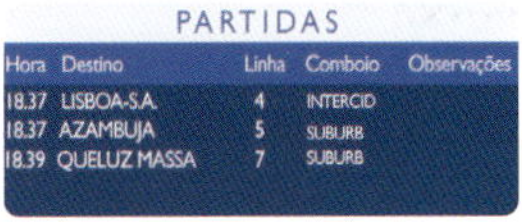

PARTIDAS

Hora	Destino	Linha	Comboio	Observações
18.37	LISBOA-S.A.	4	INTERCID	
18.37	AZAMBUJA	5	SUBURB	
18.39	QUELUZ MASSA	7	SUBURB	

Departures Board

Hora = time
Destino = destination
Linha = platform
Comboio = train (type)
Observações = further information

Modern train ticket validating machine.

Driving

Diversion

Don't be fooled. **Parque livre** means there are spaces – not that parking is free! **Parque completo** means full.

You see the name of the village or town as you enter it, and as you leave (with a red line through it).

No Parking From 9am to 7pm except for loading and unloading.

Speed Limit This is in kilometres per hour.

Payment Zone Parking must be in the same direction as the flow of traffic.

Slow Down

Motorway Toll Machine Press the red button and take a ticket.

built up area	50 km/h
normal roads	90 km/h
motorway	120 km/h

Speed Limits Cars towing trailers or caravans are subject to lower speed limits.

Green roads are major European routes. E = European, A = Motorway (**Auto-estrada**).

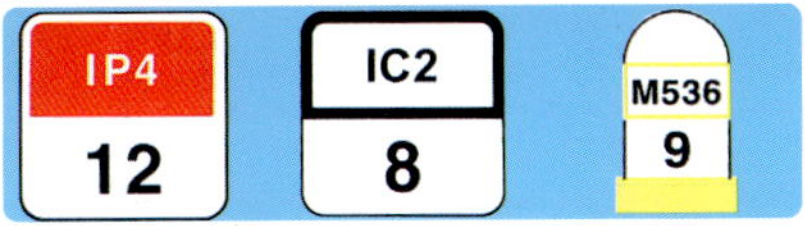

Red IP routes are main roads. IC signs are white and are for ordinary main roads and yellow M signs indicate urban highways.

General Driving Rules You drive on the right in Portugal and the alcohol limit for drivers is 0.05%. Be careful, the locals do not always comply with regulations. If there is an accident, the police will not accept ignorance of the rules as an excuse. Fines are handed out on the spot.

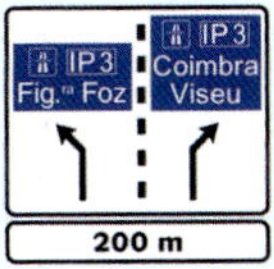

Sign For Motoway Exit **saída** = exit

Signs show which vehicles can use each lane on particular days.

Car Hire Check hire details carefully, especially your insurance.

Don't use the green **via verde** lane for paying. These are for drivers with pre-paid devices fitted who can drive straight through.

Petrol gasolina
S/Chumbo = unleaded
Gasóleo = diesel

Shopping

Shops The word for shop is **loja** (**law**-zhuh). Most small shops close between 12.30 and 2.30pm. They also close on Saturday afternoons and Sunday.

Sale

Sold Out

Lisboa Card

A Lisboa card entitles you to discounts in many shops around the city.

One of the big supermarket chains. Other big names include **Jumbo** and **Carrefour**. Larger supermarkets are generally out of town and open 7 days a week until late. You may need a coin to release the trolley (**carrinho**). Daily and weekly markets (**mercados**) are good places to buy fresh fruit and veg and are also the cheapest for clothes and shoes.

Duty Pharmacy

Details for Saturday and Sunday. Rotas are available from tourist offices and free English language newspapers.

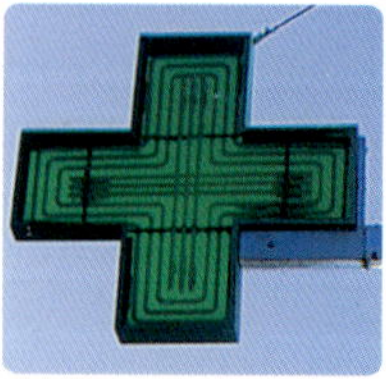

Pharmacy You can recognise a pharmacy by the green cross. If you're worried about a medical condition, ask the pharmacist for advice. Portuguese people are very health conscious and pharmacies have a large number of medicines available.

Portugal uses metric weights and measures.

Bread The general word for bread is **pão** (paooñ), although there are many kinds. Look out for maize loaves called **broa** (**braw**-uh). **Biológico(a)** = organic.

Butcher's

Without Added...
The word for 'without' is **sem** (sayñ), 'with' is **com** (kawñ).

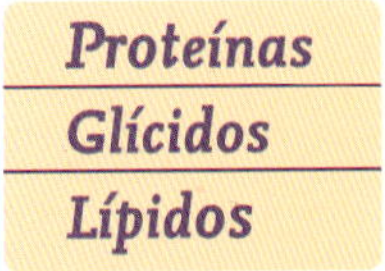

Nutrition Label
Glícidos = carbohydrates
Lípidos = fats

To Take Away

Fat

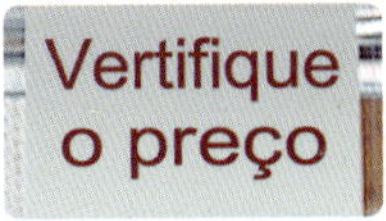

Check The Price

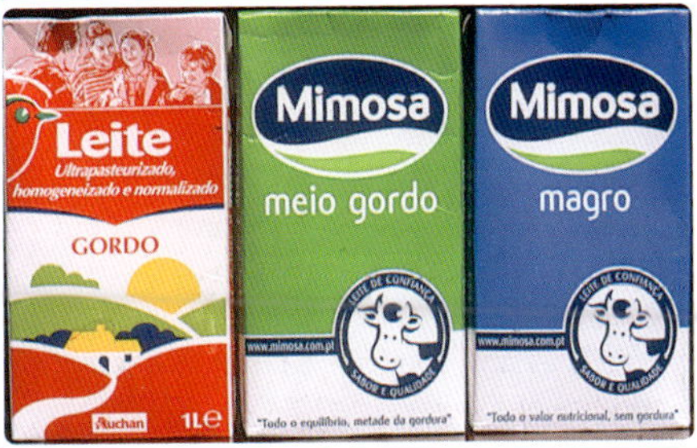

Milk Look for the colour-coding for milk. Here, red is wholemilk (**gordo**), green is semi-skimmed (**meio gordo**) and blue is skimmed (**magro**).

Keeping in touch

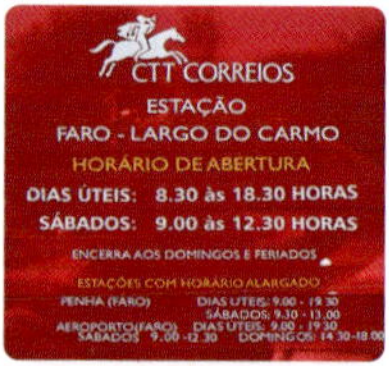

Post Office Opening Hours In large busy post offices you have to take a ticket and wait for the number to be called.

CORREIOS

Post Office Logo

Most pay phones take coins and phonecards.

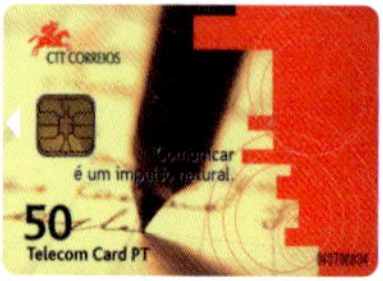

Phonecards are sold in 50 or 100 units (**impulsos**). International dialling codes are UK 00 44, Australia 00 61, USA 00 1 and Portugal 00 351.

sapo

sapo.pt is a popular search engine. **@** = **arroba** (ar-**ro**-buh)
www. = dub-lyoo dub-lyoo dub-lyoo
pon-too

Sr. e Sra. Lopes da Silva
R. da Plama, 35-2º esq.
1700-220 Lisboa
Portugal

Addressing An Envelope

Sr. e Sra. = Mr & Mrs
R. = **Rua** Street
2º esq. = 2nd floor left
Postcode and town.

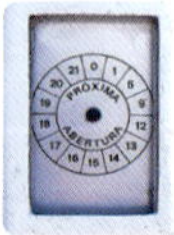

Post boxes are red for ordinary post or blue for airmail. The next-collection times may be shown on a dial.

Phone numbers are given in single digits.

21	882	03	48
dois, um	**oito, oito, dois**	**zero, três**	**quatro, oito**

Key talk

• There are three main forms of address (calling someone 'you') in Portuguese: formal **o senhor** for men, **a senhora** for women, semi-formal (**você** for both sexes) and informal **tu**.
• Stick to the formal for older people to be treated in a situation of deference and **você** for people the same age and status as yourself (until you are invited to use **tu**).

yes	**sim** seeñ
no	**não** naooñ
that's fine	**está bem** shta bayñ
please	**por favor/se faz favor** poor fa-**vawr**/suh fash fa-**vawr**
thank you	**obrigado(a)** o-bree-**ga**-doo/(-duh)
don't mention it	**de nada** duh **na**-duh
hello	**olá** o-**la**
goodbye	**adeus** a-**de**-oosh
good night	**boa noite** **baw**-uh noyt
good morning (until lunch)	**bom dia** bawñ **dee**-uh

good afternoon/ evening (until dusk)	**boa tarde** **baw**-uh tard
excuse me!	**por favor!** poor fa-**vawr**!
(to get past)	**com licença!** kawñ lee-**sen**-suh!
sorry!	**desculpe!** dush-**koolp**!
pardon?	**como?** **kaw**-moo?
a...	**um...** ('**o**' words) ooñ...
a coffee	**um café** ooñ ka-**fe**
2 coffees	**dois cafés** doysh ka-**fesh**
a...	**uma...** ('**a**' words) **oo**-muh...
a beer	**uma cerveja** **oo**-muh suhr-**vay**-zhuh
2 beers	**duas cervejas** **doo**-ush suhr-**vay**-zhush
a coffee and two beers, please	**um café e duas cervejas, por favor** ooñ ka-**fe** ee **doo**-ush suhr-**vay**-zhush, poor fa-**vawr**

• **Por favor** means 'please'. You also hear **se faz favor** (suh fash fa-**vawr**) or **faz favor** (fash fa-**vawr**).
• The easiest way to ask for something is to name it and add **por favor** (or one of the other phrases for 'please').
• Portuguese people are very polite and helpful and many speak English.

I'd like...	**queria...** **kree**-uh...
we'd like...	**queríamos...** **kreea**-moosh...

I'd like an ice cream	**queria um gelado**	**kree**-uh ooñ zhuh-**la**-doo
we'd like to visit...	**queríamos visitar...**	**kreea**-moosh vee-zee-**tar**...
do you have...?	**tem...?**	tayñ...?
do you have any milk?	**tem leite?**	tayñ layt?
do you have stamps?	**tem selos?**	tayñ **se**-loosh?
do you have a map?	**tem um mapa?**	tayñ ooñ **ma**-puh?
do you have cheese?	**tem queijo?**	tayñ **kay**-zhoo?
how much is it?	**quanto custa?**	**kwañ**-too **koosh**-tuh?
how much does ... cost?	**quanto custa o/a...?**	**kwañ**-too **koosh**-tuh oo/uh...?
how much is the cheese?	**quanto custa o queijo?**	**kwañ**-too **koosh**-tuh oo **kay**-zhoo?
how much is the ticket?	**quanto custa o bilhete?**	**kwañ**-too **koosh**-tuh oo beel-**yet**?
how much is a kilo?	**quanto custa um quilo?**	**kwañ**-too **koosh**-tuh ooñ **kee**-loo?
how much is it each?	**quanto é cada um?**	**kwañ**-too e **ka**-duh ooñ?

• To catch someone's attention use **por favor** or **desculpe** (deesh-**koolp**). In a café you can also use **faz favor** to get the waiters' attention.
• If you are trying to get past someone in a busy street, say **com licença** (kawñ lee-**sen**-suh). You also use it when entering someone's house.

where is...?	**onde é...?**	**awñd** e...?

where are...?	**onde são...?**	**awñ**-duh saooñ...?
where is the station?	**onde é a estação?**	**awñd** e uh shta-**saooñ**?
where are the toilets?	**onde são as casas de banho?**	**awñ**-duh saooñ ush **ka**-zush duh **ban**-yoo?
is/are there...?	**há...?**	a...?
is there a restaurant?	**há um restaurante?**	a ooñ rrush-to-**rañt**?
where is there a chemist?	**onde há uma farmácia?**	**awñd** a **oo**-muh far-**mas**-yuh?
are there children?	**há crianças?**	a kree-**añ**-sush?
is there a swimming pool?	**há piscina?**	a **pshee**-nuh?
there is no...	**não há...**	naooñ a...
there is no hot water	**não há água quente**	naooñ a **ag**-wuh keñt
there are no towels	**não há toalhas**	naooñ a **twal**-yush
I need...	**preciso de...**	pre-**see**-zoo duh...
I need a taxi	**preciso dum táxi**	pre-**see**-zoo dooñ **tak**-see
I need to send a fax	**preciso de mandar um fax**	pre-**see**-zoo duh mañ-**dar** ooñ faks

- The word for 'very' is **muito** (**mweeñ**-too).
- The phrase for 'pleased to meet you' is **muito prazer** (**mweeñ**-too pra-**zer**).
- The word for welcome is **bem-vindo** (bayñ-**veen**-doo). Use **bem-vinda** (bayñ-**veen**-duh) if speaking to a woman.

can I...?	**posso...?**	**po**-soo...?

can we...?	**podemos...?** poo-**de**-moosh...?
can I pay?	**posso pagar?** **po**-soo pa-**gar**?
can we go in?	**podemos entrar?** poo-**de**-moosh eñ-**trar**?
where can I...?	**onde posso...?** **awñ**-duh **po**-soo...?
where can I buy bread?	**onde posso comprar pão?** **awñ**-duh **po**-soo kawñ-**prar** paooñ?
when?	**quando?** **kwañ**-doo?
at what time...?	**a que horas...?** uh kee **o**-rush...?
when is breakfast?	**a que horas é o pequeno almoço?** uh kee **o**-rush e oo puh-**ke**-noo al-**maw**-soo?
when is dinner?	**a que horas é o jantar?** uh kee **o**-rush e oo zhañ-**tar**?
when does it open/close?	**quando abre/fecha?** **kwañ**-doo **a**-bruh/**fay**-shuh?
yesterday	**ontem** **awñ**-tayñ
today	**hoje** awzh
tomorrow	**amanhã** a-man-**yañ**
this morning	**hoje de manhã** awzh duh man-**yañ**
this afternoon	**hoje à tarde** **awzha** a tard
tonight	**hoje à noite** **awzha** noyt
is it open?	**está aberto?** shta a-**ber**-too?
is it closed?	**está fechado?** shta fuh-**sha**-doo?

- The equivalent to Mr is **Senhor**, abbreviated to **Sr**.
- The equivalent to Mrs or Ms is **Senhora**, abbreviated to **Sra**.
- The word for Miss is **Menina** (men-**ee**-nuh).
- You will also hear ladies addressed as **Dona** plus their first name. So Mrs Maria Lopes could be **Senhora Lopes** or **Dona Maria**. You don't use **Dona** with the surname.

how are you?	**como está?** **kaw**-moo shta?
fine, thank you. And you?	**bem, obrigado(a). E você?** bayñ, o-bree-**ga**-doo(-duh). ee vo-**se**?
my name is...	**chamo-me...** **sha**-moo-muh...
what is your name?	**como se chama?** **kaw**-moo suh **sha**-muh?
I don't understand	**não compreendo** naooñ kawñ-pree-**eñ**-doo
do you speak English?	**fala inglês?** **fa**-luh eeñ-**glesh**?
you have a beautiful home	**tem uma casa linda** tayñ **oo**-muh **ka**-zuh **leeñ**-duh
the meal was delicious	**a refeição estava deliciosa** uh re-fay-saooñ **shta**-vuh de-lees-**yo**-zuh
I have enjoyed myself very much	**diverti-me muito** dee-**ver**-tee-muh **mween**-too
we'd like to come back	**gostaríamos de voltar** goosh-ta-**ree**-a-mosh duh vol-**tar**
what is your address?	**qual é a sua morada?** kwal e uh **soo**-uh moo-**ra**-duh?

Money

Money - changing

- Banks are generally open from 8.30am–3pm Monday–Friday.
- Bureaux de change (**casas de câmbio**) are not as common as banks and the exchange rates are less favourable.
- The easiest way to change money is to use your bank card at an ATM dispenser – look out for the **M** (**Multibanco**) sign.
- Banks usually include the words **Banco** or **Caixa** in their name.

where can I change money?	**onde se pode trocar dinheiro?** **awñ**-duh suh pod troo-**kar** deen-**yay**-roo?
where is the bank?	**onde é o banco?** **awñd** e oo **bañ**-koo?
where is the bureau de change?	**onde é a casa de câmbio?** **awñd** e uh **ka**-zuh duh **kañ**-bee-oo?
when does the bank open?	**quando abre o banco?** **kwañ**-doo **a**-bruh oo **bañ**-koo?
when does the bank close?	**quando fecha o banco?** **kwañ**-doo **fay**-shuh oo **bañ**-koo?
I want to cash these traveller's cheques	**quero trocar estes cheques de viagem** **ke**-roo troo-**kar esh**-tush sheksh duh vee-**a**-zhayñ
what is the rate...?	**qual é o câmbio...?** kwal e oo **kañ**-bee-oo...?
for pounds	**da libra** duh **lee**-bruh
for dollars	**do dólar** doo **do**-lar

I want to change ... pounds/dollars	**quero trocar ... libras/dólares** **ke**-roo troo-**kar** ... **lee**-brush/**do**-lar-ush
where is there a cash machine?	**onde há uma caixa automática?** **awñd** a **oo**-muh **kaee**-shuh aoo-too-**ma**-tee-kuh?
I'd like small notes	**queria notas pequenas** **kree**-uh **no**-tush puh-**ke**-nush

Money - spending

- Major credit cards are widely accepted in Portugal.
- Euros (**eoo**-roosh) are used in Portugal. Euro cents are known as **cêntimos** (**sayñ**-tee-moosh).
- **Caixa** is cash desk (i.e. where you pay).
- VAT is **IVA**. Non-UK residents can claim it back.
- The word for coins is **moedas** (**mwe**-dush).

how much is it?	**quanto custa?** **kwañ**-too **koosh**-tuh?
how much will it be?	**quanto vai custar?** **kwañ**-too vaee kush-**tar**?
I would like to pay	**queria pagar** **kree**-uh pa-**gar**
we want to pay separately	**queremos pagar separadamente** **kre**-moosh pa-**gar** suh-pa-ra-duh-**meñt**
can I pay by credit card?	**posso pagar com cartão de crédito?** **po**-soo pa-**gar** kawñ kar-**taooñ** duh **kre**-dee-too?
do you accept traveller's cheques?	**aceita cheques de viagem?** a-**say**-tuh sheksh duh vee-**a**-zhayñ?
how much is it...?	**quanto é...?** **kwañ**-too e...?
per person	**por pessoa** poor **psaw**-uh

per night	**por noite**	poor noyt
per kilo	**por quilo**	poor **kee**-loo
is service included?	**está incluído serviço?**	shta eeñ-kloo-**ee**-doo suhr-**vee**-soo?
I would like a receipt, please	**queria um recibo, por favor**	**kree**-uh ooñ rruh-**see**-boo, poor fa-**vawr**
do I pay a deposit?	**deixo depósito?**	**day**-shoo duh-**po**-zee-too?
I've nothing smaller	**não tenho troco**	naooñ **tayn**-yoo **traw**-koo
keep the change	**fique com o troco**	feek kawñ oo **traw**-koo

Getting around

Airport

- Signs are generally in Portuguese and English.
- The word for airport is **aeroporto** (e-ro-**pawr**-too).
- The word for flight is **voo** (**vaw**-oo).
- Visit **www.ana.aeroportos.pt** for information on Portuguese airports.
- The national airline is called **TAP Air Portugal**.

to the airport, please	**ao aeroporto, por favor** aoo e-ro-**pawr**-too, poor fa-**vawr**
how do I get into town?	**como se vai para o centro?** **kaw**-moo suh vaee **pa**-ruh oo **señ**-troo?
where do I get a bus to the town centre?	**onde apanho um autocarro para o centro?** **awñ**-duh-**pan**-yoo ooñ o-to-**ka**-rroo **pa**-ruh o **señ**-troo?
how much is it...?	**quanto é...?** **kwañ**-too e...?
to the town centre	**para o centro** **pa**-ruh oo **señ**-troo
to the airport	**ao aeroporto** aoo e-ro-**pawr**-too
where do I check in for...?	**onde faço o check-in para...?** **awñ**-duh **fa**-soo oo chek-**een** **pa**-ruh...?
which gate is it for the flight to...?	**qual é a porta de embarque do voo para...?** kwa-**le** uh **por**-tuh deñ-**bark** doo **vaw**-oo **pa**-ruh...?
boarding will take place at gate number...	**o embarque será na porta número...** oo eñ-**bark** suh-**ra** na **por**-ta **noo**-muh-roo...

last call for passengers on flight... | **última chamada para os passageiros do voo...**
ool-tee-muh sha-**ma**-duh **pa**-ruh pa-sa-**zhay**-roosh doo **vaw**-oo...

your flight is delayed | **o seu voo está atrasado**
oo seoo **vaw**-oo shta a-tra-**za**-doo

Customs and passports

- There is no restriction by quantity or value, on goods purchased by travellers in another EU country provided they are for their own personal use (this covers gifts). Check guidelines on **www.hmrc.gov.uk**.
- EU citizens with nothing to declare can use the blue customs channels.

I have nothing to declare | **não tenho nada a declarar**
naooñ **tayn**-yoo **na**-duh uh duh-kla-**rar**

here is... | **aqui está...**
a-**kee** shta...

my passport | **o meu passaporte**
oo meoo pa-sa-**port**

here are the children's passports | **aqui estão os passaportes das crianças**
a-**kee** shtaooñ oosh pa-sa-**port**-ush duhsh kree-**an**-sush

this is the baby's passport | **este é o passaporte do bebé**
esht e oo pa-so-**port** doo be-**bay**

do I have to pay duty on this? | **é preciso pagar direitos para isto?**
e pruh-**see**-zoo pa-**gar** dee-**ray**-toosh pruh **eesh**-too?

I bought this as a gift | **comprei para oferecer**
kom-**pray pa**-ruh of-er-e-**ser**

it's for my own personal use | **é para meu uso pessoal**
e **pa**-ruh meoo **oo**-zoo puh-**swal**

we're going to... | **vamos a...**
va-moosh uh...

I'm...	**sou...** saw...
English (m/f)	**inglês/inglesa** eeñ-**glesh**/een-**gle**-zuh
Australian (m/f)	**australiano(a)** aoosh-tra-lee-**a**-noo(-nuh)
American (m/f)	**americano(a)** a-me-ree-**ka**-noo(-nuh)

Asking the way - questions

- You can catch someone's attention with **por favor** (poor fa-**vawr**) or **desculpe** (deesh-**koolp**).
- On signs **você está aqui** means 'you are here'.
- Most town centres have detailed street maps.
- **Largo** (**lar**-goo) and **praça** (**prah**-suh) mean 'square'.
- Tourist offices have a wide range of useful advice.

excuse me!	**por favor!** poor fa-**vawr**!
where is...?	**onde é...?** **awñd** e...?
where is the nearest...?	**onde é o/a ... mais próximo(a)?** **awñd** e oo/uh ... maeesh **pro**-see-moo(-muh)?
how do I get to...?	**como se vai para...?** **kaw**-moo suh vaee **pa**-ruh...?
is this the right way to...?	**a/o ... é por aqui?** oo/uh ... e poor a-**kee**?
is this the right way to the museum?	**o museu é por aqui?** oo moo-**ze**-oo e poor a-**kee**?
the...	**a/o...** oo/uh...
is it far?	**é longe?** e lawñzh?
is it far to...?	**falta muito para...?** **fal**-tuh **mweeñ**-too **pa**-ruh...?

can I walk there?	**posso ir a pé?** **po**-soo eer uh pe?
is there a bus that goes there?	**há um autocarro para lá?** a ooñ o-to-**ka**-rroo **pa**-ruh la?
we're lost	**estamos perdidos** **shta**-moosh puhr-**dee**-doosh
we're looking for...	**estamos à procura de...** **shta**-moosh a pro-**koo**-ruh duh...
can you show me on the map?	**pode-me indicar no mapa?** **pod**-muh eeñ-dee-**kar** noo **ma**-puh?

Asking the way – answers

- Keywords are 'right' **direita** (dee-**ray**-tuh), 'left' **esquerda** (**shker**-duh), 'straight on' **em frente** (ayñ freñt).
- Learn the words for 'roundabout' **a rotunda** (uh ro-**toon**-duh), 'traffic lights' **o semáforo** (oo se-**ma**-for-oo), and 'church' **a igreja** (uh ee-**gray**-zhuh).
- Portuguese distances are often under-estimated!

keep going straight ahead	**siga sempre em frente** **see**-guh sañpr ayñ freñt
you have to turn round	**tem que dar a volta** tayñ kuh dar uh **vol**-tuh
turn...	**vire ...** veer...
right	**à direita** a dee-**ray**-tuh
left	**à esquerda** a **shker**-duh
go...	**vá...** va...
straight on	**sempre em frente** señpr ayñ freñt
keep going as far as the church	**siga sempre até à igreja** **see**-guh señpr uh-**te** sa ee-**grezh**-uh

take...	**tome...** tom...
the first on the right	**a primeira à direita** uh pree-**may**-ruh a dee-**ray**-tuh
the second on the left	**a segunda à esquerda** a suh-**gooñ**-duh a **shker**-duh
the road to...	**a estrada para...** a **shtra**-duh **pa**-ruh...
follow the signs for...	**siga os sinais para...** **see**-guh oosh see-**naeesh pa**-ruh...

Bus

• Tickets and information on long-distance coach travel are available from travel agents and main bus stations. Check out countrywide National network: **www.rede-expressos.pt**, and in the Algarve, Eva Company: **www.eva-bus.net**

• On local bus journeys you pay on the bus or buy 10 tickets at a time (**uma caderneta de módulos** or **um bloco de 10 senhas**) from newspaper kiosks.

• The word for stop is **a paragem** (uh pa-**ra**-zhayñ).

• Validate your ticket in the machine behind the driver.

where is the bus station?	**onde é a estação de autocarros?** **awñd** e uh stha-**saooñ** do-to-**ka**-rroosh?
I want to go...	**quero ir...** **ke**-roo eer...
to the station	**à estação** a shta-**saooñ**
to the museum	**ao museu** aoo moo-**ze**-oo
to the Gulbenkian	**à Gulbenkian** a gulbenkian
to Rossio	**ao Rossio** aoo rroo-**see**-oo

is there a bus that goes there?	**há um autocarro para lá?** a ooñ o-to-**ka**-rroo **pa**-ruh la?
which bus do I take to go to...?	**que autocarro apanho para...?** kuh o-to-**ka**-rroo a-**pan**-yoo **pa**-ruh...?
where do I get a bus to...?	**onde apanho um autocarro para...?** **awñ**-da-**pan**-yoo ooñ o-to-**ka**-rroo **pa**-ruh...?
how often are the buses?	**que frequência têm os autocarros?** kuh fruh-**kweñ**-see-uh **tayñ**-ayñ oosh o-to-**ka**-rroosh?
when is the last bus?	**a que horas é o último autocarro?** a kee **o**-rush e oo **ool**-tee-moo o-to-**ka**-rroo?
can you tell me when to get off?	**pode-me dizer quando devo sair?** **pod**-muh dee-**zer** **kwañ**-doo **de**-voo sa**eer**?

Metro

- You can buy a 10-trip (transferable) ticket at metro stations which is cheaper than individual tickets.
- Lisbon and Oporto both have underground systems. Their websites are **www.metrolisboa.pt** and **www.metro-porto.pt**
- The Lisbon underground has four colour-coded lines and two zones. Tickets must be purchased for one or two zones.

where is the metro station?	**onde é a estação de metro?** **awñd** e uh shta-**saooñ** duh **me**-troo?
are there any special tourist tickets?	**tem um bilhete especial para turistas?** tayñ ooñ beel-**yet** shpuh-**seeal** **pa**-ruh too-**reesh**-tush?
do you have a map of the metro?	**tem um mapa do metro?** tayñ ooñ **ma**-puh doo **me**-troo?
I want to go to...	**quero ir para...** **ke**-roo eer **pa**-ruh...
can I go by metro?	**posso apanhar o metro?** **po**-soo a-pan-**yar** oo **me**-troo?
do I have to change?	**tenho que mudar?** **tayn**-yoo kuh moo-**dar**?

where?	**onde?** **awñ**-duh?
which line is it for...?	**qual é a linha para...?** kwal e uh **leen**-yuh **pa**-ruh...?
what is the next stop?	**qual é a próxima paragem?** kwal e uh **pro**-see-muh puh-**ra**-zhayñ?
which is the station for the Gulbenkian?	**qual é a estação para a Gulbenkian?** kwal e uh shta-**saooñ pa**-ruh uh gulbenkian?

Train

- Tickets for the fast **Alfa** and **Intercidades** services can be purchased at **Multibanco** ATM dispensers. Main stations in Lisbon are **Santa Apolónia** and **Oriente**.
- You must buy and validate your ticket before boarding the train. Allow plenty of time if buying your ticket at the time of travel since queuing is likely.

where is the station?	**onde é a estação?** **awñd** e uh shta-**saooñ**?
to the station, please	**à estação, por favor** a shta-**saooñ**, poor fa-**vawr**
a single to...	**um para...** ooñ **pa**-ruh...
2 singles to...	**dois para...** doysh **pa**-ruh...
a return to...	**um ida e volta para...** ooñ **ee**-duh ee **vol**-tuh **pa**-ruh...
2 returns to...	**dois ida e volta para...** **do**-eesh **ee**-duh ee **vol**-tuh **pa**-ruh...
a child's return to...	**meio bilhete, ida e volta para...** **may**-oo beel-**yet ee**-duh ee **vol**-tuh **pa**-ruh...
1st/2nd class	**primeira/segunda classe** pree-**may**-ruh/se-**gooñ**-duh klas

do I have to pay a supplement?	**paga-se suplemento?**
	pa-ga-suh soo-pluh-**meñ**-too?
is my pass valid on this train?	**este passe é valido neste comboio?**
	esht pas e **va**-lee-doo nesht kawñ-**bo**-yoo?
I would like to book...	**queria reservar...**
	kree-uh rruh-suhr-**var**...
a seat	**um lugar**
	ooñ loo-**gar**
a couchette	**uma couchette**
	oo-muh koo-**shet**

- **www.cp.pt** is the website for the Portuguese railway.
- There is a high-class sleeper service between Lisbon and Madrid known as the 'hotel-train', or '**Lusitânia-Express**'.
- The word for 'arrivals' is **chegadas**. **Partidas** means 'departures'.
- The words **linha**, **gare** and **plataforma** all mean platform.
- Train travel is efficient and extremely cheap.

could I have a timetable?	**podia dar-me um horário?**
	poo-**dee**-uh **dar**-muh ooñ o-**ra**-ree-oo?
do I need to change?	**tenho que mudar?**
	tayn-yoo kuh **moo**-dar?
where?	**onde?**
	awñ-duh?
which platform does it leave from?	**de que plataforma parte?**
	duh kuh pla-ta-**for**-muh part?
does the train to ... leave from this platform?	**é esta a plataforma do comboio para...?**
	e **esh**-tuh uh pla-ta-**for**-muh doo kawñ-**bo**-yoo **pa**-ruh...?
is this the train for...?	**é este o comboio para...?**
	e esht oo kawñ-**bo**-yoo **pa**-ruh...?
where is the left-luggage?	**onde é o depósito de bagagens?**
	awñd e oo duh-**po**-zee-too duh ba-**ga**-zhayñsh?
is this seat free?	**está livre?**
	shta **leev**-ruh?
why is there a delay?	**porque há atraso?**
	poor-**kee** a at-**ra**-zoo?

Taxi

- You can either hail a taxi or call a taxi firm. A taxi stand is called **a praça** (uh **prah**-suh).
- A green light on top, beside the word **Táxi**, means it is free. When the amber light is on it is occupied.
- A surcharge applies if luggage is placed in the boot.
- A higher rate is charged after 10pm and on weekends and public holidays.

to the airport, please	**ao aeroporto, por favor** aoo a-ro-**pawr**-too, poor fa-**vawr**
to the station, please	**à estação, por favor** a shta-**saooñ**, poor fa-**vawr**
take me to this address, please	**leve-me a esta morada, por favor** **lev**-muh uh **esh**-tuh moo-**ra**-duh, poor fa-**vawr**
how much will it cost?	**quanto vai custar?** **kwañ**-too vaee koosh-**tar**?
how much is it to the centre?	**quanto custa ao centro?** **kwañ**-too **koosh**-tuh aoo **señ**-troo?
it's too much	**é caro demais** e **ka**-roo duh-**maeesh**
where can I get a taxi?	**onde se pode arranjar um táxi?** **awñ**-duh suh pod a-rrañ-**zhar** ooñ **tak**-see?
please order me a taxi	**chame-me um táxi por favor** **sha**-muh-muh ooñ **tak**-see poor fa-**vawr**
can I have a receipt?	**pode-me dar um recibo?** **pod**-muh dar ooñ rruh-**see**-boo?
I've nothing smaller	**não tenho troco** naooñ **tayn**-yoo **traw**-koo
keep the change	**fique com o troco** feek kawñ oo **traw**-koo

Boat

- Tourist offices can give information on ferry services and boat trips in the resorts.
- If you plan to take a hire car on a ferry, check that the insurance you took out covers it.
- There is an extensive ferry boat system across the Tagus in Lisbon. In Oporto you can take a boat trip along the river Douro.

1 ticket/2 tickets	**um bilhete/dois bilhetes** ooñ beel-**yet**/doysh beel-**yetsh**
single/round trip	**de ida/de ida e volta** **dee**-duh/**dee**-duh ee **vol**-tuh
is there a tourist ticket?	**há bilhete para turistas?** a beel-**yet pa**-ruh too-**reesh**-tush?
are there any boat trips?	**há excursões de barco?** a shkoor-**soyñsh** duh **bar**-koo?
how long is the trip?	**quanto tempo dura a viagem?** **kwañ**-too **tem**-poo **doo**-ruh a **veea**-zhayñ?
when is the next boat?	**a que horas parte o próximo barco?** a kee **o**-rush part oo **pro**-see-moo **bar**-koo?
when is the next ferry?	**a que horas parte o próximo ferry-boat?** a kee **o**-rush part oo **pro**-see-moo ferry-boat?
when is the first/last boat?	**a que horas é o primeiro/último barco?** a kee **o**-rush e oo pree-**may**-roo/**ool**-tee-moo **bar**-koo?
when does the boat leave?	**quando parte o barco?** **kwañ**-doo part oo **bar**-koo?
do you have a timetable?	**tem um horário?** tayñ ooñ o-**ra**-ree-oo?
is there a restaurant on board?	**o barco tem restaurante?** oo **bar**-koo tayñ rrush-to-**rañt**?
can we hire a boat?	**podemos alugar um barco?** po-**de**-moosh a-loo-**gar** ooñ **bar**-koo?

Car

Driving

- Speed limits are enforced. There are radar controls.
- Drivers must always carry their licence, passport, logbook or rental agreement and an insurance certificate.
- Seat belts are compulsory in both front and back, although most people do not use the back ones. However, it pays to obey the rules.
- Tolls are payable on motorways and Lisbon bridges. Do not use the lane marked **Via Verde**.

can I park here?	pode-se estacionar aqui? **pod**-suh shtas-yoo-**nar** a-**kee**?
where can I park?	onde posso estacionar? **awñ**-duh **po**-soo shtas-yoo-**nar**?
is there a car park?	há um parque de estacionamento? a ooñ park duh shtas-yoo-na-**meñ**-too?
do I need a parking disc?	é preciso uma licença de estacionamento? e pruh-**see**-zoo **oo**-muh lee-**señ**-suh duh shtas-yoo-na-**meñ**-too?
where can I get a parking disc?	onde posso comprar uma licença de estacionamento? **awñ**-duh **po**-soo kawñ-**prar oo**-muh lee-**señ**-suh duh shtas-yoo-na-**meñ**-too?
how long can I park here?	quanto tempo posso estacionar aqui? **kwañ**-too **teñ**-poo **po**-soo shtas-yoo-**nar** a-**kee**?
we're going to...	vamos a... **va**-moosh uh...
what's the best route?	qual é o melhor caminho? kwa-**le** oo mel-**yor** ka-**meen**-yoo?

how do I get to the motorway?	**como se vai para a auto-estrada?** **kaw**-moo suh vaee **pa**-ruh uh ow-too-**shtra**-duh?
which exit is it for...?	**qual é a saída para...?** kwa-**le** uh sa-**ee**-duh **pa**-ruh...?

Petrol

• Petrol stations in the country may close between 12 and 3pm. Always keep an eye on your fuel level.
• Pumps are colour-coded – green and blue are generally lead-free. Black is for diesel.
• In smaller areas petrol stations are attended.
• **s/chumbo** = **sem chumbo** = unleaded.
• The word for petrol is **a gasolina** (uh ga-zoo-**lee**-nuh). Do not confuse it with the word for diesel (**gasóleo**).
• Larger stations have credit card and pre-pay machines.

is there a petrol station near here?	**há uma estação de serviço aqui perto?** a **oo**-muh shta-**saooñ** duh suhr-**vee**-soo a-**kee per**-too?
fill it up, please	**encha, por favor** **eñ**-shuh, poor fa-**vawr**
...euros worth of unleaded	**...euros de gasolina sem chumbo** ...**eoo**-roosh duh ga-zoo-**lee**-nuh sayñ **shoom**-boo
pump number...	**bomba número...** **bawñ**-buh **noo**-muh-roo...
that is my car	**esse é o meu carro** ess e oo meoo **ka**-rroo
where is the air line?	**onde está o ar?** **awñ**-duh shta oo ar?
where is the water?	**onde está a água?** **awñ**-duh shta a **ag**-wuh?
please check...	**pode verificar...** pod vuh-ree-fee-**kar**...

the oil | **o óleo**
oo **o**-lee-oo

the water | **a água**
uh **ag**-wuh

the tyre pressure | **a pressão dos pneus**
a pruh-**saooñ** doosh pneoosh

which pump? | **que bomba?**
kuh **bawñ**-buh?

can I pay by credit card? | **posso pagar com cartão de crédito?**
po-soo pa-**gar** kawñ kar-**taooñ** duh **kre**-dee-too?

Problems/breakdown

- If you break down on a major road, use one of the orange SOS telephones. State whether you're entitled to breakdown cover. English is understood.
- If you break down on the motorway put on your hazard lights and place a warning triangle about 100m behind the car. Make sure you put on the fluorescent jacket (compulsory in all cars).
- If you have an accident, contact the police immediately. On the motorway, call 808 508 508, or dial 112. However, make sure of all relevant details with your insurance, beforehand.

I've broken down | **o meu carro está avariado**
oo meoo **ka**-rroo shta a-va-ree-**a**-doo

what do I do? | **o que devo fazer?**
o kuh **de**-voo fa-**zer**?

I'm on my own (female) | **estou sozinha**
shtaw saw-**zeen**-yuh

there are children in the car | **há crianças no carro**
a kree-**añ**-sush noo **ka**-rroo

where is there a garage near here? | **onde há uma oficina aqui perto?**
awñd a **oo**-muh o-fee-**see**-nuh a-kee **per**-too?

is it serious? | **é grave?**
e grav?

can you repair it?	**pode arranjá-lo?** pod a-rrañ-**zha**-loo?
how much will it cost?	**quanto vai custar?** **kwañ**-too vaee kush-**tar**?
when will it be ready?	**quando estará pronto?** **kwañ**-doo shta-**ra prawñ**-too?
the car won't start	**o carro não pega** oo **ka**-rroo naooñ **pe**-guh
the engine is overheating	**o motor está a aquecer demais** oo moo-**tawr** shta a a-ke-**ser** duh-**maeesh**
it's not working	**não anda** naooñ **añ**-duh
the battery is flat	**a bateria está descarregada** uh ba-tuh-**ree**-uh shta dush-ka-rruh-**ga**-duh
I have a flat tyre	**tenho um furo** **tayn**-yoo ooñ **foo**-roo
have you the parts?	**tem as peças?** tayñ ush **pe**-sush?
can you replace the windscreen?	**pode substituir o pára-brisas?** pod sub-shtee-**tweer** oo pa-ra-**bree**-zush?

Car hire

- Cars can be hired at airports and in towns and resorts.
- Age restrictions vary so it is worth comparing different companies.
- Check the car hire policy carefully – what you do in case of problems and whether you can take the car over the border or on ferries.
- If you need to return a full tank, check where the nearest petrol station is.

I would like to hire a car	**queria alugar um carro** **kree**-uh a-loo-**gar** ooñ **ka**-rroo
for one day	**para um dia** **pa**-ruh ooñ **dee**-uh
for ... days	**para ... dias** **pa**-ruh ... **dee**-ush

I want...	**quero...** **ke**-roo...
a large car	**um carro grande** ooñ **ka**-rroo grañd
a small car	**um carro pequeno** ooñ **ka**-rroo puh-**ke**-noo
an automatic	**um carro automático** ooñ **ka**-rroo aoo-too-**ma**-tee-koo
how much is it?	**quanto é?** **kwañ**-too e?
is fully-comprehensive insurance included in the price?	**inclui o seguro contra todos os riscos?** eeñ-**kloo**-ee oo suh-**goo**-roo **kawñ**-truh **to**-doosh oosh **rreesh**-koosh?
what do I do if I break down?	**o que devo fazer se o carro avariar?** o kuh **de**-voo fa-**zer** soo **ka**-rroo a-va-ree-**ar**?
when must I return the car by?	**a que horas tenho de devolver o carro?** uh kee **o**-rush **tayn**-yoo kuh duh-vol-**ver** oo **ka**-rroo?
please show me the controls	**podia mostrar-me os comandos?** po-**dee**-uh moosh-**trar**-muh oosh koo-**mañ**-doosh?
where are the documents?	**onde estão os documentos?** **awñ**-duh shtaooñ oosh do-koo-**meñ**-toosh?
where is the nearest petrol station?	**onde é a estação de serviço mais próxima?** **awñd** e uh shta-**saooñ** duh suhr-**vee**-soo maeesh **pro**-see-muh?

Shopping

Shopping - holiday

- Shops open from 9am-7pm. In smaller towns there is usually a lunch break between 1 and 3pm but they stay open later.
- Big shopping centres on the outskirts of major towns open from 10am-11pm seven days a week.
- Normal shops are usually closed on Saturday afternoons and Sundays.

do you sell...?	**vende...?** **veñ**-duh...?
stamps	**selos** **se**-loosh
batteries for this camera	**pilhas para esta máquina** **peel**-yush **pa**-ruh **esh**-tuh **ma**-kee-nuh
where can I buy...?	**onde posso comprar...?** **awñ**-duh **po**-soo kawñ-**prar**...?
matches	**fósforos** **fosh**-foo-roosh
films	**rolos** **rraw**-loosh
10 stamps	**dez selos** desh **se**-loosh
for postcards	**para postais** **pa**-ruh poosh-**taeesh**
to Britain	**para a Grã-Bretanha** **pa**-ruh uh grañ-bruh-**tan**-yuh
to United States	**os Estados Unidos** oosh **shta**-doosh oo-**nee**-doosh

to Australia	**a Austrália**	uh aoosh-**tra**-lee-yuh
a colour film	**um rolo a cores**	ooñ **rraw**-loo uh **kaw**-rush
a tape for this video camera	**uma cassette para esta câmara de vídeo**	**oo**-muh ka-**set pa**-ruh **esh**-tuh **ka**-ma-ruh duh **vee**-deeoo
I'm looking for a present	**estou à procura dum presente**	shtaw a pro-**koo**-ruh dooñ pruh-**señt**
have you anything cheaper?	**não tem nada mais barato?**	naooñ tayñ **na**-duh maeesh ba-**ra**-too?
it's a gift	**é para oferta**	e **pa**-ruh o-**fer**-tuh
please could you wrap it up?	**podia embrulhá-lo?**	poo-**dee**-uh eñ-brool-**ya**-loo?
is there a market?	**há algum mercado?**	a al-**gooñ** muhr-**ka**-doo?
when?	**quando?**	**kwañ**-doo?

Shopping - clothes

- The cheapest places are at weekly/monthly markets, also at some large supermarkets.
- The word for 'discount' is **desconto** (deesh-**koñ**-too).
- Tourists in Lisbon can claim a range of discounts by using the **Lisboa Card**, sold at Tourist Offices.
- Lisbon, in particular, has become a fashion mecca, with names such as Ana Salazar and the popular store, **Zara**. Look out for shoes and other leather goods as well.

can I try this on?	**posso experimentar?**	**po**-soo shpuh-ree-meñ-**tar**?
where are the changing rooms?	**onde é o gabinete de provas?**	**awñd** e oo ga-bee-**net** duh **pro**-vush?

it's too big — **fica-me grande**
fee-ka-muh grand

have you a smaller size? — **tem uma medida mais pequena?**
tayñ **oo**-muh muh-**dee**-duh maeesh puh-**ke**-nuh?

it's too small — **fica-me pequeno**
fee-ka-muh puh-**ke**-noo

have you a larger size? — **tem uma medida maior?**
tayñ **oo**-muh muh-**dee**-duh maee-**or**?

it's too expensive — **é caro demais**
e **ka**-roo duh-**maeesh**

I'm just looking — **estou só a ver**
shtaw so a ver

I'll take this one — **levo este**
le-voo esht

I take a size ... shoe — **calço o número...**
kal-soo oo **noo**-muh-roo...

what shoe size are you? — **que número calça?**
kuh **noo**-muh-roo **kal**-suh?

does it fit? — **serve-lhe?**
ser-vuhl-yuh?

Shopping – food

- You can buy fresh fruit, vegetables and other local produce from the market, **mercado** (mer-**ka**-doo). They are usually open in the mornings. But mini-markets and supermarkets are plentiful and sell everything from fresh produce to frozen foods. Mega shopping centres offer all sorts of shops, including supermarkets.
- In tourist resorts markets may stay open until late afternoon.
- The word **biológico** on labels indicates organic produce.

where can I buy...? — **onde posso comprar...?**
awñ-duh **po**-soo kawñ-**prar**...?

fruit — **fruta**
froo-tuh

bread	**pão**	paooñ
where is...?	**onde é...?**	**awñd** e...?
the supermarket	**o supermercado**	oo soo-per-muhr-**ka**-doo
the baker's	**a padaria**	uh pa-da-**ree**-uh
where is the market?	**onde é o mercado?**	**awñd** e oo muhr-**ka**-doo?
which day is the market on?	**que dia é o mercado?**	kuh **dee**-uh e oo muhr-**ka**-doo?
it's my turn next	**sou eu a seguir**	saw eoo a suh-**geer**
that's enough	**chega**	**she**-guh
a litre of...	**um litro de...**	ooñ **lee**-troo duh...
milk	**leite**	layt
beer	**cerveja**	suhr-**vay**-zhuh
a bottle of...	**uma garrafa de...**	**oo**-muh ga-**rra**-fuh duh...
water	**água**	**ag**-wuh
wine	**vinho**	**veen**-yoo
olive oil	**azeite**	a-**zayt**
a can of...	**uma lata de...**	**oo**-muh **la**-tuh duh...
coke	**coca-cola**	ko-ka-**ko**-luh
tonic water	**água tónica**	**ag**-wuh **to**-nee-kuh

a carton of...	**um pacote de...** ooñ pa-**kot** duh...
orange juice	**sumo de laranja** **soo**-moo duh luh-**rañ**-zhuh

• Milk is **leite** (layt). It is generally colour-coded: full fat = **gordo** (red), semi-skimmed = **meio gordo** (green) and skimmed = **magro** (blue).
• The word for 'bread' is **pão** (paooñ). There are many kinds of bread. Look out for maize loaves called **broa** (**bro**-uh).
• **Gordura** = fat

100 grams of...	**cem gramas de...** sayñ **gra**-mush duh...
cheese	**queijo** **kay**-zhoo
olives	**azeitonas** a-zay-**taw**-nush
half a kilo of...	**meio quilo de...** **may**-oo **kee**-loo duh...
sausages	**salsichas** sal-**see**-shush
mushrooms	**cogumelos** kaw-goo-**me**-loosh
a kilo of...	**um quilo de...** ooñ **kee**-loo duh...
potatoes	**batatas** ba-**ta**-tush
apples	**maçãs** ma-**sañsh**
8 slices of...	**oito fatias de...** **oy**-too fa-**tee**-ush duh...
cooked ham	**fiambre** fee-**añ**-bruh
cured ham	**presunto** pruh-**zooñ**-too

a loaf of bread	**um pão** ooñ paooñ
three yogurts	**três iogurtes** tresh yo-**goor**-tush
half a dozen eggs	**meia dúzia de ovos** **may**-uh **doo**-zee-uh **do**-voosh
a packet of...	**um pacote de...** ooñ pa-**kot** duh...
biscuits	**bolachas** boo-**la**-shush
sugar	**açúcar** a-**soo**-kar
a tin of tomatoes	**uma lata de tomates** **oo**-muh **la**-tuh duh too-**ma**-tush
a jar of jam	**um frasco de doce** ooñ **frash**-koo duh daw-suh
what would you like?	**o que deseja?** oo kuh duh-**zay**-zhuh?
anything else?	**mais alguma coisa?** maeesh al-**goo**-muh **koy**-zuh?

Daylife

Sightseeing

- If spending time in Lisbon, a **Lisboa Card** entitles you to a range of discounts. You can buy them at tourist offices.
- Most museums are closed on Mondays and close for lunch between 12 and 2.30pm.
- Lisbon's 'artshuttle' bus ferries visitors around the city to places of cultural interest. The **Lisboa Card** lets you travel free.

where is the tourist office?	**onde é o centro de turismo?** **awñd** e oo **señ**-troo duh too-**reezh**-moo?
we'd like to visit...	**queríamos visitar...** **kreea**-moosh vee-zee-**tar**...
have you any leaflets?	**tem folhetos?** tayñ fool-**ye**-toosh?
do you have a town guide?	**tem um guia da cidade?** tayñ ooñ **gee**-uh duh see-**dad**?
when can we visit...?	**quando podemos visitar...?** **kwañ**-doo poo-**de**-moosh vee-zee-**tar**...?
what day does it close?	**que dia fecha?** kuh **dee**-uh **fay**-shuh?
is it open to the public?	**está aberto ao público?** shta a-**ber**-too aoo **poo**-blee-koo?
we'd like to go to...	**queríamos ir para...** **kreea**-moosh eer **pa**-ruh...
are there any excursions?	**há excursões organizadas?** a shkoor-**soyñsh** or-ga-nee-**za**-dush?
when does it leave?	**a que horas parte?** a kee **o**-rush part?

where does it leave from?	**de onde parte?** dawñd part?
how much is it to get in?	**quanto é a entrada?** **kwañ**-too e uh eñ-**tra**-duh?
is there a reduction for...?	**fazem desconto para...?** **fa**-zayñ desh-**kawñ**-too **pa**-ruh...?
children/students/ seniors	**crianças/estudantes/terceira idade** kree-**añ**-sush/shtoo-**dañ**-tush/tuhr-**say**-ruh ee-**dad**

Beach

• A green flag flying at the beach means it is safe to swim, a yellow flag = not recommended, a red flag = dangerous.
• Beaches which meet European standards of cleanliness fly a blue flag.
• In public indoor swimming pools you are required to wear a swimming cap.

is there a quiet beach?	**há uma praia sossegada?** a **oo**-muh **pra**-yuh saw-suh-**ga**-duh?
how do I get there?	**como é que se vai para lá?** kaw-**me** kuh suh vaee pruh la?
is there a swimming pool?	**há piscina?** a **pshee**-nuh?
is there a lifeguard?	**há salva-vidas?** a **sal**-vuh-**vee**-dush?
can we swim in the river?	**pode-se nadar no rio?** pod-suh na-**dar** noo **rree**-oo?
is it safe to swim here?	**pode-se nadar aqui?** pod-suh na-**dar** a-**kee**?
is the water clean?	**a água é limpa?** a **ag**-wuh e **leeñ**-puh?
is it deep?	**é funda?** e **fooñ**-duh?

is the water cold?	**a água está fria?**	a **ag**-wuh shta **free**-uh?
is it dangerous?	**é perigoso?**	e pree-**gaw**-zoo?
are there currents?	**há correntes?**	a koo-**rreñ**-tush?
where can we...?	**onde se pode...?**	**awñ**-duh suh pod...?
windsurf	**fazer windsurf**	fa-**zer** windsurf
waterski	**fazer esqui aquático**	fa-**zer** shkee a-**kwa**-tee-koo
can I hire...?	**posso alugar...?**	**po**-soo a-loo-**gar**...?
a beach umbrella	**um chapéu de praia**	ooñ sha-**peoo** duh **pra**-yuh
a jetski	**um jet-ski**	ooñ **zhet**-skee

Sport

• Tourist offices have information on sports activities in their area. Check out **www.visitportugal.com**, for all kinds of useful data, including sports.
• Horse riding is popular in Portugal.
• The annual horse fair at **Golegã** takes place in the **Ribatejo** in November.
• Check also other sports, such as fishing, hunting, surfing and sailing.

where can we...?	**onde se pode...?**	**awñ**-duh suh pod...?
play tennis	**jogar ténis**	zhoo-**gar te**-neesh
play golf	**jogar golfe**	zhoo-**gar** golf

go swimming	**nadar**	nuh-**dar**
hire bikes	**alugar bicicletas**	a-loo-**gar** bee-see-**kle**-tush
go fishing	**pescar**	push-**kar**
go riding	**andar a cavalo**	añ-**dar** uh ka-**va**-loo
how much is it...?	**quanto é...?**	**kwañ**-too e...?
per hour/day	**por hora/dia**	poor **o**-ruh/**dee**-uh
how do I book a court?	**como se aluga um campo?**	**kaw**-moo see a-**loo**-guh ooñ **kañ**-poo?
do you hire rackets?	**alugam raquetas?**	a-**loo**-gaooñ rra-**ketush**
do I need walking boots?	**preciso de botas de alpinismo?**	pruh-**see**-zoo duh **bo**-tush?
is there a football match?	**há algum jogo de futebol?**	a al-**gooñ zhaw**-goo duh foot-**bol**?
do I need a fishing permit?	**é preciso uma liçenca de pesca?**	e pre-**see**-zoo **oo**-muh lee-**señ**-suh duh **pesh**-kuh?
where is there a sports shop?	**onde há uma loja de artigos de desporto?**	**awñd** a **oo**-muh **lo**-zhuh dee-ar-**tee**-goosh duh dush-**pawr**-too?

Golf

• There are many good golf courses in Portugal, particularly in the Algarve. Visit **www.portugalgolf.pt.**

• The Portuguese tourist office website, **www.visitportugal.com**, also has information on golf and sound general information.

• Away from the Algarve, a number of world-class courses are found around the Lisbon area.

is there a golf club near here?	**há um clube de golfe aqui perto?** a ooñ kloob duh golf **a**-kee **per**-too?
how much is a round?	**quanto custa uma volta?** **kwañ**-too **koosh**-tuh **oo**-muh **vol**-tuh?
do you need to be a member to play here?	**é preciso ser membro para jogar?** e pruh-**see**-zoo ser **meñ**-broo **pa**-ruh zhoo-**gar**?
can I hire...?	**pode-se alugar...?** **pod**-suh a-loo-**gar**...?
golf clubs	**tacos de golfe** **ta**-koosh duh golf
a caddie	**um caddie** ooñ caddie
a buggy	**um buggy** ooñ buggy
can we book tee-off times?	**é possível reservar a hora de tee-off?** e poo-**see**-vel rruh-suhr-**var** uh **o**-ruh duh tee-off?
where do I go to tee up?	**onde está o primeiro tee?** **awñ**-duh shta oo pree-**may**-roo tee?
what par is this hole?	**qual é o par deste buraco?** kwal e oo par desht boo-**ra**-koo?
it's in the bunker	**está no bunker** shta noo bunker
what is your handicap?	**qual é o seu handicap?** kwal e oo seoo handicap?
my handicap is...	**o meu handicap é...** oo meoo handicap e...

Nightlife

Nightlife - popular

• Portuguese people tend to dine late and then go out about 10pm. An evening out, after dinner, may consist of going to a bar or café with friends, to the cinema, theatre or a disco.
• **Fado** is Portuguese folk songs which are often melancholic and sad, and is popular in the Lisbon area. A very good site for a wide range of information is **www.portugalvirtual.pt**.

what is there to do at night? — **o que se pode fazer à noite?**
oo kuh suh pod fa-**zer** a noyt?

where is there a good bar round here? — **onde há um bom bar por aqui?**
awñd a ooñ bawñ bar poor a-**kee**?

which is a good disco? — **qual é uma boa discoteca?**
kwal e **oo**-muh **baw**-uh deesh-koo-**te**-kuh?

where can we hear live music? — **onde se pode ouvir música ao vivo?**
awñ-duh suh pod aw-**veer moo**-zee-kuh aoo **vee**-voo?

is it expensive? — **é caro?**
e **ka**-roo?

where can we hear fado/classical music? — **onde se pode ouvir fado/música clássica?**
awñ-duh suh pod aw-**veer fa**-doo/**moo**-zee-kuh **kla**-see-kuh?

where do local people go at night? — **onde é que a gente daqui vai à noite?**
awñd e kuh zheñt duh-**kee** vaee a noyt?

is it a safe area? — **é uma zona segura?**
e **oo**-muh **zo**-nuh suh-**goo**-ruh?

are there any concerts on?	**há algum concerto por aqui?** a al-**gooñ** kawñ-**ser**-too poor a-**kee**?
do you want to dance?	**quer dançar comigo?** ker dañ-**sar** coo-**mee**-goo?
my name is...	**chamo-me...** **sha**-moo-muh...
what's your name?	**como se chama?** **kaw**-moo suh **sha**-muh?

Nightlife - cultural

- There are many drama, dance and music summer festivals.
- The tourist office can give information on local events.
- In Portugal it is customary to show films in their original versions with subtitles. Cinema is very cheap.
- Lisbon, Oporto and other larger cities have a wide range of cultural activities.

is there a list of cultural events?	**há um guia de eventos culturais?** a ooñ **gee**-yuh de-**veñ**-toosh kool-too-**raeesh**?
what's on?	**qual é o programa?** kwal e oo pro-**gra**-muh?
when is the local festival?	**quando é que são as festas da zona?** **kwañ**-doo e kuh saooñ ush **fesh**-tush duh **zaw**-nuh?
we want to go...	**queremos ir...** **kre**-moosh eer...
to the theatre	**ao teatro** aoo tee-**at**-roo
to the opera	**à ópera** a **o**-puh-ruh
to the ballet	**ao ballet** aoo ba-**le**
to a concert	**a um concerto** uh ooñ kawñ-**ser**-too

do I need to get tickets in advance?	**é preciso comprar bilhetes com antecedência?** e pruh-**see**-zoo kawñ-**prar** beel-**yetsh** kawñ añ-tuh-suh-**deñ**-see-uh?
how much are the tickets?	**quais são os preços dos bilhetes?** kwaeesh saooñ oosh **pre**-soosh doosh?
2 tickets...	**dois bilhetes...** doysh beel-**yetsh**...
for tonight	**para esta noite** **presh**-tuh noyt
for tomorrow	**para amanhã** pa-ra-man-**yañ**
for 5th August	**para o cinco de Agosto** **pa**-ruh oo **seeñ**-koo duh-**gawsh**-too

Accommodation

Hotel

- Tourist offices have lists of hotels and other accommodation, also check **www.portugal-hotels.com**. A **pousada** is a luxurious hotel which is often a converted palace, monastery or other historic building. Check out **www.pousadas.pt**.
- Guesthouses (**pensão** or **residência**) usually offer breakfast only. **Turismo de habitação** is when you stay as a guest in a Portuguese home. A useful website is **www.portugal-villa.com**.

have you a room for tonight?	**tem um quarto para esta noite?** tayñ ooñ **kwar**-too pa-**resh**-tuh noyt?
a room	**um quarto** ooñ **kwar**-too
single	**individual** eeñ-dee-vee-**dwal**
double	**de casal** duh kuh-**zal**
family	**de família** duh fa-**meel**-yuh
with a shower	**com chuveiro** kawñ shoo-**vay**-roo
with a toilet (ie. ensuite)	**com casa de banho** kawñ **ka**-suh duh **ban**-yoo
how much is it per night?	**quanto é por noite?** **kwañ**-too e poor noyt?
is breakfast included?	**inclui pequeno almoço?** eeñ-**kloo**-ee puh-**ke**-noo al-**maw**-soo?
I booked a room	**reservei um quarto** ruh-suhr-**vay** ooñ **kwar**-too

my name is...	**chamo-me...**	**sha**-moo-muh...
I'd like to see the room	**queria ver o quarto**	**kree**-uh ver oo **kwar**-too
have you anything cheaper?	**não tem nada mais barato?**	naooñ tayñ **na**-duh maeesh buh-**ra**-too?
I would like a room with three beds	**queria um quarto com três camas**	**kree**-uh ooñ **kwar**-too kawñ tresh **ka**-mush
can I leave this in the safe?	**posso deixar isto no cofre?**	**po**-soo day-**shar eesh**-too noo **kof**-ruh?
can I have my key, please?	**queria a chave, por favor**	**kree**-uh uh shav, poor fa-**vawr**
are there any messages for me?	**há algum recado para mim?**	a al-**gooñ** rruh-**ka**-doo pruh meeñ?
come in!	**entre!**	**eñ**-truh!
please come back later	**volte mais tarde, por favor**	volt maeesh tard, poor fa-**vawr**
I'd like breakfast in my room	**queria o pequeno almoço no quarto**	**kree**-uh oo puh-**ke**-noo al-**maw**-soo noo **kwar**-too
please bring...	**por favor traga-me...**	poor fa-**vawr tra**-ga-muh...
toilet paper	**papel higiénico**	pa-**pel** ee-zhee-**e**-nee-koo
soap	**sabonete**	sa-boo-**net**
clean towels	**toalhas limpas**	**twal**-yush **leeñ**-push
a glass	**um copo**	ooñ **ko**-poo
could you clean...?	**podia limpar...?**	poo-**dee**-uh leeñ-**par**...?
my room	**o meu quarto**	oo meoo **kwar**-too
the bath	**a banheira**	uh ban-**yay**-ruh

please call me...	**podia-me chamar...** poo-**dee**-a-muh sha-**mar**...
at 8 o'clock	**às oito horas** azh **oy**-too **o**-rush
do you have a laundry service?	**tem serviço de lavandaria?** tayñ suhr-**vee**-soo duh la-vañ-duh-**reea**?
we're leaving tomorrow	**vamos embora amanhã** **va**-moosh eñ-**bo**-ra-man-yañ
could you prepare the bill?	**faça a conta, por favor?** **fa**-suh uh **kawñ**-tuh, poor fa-**vawr**?

Self-catering

• The voltage in Portugal is 220. Plugs have two round pins and you should take an adaptor if you plan to take any electrical appliances with you.
• In self-catering accommodation gas for cooking is usually bottled. Check you understand how the bottle connects and what you need to do if it runs out.

which is the key for this door?	**qual é a chave desta porta?** kwal e uh shav **desh**-tuh **por**-tuh?
please show me how this works	**podia mostrar-me como é que isto funciona?** poo-**dee**-a moosh-**trar**-muh kaw-**me**-keesh-too fooñ-see-**aw**-nuh?
how does ... work?	**como é que o/a ... funciona?** kaw-**me** kee oo/uh ... fooñ-see-**aw**-nuh?
the waterheater	**o esquentador** oo shkeñ-ta-**dawr**
the washing machine	**a máquina de lavar roupa** uh **ma**-kee-nuh duh luh-**var rraw**-puh
the cooker	**o fogão** oo foo-**gaooñ**
is there always hot water?	**há sempre água quente?** a **semp**-ruh **ag**-wuh keñt?

who do I contact if there are any problems? **quem é que devo contactar no caso de haver problemas?**
kayñ e kuh **de**-voo kawñ-tak-**tar** noo **ka**-zoo da-**ver** proo-**ble**-mush?

we need extra... **precisamos de mais...**
pruh-see-**za**-moosh de maeesh...

cutlery **talheres**
tal-**ye**-rush

sheets **lençóis**
leñ-**soysh**

the gas has run out **acabou-se o gás**
a-kuh-**baws** oo gazh

where are the fuses? **onde estão os fusíveis?**
awñ-duh shtaooñ oosh foo-**zee**-vaysh?

what do I do? **o que devo fazer?**
o kuh **de**-voo fa-**zer**?

where do I put out the rubbish? **onde é que se põe o lixo?**
awñd e kuh suh poyñ oo **lee**-shoo?

Camping and caravanning

- There are many sites along the coast, fewer inland.
- Camping outside approved sites is possible except in the Algarve where this is strictly prohibited.
- If towing a caravan or trailer you need an international camping carnet available from the Caravan Club.
- Campsites are classified 4 to 1 star and R for rural.

we're looking for a campsite **procuramos um parque de campismo**
pro-koo-**ra**-moosh ooñ park duh kañ-**peezh**-moo

have you a list of campsites? **tem uma lista de parques de campismo?**
tayñ **oo**-muh **leesh**-tuh duh **par**-kush duh kañ-**peezh**-moo?

where is the campsite? **onde é o parque de campismo?**
awñd e oo park duh kañ-**peezh**-moo?

have you any vacancies?	**tem lugares vagos?**	tayñ loo-**ga**-rush **va**-goosh?
how much is it per night?	**quanto custa por noite?**	**kwañ**-too **koosh**-tuh poor noyt?
we'd like to stay for ... nights	**gostaríamos de ficar ... noites**	goosh-ta-**reea**-moosh duh fee-**kar** ... noytsh
is the campsite near the beach?	**o parque de campismo fica perto da praia?**	oo park duh kañ-**peezh**-moo **fee**-kuh **per**-too duh **pra**-yuh?
it is very muddy here	**há muita lama aqui**	a **mweeñ**-tuh **la**-muh uh-**kee**
is there another site?	**há outro parque?**	a **aw**-troo park?
is there a shop on the site?	**há uma loja no parque?**	a **oo**-muh **lo**-zhuh noo park?
can we camp here?	**podemos acampar aqui?**	poo-**de**-moosh a-kañ-**par** a-**kee**?
can we park our caravan here?	**podemos estacionar a nossa caravana aqui?**	poo-**de**-moosh shtas-yoo-**nar** uh **no**-suh ka-ruh-**va**-nuh a-**kee**?

Different travellers

Children

• The word for children is **crianças** (kree-**an**-sush).
• Children are welcome in Portuguese restaurants and you can order children's portions or half portions.
• Children under 12 are not allowed to travel in the front of a car unless in an approved seat or harness.
• On public transport children under 5 don't pay.

a child's ticket	**um bilhete de criança** ooñ beel-**yet** duh kree-**añ**-suh
is there a reduction for children?	**fazem descontos para crianças?** **fa**-zayñ dush-**kawñ**-toosh **pa**-ruh kree-**añ**-sush?
do you have a children's menu?	**tem uma ementa para crianças?** tayñ **oo**-muh ee-**meñ**-tuh **pa**-ruh kree-**añ**-sush?
do you have...?	**tem...?** tayñ...?
a high chair	**uma cadeira de bebé** **oo**-muh kuh-**day**-ruh duh be-**be**
a cot	**um berço** ooñ **ber**-soo
is it ok to bring children here?	**é possível trazer as crianças?** e poo-**see**-vel tra-**zer** ush kree-**añ**-sush?
what is there for children to do?	**o que há para as crianças fazerem?** oo kee a **pa**-ruh ush kree-**añ**-sush fa-**ze**-rayñ?
is it safe to give to children?	**pode-se dar às crianças?** **pod**-suh dar azh kree-**añ**-sush?
is it dangerous?	**é perigoso?** e pree-**gaw**-zoo?

I have two children	**tenho duas crianças**	
	tayn-yoo **doo**-ush kree-**añ**-sush	
he/she is 10 years old	**ele/ela tem dez anos**	
	el/ela tayñ dezh **a**-noosh	
do you have children?	**tem filhos?**	
	tayñ **feel**-yoosh?	

Special needs

- Tourist offices can supply a list of hotels with facilities for the disabled.
- The organisation **Secretariado Nacional de Reabilitação** publishes a guide to disabled facilities throughout Portugal. Check **www.snripd.pt**.
- Lisbon and Oporto have a special dial-a-ride bus for the disabled. Ask for details at the tourist office.

is it possible to visit ...with a wheelchair?	**é possível visitar ... com uma cadeira de rodas?**
	e poo-**see**-vel vee-zee-**tar** ... kawñ **oo**-muh ka-**day**-ruh duh **rro**-dush?
do you have toilets for the disabled?	**tem casa de banho para deficientes?**
	tayñ **ka**-zuh duh **ban**-yoo **pa**-ruh duh-fee-see-**eñtsh**?
I need a bedroom on the ground floor	**preciso dum quarto no rés-do-chão**
	pruh-**see**-zoo dooñ **kwar**-too noo rrezh-doo-**shaooñ**
is there a lift?	**há elevador?**
	a ee-luh-va-**dawr**?
where is the lift?	**onde é o elevador?**
	awñd e oo ee-luh-va-**dawr**?
I can't walk far	**não posso andar muito**
	naooñ **po**-soo añ-**dar mweeñ**-too
are there many steps?	**há muitos degraus?**
	a **mweeñ**-toosh duh-**gra**-oosh?

is there an entrance for wheelchairs? **há uma entrada para cadeiras de rodas?**
a **oo**-muh eñ-**tra**-duh **pa**-ruh ka-**day**-rush duh **rro**-dush?

can I travel on this train with a wheelchair? **posso viajar neste comboio com cadeira de rodas?**
po-soo veea-**zhar** nesht kawñ-**bo**-yoo kawñ ka-**day**-ruh duh **rro**-dush?

is there a reduction for the disabled? **há desconto para deficientes?**
a dush-**kawñ**-too **pa**-ruh duh-fee-see-**eñtsh**?

Exchange visitors

- These phrases are intended for families hosting Portuguese-speaking visitors. We have used the familiar **tu** form.
- Portuguese people generally eat dinner quite late (8pm).
- Eating in front of the TV is practically unheard of in Portugal!

what would you like for breakfast? **o que queres para o pequeno almoço?**
oo kuh **ke**-rush **pa**-ruh oo puh-**ke**-noo al-**maw**-soo?

do you eat...? **comes...?**
kaw-mush...?

what would you like to eat? **o que queres comer?**
oo kuh **ke**-rush kaw-**mer**?

what would you like to drink? **o que queres beber?**
oo kuh **ke**-rush buh-**ber**?

did you sleep well? **dormiste bem?**
door-**meesh**-tuh bayñ?

would you like to take a shower? **queres tomar banho?**
ke-rush taw-**mar ban**-yoo?

what would you like to do today? **o que queres fazer hoje?**
oo kuh **ke**-rush fa-**zer** awzh?

would you like to go shopping? **queres ir às compras?**
ke-ruh-sheer azh **kawñ**-prush?

I will pick you up at... **vou-te buscar às...**
vaw-tuh **boosh**-kar azh...

did you enjoy yourself?	**divertiste-te?**	dee-vuhr-**teesh**-tuh-tuh?
take care	**tem cuidado**	tayñ kwee-**da**-doo
please be back by...	**por favor volta antes de...**	poor fa-**vawr vol**-tuh **añ**-tush duh...
we'll be in bed when you get back	**estaremos na cama quando voltares**	shta-**re**-moosh nuh **ka**-muh **kwañ**-doo vol-**ta**-rush

• These phrases are intended for those people staying with Portuguese-speaking families.
• If invited to a Portuguese family for a meal take flowers or chocolates. Be prepared for huge quantities of food.
• It is polite to say **com licença** (koñ lee-**sen**-suh) when entering someone's house.

I like...	**gosto de....**	**gosh**-too duh...
I don't like...	**não gosto de...**	naooñ **gosh**-too duh...
that was delicious	**estava uma delícia**	**shta**-vuh **oo**-muh duh-**lee**-see-uh
thank you very much	**muito obrigado(a)**	**mweeñ**-too o-bree-**ga**-doo(-duh)
may I phone home?	**posso telefonar para casa?**	**po**-soo tuh-luh-foo-**nar pa**-ruh **ka**-zuh?
could you take me by car?	**podia-me levar de carro?**	poo-**dee**-uh-muh luh-**var** duh **ka**-rroo?
could I have a key?	**podia dar-me uma chave?**	poo-**dee**-uh **dar**-muh **oo**-muh shav?
could I borrow...?	**podia-me emprestar...?**	poo-**dee**-uh-muh eñ-prush-**tar**...?
an iron	**um ferro**	ooñ **fe**-rroo
a hairdryer	**um secador de cabelo**	ooñ se-ka-**dawr** duh ka-**be**-loo

what time do you get up?	**a que horas se levanta?** a kee **o**-rush suh luh-**vañ**-tush?
please would you call me at...	**podia-me chamar às...** poo-**dee**-uh-muh shuh-**mar** azh...
I'm staying with...	**estou a ficar na casa de...** shtaw uh fee-**kar** nuh **ka**-zuh duh...
thanks for everything	**obrigado(a) por tudo** o-bree-**ga**-doo(-duh) poor **too**-doo
I've had a great time	**diverti-me imenso** dee-vuhr-**tee**-muh ee-**meñ**-soo

Difficulties

Problems

- Many Portuguese people speak good English so you should not encounter too many language difficulties.
- Beware of pickpockets and bag-snatchers particularly in tourist areas and crowded places.
- Traffic fines, **multas** (**mool**-tush), have to be paid on the spot by non-residents.

can you help me, please?	**pode-me ajudar, por favor?** **pod**-muh-zhoo-**dar**, poor fa-**vawr**?
I don't speak Portuguese	**não falo português** naooñ **fa**-loo poor-too-**gesh**
do you speak English?	**fala inglês?** **fa**-luh eeñ-**glesh**?
does anyone speak English?	**há alguém que fale inglês?** a al-**gayñ** kuh fal eeñ-**glesh**?
I'm lost	**perdi-me** per-**deem**
how do I get to...?	**como se vai para...?** **kaw**-moo suh vaee **pa**-ruh...?
I need to get to...	**preciso de ir a...** pre-**see**-zoo deer uh...
I'm late	**estou atrasado(a)** shtaw a-tra-**za**-doo(-duh)
I've missed...	**perdi...** per-**dee**...
my connection	**a minha ligação** uh **meen**-yuh lee-ga-**saooñ**

my plane	**o avião** oo a-vee-**aooñ**
I've lost...	**perdi...** per-**dee**...
my passport	**o passaporte** oo pa-sa-**port**
my wallet	**o porta-moedas** oo por-ta-**mwe**-dush
my luggage has not arrived	**a minha bagagem não chegou** uh **meen**-yuh ba-**ga**-zhayñ naooñ shuh-**gaw**
I've left my bag...	**deixei a mala...** day-**shay** uh **ma**-luh...
leave me alone!	**deixe-me em paz!** **daysh**-mayñ pazh!
go away!	**vá-se embora!** va-señ-**bo**-ruh!

Complaints

- The Portuguese expect to receive good service and quality.
- If you find something is not up to standard, do not be afraid to complain. Portuguese people complain when things are not to their liking.
- Restaurants and hotels, and some larger shops have complaints books – **livros de queixas**.

the light	**a luz** uh loozh
the air conditioning	**o ar condicionado** oo ar kawñ-dees-yoo-**na**-doo
...doesn't work	**...não trabalha** ...naooñ tra-**bal**-yuh
the room is dirty	**o quarto está sujo** oo **kwar**-too shta **soo**-zhoo
the bath is dirty	**a banheira está suja** uh ban-**yay**-ruh shta **soo**-zhuh

there is no...	**não há...** naooñ a...
toilet paper	**papel higiénico** pa-**pel** ee-zhee-**e**-nee-koo
hot water	**água quente** **ag**-wuh keñt
it is too noisy	**há muito ruído** a **mweeñ**-too **rrwee**-doo
it is too small	**é muito pequeno** e **mweeñ**-too puh-**ke**-noo
this isn't what I ordered	**isto não é o que eu pedi** **eesh**-too naooñ e oo kee eoo puh-**dee**
I want to complain	**quero apresentar uma queixa** **ke**-roo a-pruh-señ-**tar oo**-muh **kay**-shuh
there is a mistake	**há um erro** a ooñ **e**-rroo
we've been waiting for a very long time	**estamos à espera há muito tempo** **shta**-moosh a **shpe**-ruh a **mweeñ**-too **teñ**-poo
this is broken	**isto está partido** **eesh**-too shta par-**tee**-doo
can you repair it?	**pode arranjá-lo?** pod a-rrañ-**zha**-loo?

Emergencies

- The number 112 connects you to the three emergency services: **Polícia**, **Bombeiros** (fire brigade) and **Ambulância**.
- You will be able to speak in English when accessing the emergency number.
- You must report any theft or loss at a police station as soon as possible and obtain a police report, to show to your insurance company.

help!	**socorro!** soo-**kaw**-rroo!

can you help me?	**pode-me ajudar?** **pod**-muh-zhoo-**dar**?
there's been an accident	**houve um acidente** awv ooñ a-see-**deñt**
someone is injured	**há um ferido** a ooñ fuh-**ree**-doo
call...	**chame...** sham...
the police	**a polícia** uh poo-**lees**-yuh
an ambulance	**uma ambulância** oo-mañ-boo-**lañ**-see-uh
we're on our way	**vamos lá ter** **va**-moosh la ter
he was driving too fast	**ele estava a conduzir rápido demais** el **shta**-vuh uh kawñ-doo-**zeer rra**-pee-doo duh-**maeesh**
where's the police station?	**onde é a esquadra?** **awñd** e uh **shkwa**-druh?
I want to report a theft	**quero participar um roubo** **ke**-roo par-tee-see-**par** ooñ **raw**-boo
I need a report for my insurance	**preciso dum relatório para o meu seguro** **pre**-see-zoo dooñ ruh-la-**tor**-yoo **pa**-ruh oo meoo suh-**goo**-roo
I've been robbed	**fui roubado(a)** fooee rraw-**ba**-doo(-duh)
I've been attacked	**fui agredido(a)** fooee a-gruh-**dee**-doo(-duh)
I've been raped	**fui violado(a)** fooee vee-oo-**lah**-doo(-duh)
my car has been broken into	**assaltaram-me o carro** a-sal-**ta**-raooñ-muh oo **ka**-rroo
my car has been stolen	**roubaram-me o carro** rraw-**ba**-raooñ-muh oo **ka**-rroo
that man keeps following me	**aquele homem está-me a seguir** a-**kel o**-mayñ **shta**-muh suh-**geer**

how much is the fine?	**quanto é a multa?** **kwañ**-too e uh **mool**-tuh?
I don't have enough	**não tenho o suficiente** naooñ **tayn**-yoo oo soo-fees-**yeñt**
can I pay at the police station?	**posso pagar na esquadra?** **po**-soo pa-**gar** nuh **shkwa**-druh?
I would like to phone my embassy	**gostava de telefonar à minha embaixada** goosh-**ta**-vuh duh tuh-luh-foo-**nar** a **meen**-yuh eñ-baee-**sha**-duh
where is the British Consulate?	**onde é que fica o consulado britânico?** **awñd** e kuh **fee**-kuh oo kawñ-soo-**la**-doo bree-**tañ**-nee-koo?
I have no money	**não tenho dinheiro nenhum** naooñ **tayn**-yoo deen-**yay**-roo nayn-**yooñ**

Health

• EU citizens are entitled to free emergency care in Portugal. You must have a European Health Insurance Card (available from **www.dh.gov.uk/travellers**). You will still need a medical insurance policy to cover non-emergency treatment. Pharmacies can provide advice on any health matters and deal with minor problems.
• Many medicines obtainable only by prescription at home, can be bought over the counter, following the phamacist's advice. They are highly qualified.

have you something for...?	**tem algo para...?** tayñ **al**-goo **pa**-ruh...?
travel sickness	**o enjoo** oo eñ-**zhaw**-oo
diarrhoea	**a diarreia** uh deea-**rray**-uh
is it safe for children to take?	**pode-se dar às crianças?** **pod**-suh dar azh kree-**añ**-sush?
I don't feel well	**não me sinto bem** naooñ muh **seen**-too bayñ
I need a doctor	**preciso dum médico** pruh-**see**-zoo dooñ **me**-dee-koo
I'm taking these drugs	**estou a tomar estes medicamentos** shtaw a too-**mar esh**-tush muh-dee-ka-**meñ**-toosh
my son/ my daughter is ill	**o meu filho/a minha filha está doente** oo meoo **feel**-yoo/uh **meen**-yuh **feel**-yuh shta doo-**eñt**
he/she has a temperature	**ele/ela tem febre** el/**e**-la tayñ **feb**-ruh

I have high blood pressure	**tenho a tensão alta** **tayn**-yoo uh teñ-**saooñ al**-tuh
I'm pregnant	**estou grávida** shtaw **gra**-vee-duh
I'm on the pill	**tomo a pílula** **to**-moo uh **pee**-loo-luh
I'm allergic to penicillin	**sou alérgico(a) à penicilina** saw a-**ler**-zhee-koo(-kuh) a pe-nee-see-**lee**-nuh
my blood group is...	**o meu grupo sanguíneo é...** oo meoo **groo**-poo sañ-**gwee**-neeoo e...
I'm breastfeeding	**estou a amamentar** shtaw uh a-ma-meñ-**tar**
is it safe to take?	**tem contra-indicações?** tayñ kawñ-tra-eeñ-dee-ka-**soyñsh**?
will he/she have to go to hospital?	**tem que ir para o hospital?** tayñ keer **pa**-ruh oo osh-pee-**tal**?
I need to go to casualty	**preciso de ir às urgências** pre-**see**-zoo deer azh oor-**zheñ**-see-ush
where is the hospital?	**onde é o hospital?** **awñd** e oo osh-pee-**tal**?
when are visiting hours?	**quais são as horas de visita?** kwaeesh saooñ ush **o**-rush duh vee-**zee**-tuh?
which ward?	**qual é a enfermaria?** kwal e uh eñ-fuhr-ma-**ree**-uh?
I need to see a dentist	**preciso dum dentista** pre-**see**-zoo dooñ deñ-**teesh**-tuh
I have toothache	**tenho uma dor de dentes** **tayn**-yoo **oo**-muh dawr duh dentsh
the filling has come out	**caiu-me o chumbo** ka-**eeoo**-muh oo **shooñ**-boo
it hurts	**dói-me** **doy**-muh
my dentures are broken	**a dentadura está partida** uh den-ta-**doo**-ruh shta par-**tee**-duh
can you repair them?	**podia repará-la?** poo-**dee**-uh rruh-pa-**ra**-luh?
I have an abscess	**tenho um abcesso** **tayn**-yoo ooñ ab-**se**-soo

Business

- Office hours vary but most offices open at 9am, have a lunch hour (usually from 1–3pm) and close at 6 or 7 in the evening.
- Government offices open to the public from 9am–1pm.
- Business lunches are important for sealing deals, and may be quite long.

I'm...	sou... saw...
here's my card	aqui tem o meu cartão a-**kee** tayñ oo meoo kar-**taooñ**
I'm from Jones Ltd	sou de Jones Limitada saw duh Jones lee-mee-**ta**-duh
I'd like to arrange a meeting with Mr/Ms...	gostaria de ter uma reunião com o Senhor/a Senhora... goosh-ta-**ree**-yuh duh ter **oo**-muh rreoo-nee-**aooñ** kawñ oo suhn-**yawr**/ uh suhn-**yaw**-ruh...
could we meet at a restaurant?	podíamos nos encontrar num restaurante? poo-**dee**-uh-moosh nooz eñ-kawñ-**trar** nooñ rrush-to-**rañt**?
I will confirm by fax	confirmarei por fax kawñ-feer-ma-**ray** poor faks
I'm staying at Hotel...	estou no Hotel... shtaw noo o-**tel**...
how do I get to your office?	como se vai ao seu escritório? **kaw**-moo suh vaee aoo seoo shkree-**to**-reeoo?

here is some information about my company	**aqui tem informação sobre a minha empresa**	a-**kee** tayñ eeñ-foor-muh-**saooñ saw**-bruh uh **meen**-yuh eñ-**pre**-zuh
where can I plug in my laptop?	**onde é que posso ligar o meu portátil?**	**awñd** e kuh **po**-soo lee-**gar** oo meoo por-**ta**-teel?
what is your website/ e-mail address?	**qual é o seu endereço electrónico/ o seu e-mail?**	kwal e oo seoo eñ-**dre**-soo e-lek-**tro**-nee-koo/ oo seoo e-mail?
do you have an appointment?	**tem encontro marcado?**	tayñ eñ-**kawñ**-troo mar-**ka**-doo?
I have an appointment with...	**tenho um encontro marcado com...**	**tayn**-yoo ooñ eñ-**kawñ**-troo mar-**ka**-doo kawñ...
at ... o'clock	**às ... horas**	azh ... **o**-rush
I'm delighted to meet you	**prazer em conhecê-lo(la)**	pra-**zer** ayñ kawñ-yuh-**se**-loo(-luh)
my Portuguese isn't very good	**não falo muito bem português**	naooñ **fa**-loo **mweeñ**-too bayñ poor-too-**gesh**
what is the name of the managing director?	**como é que se chama o director geral?**	kaw-**me** kuh suh **sha**-muh oo dee-rek-**tawr** zhuh-**ral**?
I would like some information about the company	**queria informação sobre a companhia**	**kree**-uh eeñ-foor-ma-**saooñ saw**-bruh uh kawñ-pan-**yee**-uh
do you have a press office?	**tem um departamento de imprensa?**	tayñ ooñ duh-puhr-ta-**meñ**-too deeñ-**preñ**-suh?
I need an interpreter	**preciso dum intérprete**	pre-**see**-zoo dooñ eeñ-**ter**-pruh-tuh
could you photocopy this for me?	**podia fotocopiar-me isto?**	poo-**dee**-uh fo-to-koo-pee-yar-**meesh**-too?
is there a business centre?	**há um centro de negócios?**	a ooñ **señ**-troo duh nuh-**gos**-yoosh?

Phoning

- You can rent a phone or buy SIM cards to use in your own phone at Portuguese airports.
- Coin-operated phones can be hard to find, but card-operated ones are becoming much more common.
- You can buy phonecards from post offices, newsstands and tobacconists.
- To call abroad, dial 00 before the country code (UK 44, Portugal 351, US 1, Australia 61).

a phonecard	um cartão credifone ooñ kar-**taooñ** kre-dee-**fon**
for 10/20 Euros	de 10/20 euros duh desh/veent **eoo**-roosh
I want to make a phone call	quero fazer uma chamada telefónica **ke**-roo fa-**zer oo**-muh sha-**ma**-duh tuh-luh-**fo**-nee-kuh
I want to make a reverse charge call	quero fazer uma chamada a cobrar no destinatário **ke**-roo fa-**zer oo**-muh sha-**ma**-duh a koo-**brar** noo dush-tee-na-**ta**-ree-yoo
can I speak to...?	posso falar com...? **po**-soo fa-**lar** kawñ...?
this is...	daqui fala... da-**kee fa**-luh...
Senhor Lopes, please	o Senhor Lopes, por favor oo suhn-**yawr lop**-sh, poor fa-**vawr**
I'll call back later	chamo mais tarde **sha**-moo maeesh tard
can you give me an outside line, please	dê-me uma linha, por favor **de**-muh **oo**-muh **leen**-yuh, poor fa-**vawr**
hello	estou/sim shtaw/seeñ

who is calling?	**quem fala?**	kayñ **fa**-luh?
it's engaged	**está impedido**	shta eeñ-puh-**dee**-doo
please try again later	**por favor, volte a tentar mais tarde**	poor fa-**vawr**, **volt** uh teñ-**tar** maeesh tard
I'll text you	**mando-lhe uma mensagem/um SMS**	**man**-doo lyuh **oo**-muh men-**sa**-zhayñ/ooñ SMS
Could you text me?	**podai-me mandar uma mensagem/ um SMS**	po-**dee**-uh muh man-**dar** **oo**-muh men-**sa**-zhayñ/ooñ SMS

E-mail/fax

- Internet cafés are on the increase. Visit **www.cybercafes.com** to find the nearest one.
- Post offices with **Netpost** have internet access, as well as public libraries.
- www. is (dublyoo dublyoo dublyoo pon-too).
- The Portuguese for @ is **arroba** (ar-**roh**-buh).
- The ending for Portuguese websites is **.pt**.
- **sapo.pt** is a popular Portuguese search engine.

I would like to send an e-mail	**queria mandar um e-mail**	**kree**-uh mañ-**dar** ooñ e-mail
what's your e-mail address?	**qual é o seu endereço de e-mail?**	kwal e oo seoo eñ-**dre**-soo duh e-mail?
my e-mail address is...	**o meu endereço de e-mail é...**	oo meoo eñ-**dre**-soo duh e-mail e...
how do you spell it?	**como se escreve?**	**kaw**-moo suh shkrev?
all one word	**uma palavra só**	**oo**-muh pa-**la**-vruh so
all lower case (small letters)	**tudo em letras minúsculas**	**too**-doo ayñ **le**-truhsh mee-**nush**-koo-luhsh

did you get my e-mail?	**recebeu o meu e-mail?**	ruh-suh-**beoo** oo meoo e-mail?
I would like to send a fax	**queria mandar um fax**	**kree**-uh mañ-**dar** ooñ faks
what's your fax number?	**qual é o seu número de fax?**	kwal e oo seoo **noo**-muh-roo duh faks?
did you get my fax?	**recebeu o meu fax?**	rruh-suh-**beoo** oo meoo faks?
do you have a fax?	**tem fax?**	tayñ faks?
can I send a fax from here?	**posso mandar um fax daqui?**	**po**-soo mañ-**dar** ooñ faks da-**kee**?

Internet/cybercafé

• It is possible to find cybercafés in larger towns, particularly in the Algarve area. Some libraries have access but this is an area that is still developing. Most offices of the Portuguese Telecom Company (Telecom PT) offer Internet access.

• The most popular search engines are: **Altavista**, **Terra Vista**, **Portugalnet**, and **Portal de Portugal**.

• Popular sites of general interest are: **www.sapo.pt** and **www.clix.pt**.

I'd like to check my email	**queria aceder ao meu email**	**kree**-uh a-suh-**der** aoo **me**oo email
how much is it... for 15 minutes/ for one hour/ to print something out?	**quanto é ... por 15 minutos/ por uma hora/para imprimir?**	**kwan**-too e ... por keeñz mee-**noo**-toosh/ por **oo**-muh **o**-ruh/**pa**-ruh eem-pree-**mee**r?
I'd like to put these photos onto CD	**queria transferir estas fotos para um CD**	**kree**-uh transh-fuhr-**reer esh**t-uhsh **fo**-toosh **pa**-ruh ooñ CD

could you print it out?	podia imprimi-lo (la)? po-**dee**-uh eem-pree-**mee**-loo(luh)?
where can I buy a memory stick?	onde é que posso comprar um cartão memória? **awñd** e kuh **po**-soo com-**prar** ooñ car-**towñ** me-**mo**-ree-yuh?
could you help me please?	podia-me ajudar por favor? po-**dee**-uh-muh a-zhoo-**dar** poor fa-**vawr**?
it doesn't work	não funciona naooñ fun-see-**o**-nuh
this computer has crashed	este computador falhou esht com-poo-ta-**dor** fal-**yoh**

Practical info

Numbers

0	**zero**	**ze**-roo
1	**um (uma)**	ooñ (**oo**-muh)
2	**dois (duas)**	doysh (**doo**-ush)
3	**três**	tres
4	**quatro**	**kwa**-troo
5	**cinco**	**seeñ**-koo
6	**seis**	saysh
7	**sete**	set
8	**oito**	**oy**-too
9	**nove**	nov
10	**dez**	desh
11	**onze**	awñz
12	**doze**	dawz
13	**treze**	trez
14	**catorze**	ka-**tawrz**
15	**quinze**	keeñz
16	**dezasseis**	dzuh-**saysh**
17	**dezassete**	dzuh-**set**
18	**dezoito**	**dzoy**-too
19	**dezanove**	dzuh-**nov**
20	**vinte**	veent
21	**vinte e um**	veeñ-tee-**ooñ**
22	**vinte e dois**	veeñ-tee-**doysh**
30	**trinta**	treeñ-tuh
40	**quarenta**	kwa-**reñ**-tuh
50	**cinquenta**	seeñ-kw**eñ**-tuh
60	**sessenta**	suh-**señ**-tuh
70	**setenta**	suh-**teñ**-tuh

80	**oitenta**	oy-**teñ**-tuh
90	**noventa**	naw-**veñ**-tuh
100	**cem/cento**	sayñ/**señ**-too
110	**cento e dez**	**señ**-too ee desh
150	**cento e cinquenta**	**señ**-too ee seeñ-kw**eñ**-tuh
200	**duzentos**	doo-**zeñ**-toosh
500	**quinhentos**	keen-**yeñ**-toosh
1,000	**mil**	meel
1,000,000	**um milhão**	ooñ meel-**yaooñ**
1st	**primeiro(a)**	pree-**may**-roo(uh)
2nd	**segundo(a)**	suh-**gooñ**-doo(uh)
3rd	**terceiro(a)**	tuhr-**say**-roo(uh)
4th	**quarto(a)**	**kwar**-too(uh)
5th	**quinto(a)**	**keeñ**-too(uh)
6th	**sexto(a)**	**saysh**-too(uh)
7th	**sétimo(a)**	**se**-tee-moo(uh)
8th	**oitavo(a)**	oy-**ta**-voo(uh)
9th	**nono(a)**	**naw**-noo(uh)
10th	**décimo(a)**	**de**-see-moo(uh)

Days and months

Monday	**segunda-feira**	se-**gooñ**-duh-**fay**-ruh
Tuesday	**terça-feira**	**ter**-suh-**fay**-ruh
Wednesday	**quarta-feira**	**kwar**-tuh-**fay**-ruh
Thursday	**quinta-feira**	**keeñ**-tuh-**fay**-ruh
Friday	**sexta-feira**	**saysh**-tuh-**fay**-ruh
Saturday	**sábado**	**sa**-ba-doo
Sunday	**domingo**	daw-**meeñ**-goo

January	**Janeiro**	zhuh-**nay**-roo
February	**Fevereiro**	fuhv-**ray**-roo
March	**Março**	**mar**-soo
April	**Abril**	ab-**reel**
May	**Maio**	**maee**-oo
June	**Junho**	**zhoon**-yoo

July	**Julho**	**zhool**-yoo
August	**Agosto**	a-**gosh**-too
September	**Setembro**	suh-**tayñ**-broo
October	**Outubro**	aw-**toob**-roo
November	**Novembro**	nov-**ayñ**-broo
December	**Dezembro**	duh-**zayñ**-broo

what's the date?	**qual é a data?** kwal e uh **da**-tuh?
which day?	**que dia?** kuh **dee**-uh?
week	**semana** suh-**ma**-nuh
month	**mês** mesh
year	**ano** **a**-noo
March 5th	**o cinco de Março** oo **seeñ**-koo duh **mar**-soo
July 6th	**o seis de Julho** oo saysh duh **zhool**-yoo
on Saturday	**no sábado** noo **sa**-ba-doo
on Saturdays	**aos sábados** aoosh **sa**-ba-doosh
every Saturday	**todos os sábados** **taw**-doosh oosh **sa**-ba-doosh
this Saturday	**este sábado** esht **sa**-ba-doo
next Saturday	**o próximo sábado** oo **pro**-see-moo **sa**-ba-doo
last Saturday	**o sábado passado** o **sa**-ba-doo pa-**sa**-doo
next week	**a semana que vem** uh suh-**ma**-nuh kuh vayñ
last month	**o mês passado** oo mesh pa-**sa**-doo

Time

- Note that throughout Europe the 24-hour clock is used much more widely than in the UK.
- am = **da manhã** (duh man-**yañ**).
- pm = **da tarde** (duh tard).
- until = **até** (**a**-te).
- Portugal operates on the same time as the UK.

what time is it, please?	**que horas são, por favor?** kee **o**-rush saooñ, poor fa-**vawr**?
am	**da manhã** duh man-**yañ**
pm	**da tarde** duh tard
it's 1 o'clock	**é uma hora** e **oo**-muh **o**-ruh
it's 2/3 o'clock	**são duas/três horas** saooñ **doo**-ush/tresh **o**-rush
it's half past 8	**são oito e meia** saooñ **oy**-too ee **may**-uh
it is half past 10	**são dez e meia** saooñ desh ee **may**-uh
in an hour	**dentro de uma hora** **deñ**-troo dee **oo**-muh **o**-ruh
in half an hour	**dentro de meia hora** **deñ**-troo duh **may**-uh **o**-ruh
a quarter of an hour	**um quarto de hora** ooñ **kwar**-too **do**-ruh
three quarters of an hour	**três quartos de hora** tresh **kwar**-toosh **do**-ruh
until 8 o'clock	**até às oito** a-**te** azh **oy**-too
until 4 o'clock	**até às quatro** a-**te** azh **kwa**-troo

at 10 am	**às dez horas** azh dez **o**-rush
at 2200	**às vinte e duas horas** azh **veeñ**-tee **doo**-ush **o**-rush
at midday	**ao meio-dia** aoo may-oo-**dee**-uh
at midnight	**à meia-noite** a may-uh-**noyt**
soon	**em breve** ayñ brev
later	**mais tarde** maeesh tard

Eating out

Portuguese cuisine is varied and distinctive. Anyone expecting to find an extension of Spanish food with **paellas** and suchlike, will be surprised to discover that Portuguese food is very different.

Every province has its own gastronomic specialities but there are various national culinary preferences found throughout Portugal, such as the use of **bacalhau** (salt cod) under many delicious guises, as well as **peixe** (fish) and **marisco** (shellfish), especially along the extensive coastline.

Pork is the most popular meat in Portugal, fresh or cured, in the form of the excellent **presunto** (cured ham) and many kinds of spicy **chouriços** (smoked spicy sausages) which are delicious both raw or cooked. Lamb, kid, poultry and game are also very common all over the country. Garlic and fragrant fresh coriander are essential ingredients of many Portuguese dishes.

The Portuguese are very fond of bread and bake a great variety, using mixed flours (wheat, rye and maize). Many national specialities are actually based on **açordas** (cooked bread) served in place of potatoes or rice, or as a main dish when mixed with all sorts of seafood or meats and seasoned with herbs and garlic. The result is delicious even if the appearance of such dishes might not be too sophisticated.

Breakfast (**pequeno almoço**) is usually white coffee, **pão** (bread) or **torradas** (toast) and butter, and honey or jam. Lunch and dinner (**almoço** and **jantar**) may be similar. A light lunch could include **sopa e um pãozinho** or **papo-seco** (soup and a roll). A more leisurely dinner might include soup or another **entrada** (starter) and **prato principal** (main dish) with fish or meat. This will include vegetables in some form and rice or potatoes (often chips), but there will also be a salad option. **Sobremesa** (dessert) generally follows. This may be cheese and biscuits, fruit, a pudding or ice-cream, followed by **bica** or **café** (strong black coffee).

Ordering drinks

- Drinks are served either cold from the fridge, **fresco** (**fresh**-koo), or at room temperature, **natural** (na-too-**ral**)
- There are many variations of coffee, both black and white. **Um galão** (ooñ guh-**laooñ**) is a large milk coffee served in a tall glass.
- To avoid getting hot milk served with your tea, make sure you ask for **leite frio** (layt **free**-oo).

a black coffee	**um café** ooñ ka-**fe**
a white coffee	**um café com leite** ooñ ka-**fe** kawñ layt
2 white coffees	**dois cafés com leite** doysh ka-**fes** kawñ layt
a tea	**um chá** ooñ sha
with milk	**com leite** kawñ layt
with lemon	**com limão** kawñ lee-**maooñ**
a beer	**uma cerveja** **oo**-muh suhr-**vay**-shuh
large	**grande** **grañ**-duhv
small	**pequena** puh-**ke**-na
a bottle of mineral water	**uma garrafa de água mineral** **oo**-muh ga-**rra**-fuh **dag**-wuh mee-nuh-**ral**

a port	**um vinho do porto**	
	ooñ **veen**-yoo doo **por**-too	
a hot chocolate, please	**um chocolatequente, se faz favor**	
	ooñ sho-ko-**lat** keñt, suh fash fa-**vawr**	
sparkling	**com gás**	
	kawñ gash	
still	**sem gás**	
	sayñ gash	
the wine list, please	**a lista de vinhos, por favor**	
	uh **leesh**-tuh duh **veen**-yoosh, poor fa-**vawr**	
a glass of red wine	**um copo de vinho tinto**	
	ooñ **kaw**-poo duh **veen**-yoo **teeñ**-too	
a glass of white wine	**um copo de vinho branco**	
	ooñ **kaw**-poo duh **veen**-yoo **brañ**-koo	
a bottle of wine	**uma garrafa de vinho**	
	oo-muh guh-**rra**-fuh duh **veen**-yoo	
red	**tinto**	
	teeñ-too	
white	**branco**	
	brañ-koo	
would you like a drink?	**quer uma bebida?**	
	ker **oo**-muh buh-**bee**-duh?	
what will you have?	**o que quer tomar?**	
	o kuh ker too-**mar**?	

Ordering food

- By law, Portuguese restaurants must display prices outside.
- Many restaurants close on Sunday or Monday. Check beforehand if there is one you particularly want to visit.
- Many restaurants offer a set menu, **ementa turística** (ee-**men**-tuh too-**rees**-tee-kuh), which is usually good value.
- Portions are invariably huge, and many menus offer a half-portion, **meia dose** (**may**-uh daws)
- **Prato do dia** (**pra**-too doo **dee**-uh) is 'dish of the day'.

I'd like to book a table	**queria reservar uma mesa**	**kree**-uh ruh-zuhr-**var oo**-muh **me**-zuh
for ... people	**para ... pessoas**	**pa**-ruh ... puh-**saw**-ush
for tonight	**para esta noite**	**presh**-tuh noyt
at 8pm	**às oito horas**	ash **oy**-too **o**-rush
the menu, please	**a ementa, por favor**	uh ee-**men**-tuh, poor fa-**vawr**
is there a dish of the day?	**há um prato do dia?**	a ooñ **pra**-too doo **dee**-uh?
have you a set-price menu?	**tem a ementa do dia?**	tayñ uh ee-**men**-tuh doo **dee**-uh?
I'll have this	**quero isto**	**ke**-roo **eesh**-too
what do you recommend?	**o que recomenda?**	oo kuh ruh-koo-**meñ**-duh?
I don't eat meat	**não como carne**	naooñ **kaw**-moo karn
do you have any vegetarian dishes?	**tem algum prato vegetariano?**	tayñ al-**gooñ pra**-too vuh-zhuh-tuh-ree-**a**-noo?
excuse me!	**faz favor!**	fash fa-**vawr**!
more bread	**mais pão**	maeesh paooñ
more water	**mais água**	maeesh **ag**-wuh
the bill, please	**a conta, por favor**	uh **kawn**-tuh, poor fa-**vawr**
enjoy your meal!	**bom apetite!**	bawñ a-puh-**teet**!

Special requirements

- Bread is served at every meal in Portugal, along with butter.
- **Gordo** = full fat, **meio gordo** = half fat or semi skimmed (for milk), **magro** = low fat (or skimmed for milk).
- On food nutrition labels **glícidos** are carbohydrates; **lípidos** are fats.
- Decaffeinated is **descafeinado** (dush-ka-fay-**na**-doo).

I'm vegetarian	**sou vegetariano(a)** saw vuh-zhay-tuh-ree-**a**-noo(-nuh)
I don't eat fish/ shellfish	**não como peixe/marisco** naooñ **kaw**-moo paysh/muh-**reesh**-koo
I'm allergic to shellfish	**sou alérgico(a) a marisco** saw a-**ler**-zhee-koo(-kuh) uh muh-**reesh**-koo
I am on a diet	**estou de dieta** shtaw duh dee-**eh**-tuh
I am allergic to peanuts	**sou alérgico(a) a amendoins** saw a-**ler**-zhee-koo(-kuh) uh a-mayñ-doh-**eeñsh**
I can't eat liver	**não posso comer fígado** naooñ **pos**-soo kaw-**mer fee**-guh-doo
I don't drink alcohol	**não tomo bebidas alcoólicas** naooñ **taw**-moo buh-**bee**-dush al-koo-**ol**-ee-kush
what is this made with?	**de que é feito?** duh kuh e **fay**-too?
is it raw?	**está cru?** shta kroo?

Eating photoguide

Eating places

Cafés are open all day and serve snacks and simple meals.

Casa de Pasto
Simple, traditional, cheap restaurant offering good value meals at lunchtimes.

Cake Shop Serves light meals and mouth-watering cakes.

Restaurant With Outside Bar
esplanada = open air. Lunch is usually between 12.30 and 2.30pm. Dinner is usually from 7 until 9 or 9.30pm. Menus and prices must be displayed outside. Many restaurants close on Sunday or Monday.

Casa das tostas
A snackbar selling toasted sandwiches, a popular snack. Cheese and ham toasties are a speciality.

Tea is **Chá** and is usually served weak and black. Ask for cold milk, **leite frio** (layt **free**-oo), or you may be served hot milk. For a refreshing caffeine-free drink, ask for a **chá de limão** (sha duh lee-**maooñ**), boiling water poured over lemon rind.

Shellfish Restaurant **Marisqueira** is a shellfish restaurant. Most restaurants include shellfish dishes on their menus.

King prawns
lagostins

Beer in Portugal is lager. A small glass of draught beer is **um fino** or **uma imperial**. A pint-sized glass is **uma caneca** and a litre, **uma girafa**.

Appetisers
You are often served fairly substantial appetisers (**Acepipes**) before your meal arrives. Take care not to order too much!

Beerhouse Beerhouses (**Cervejaria**) serve lager and savoury dishes. Some are well-known for their steak (**bife**), often served with a fried egg on top, plenty of gravy-like sauce and very good chips.

Bifes Do Lombo
fillet steak

Churrasqueira Restaurant serving barbecued food, mainly chicken, and often with a take-away (**para fora**) service. **Frango** is a young chicken. A popular dish is **frango à piri-piri** (barbecued chicken in a chilli sauce).

Bolo de arroz
Portuguese people have a sweet tooth and are partial to a mid-morning coffee and a cake (**bolo**). **Bolo de arroz** (rice cake) is often eaten at breakfast.

Sandwiches (**sandes**) are often made with cheese (**queijo**), cooked ham (**fiambre**) or cured ham (**presunto**).

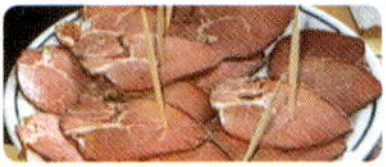

Cooked Ham

Presunto
Cured ham

Queijo Small cheeses made with sheep/goats milk are often served as a starter to go with bread and rolls.

Coffee For a small, strong, espresso-like coffee ask for **um café** or **uma bica**. A regular-sized white coffee is **um café com leite** or **uma meia de leite**. That same size cup of black coffee is **um duplo** – a double. A large white coffee (similar to a 'latte') is called **um galão**, and is served in a tall glass.

Reading the menu

EMENTA menu

Entradas starters

Acepipes appetisers

Sopas soups

Peixe e Marisco fish and shellfish

Pratos de Carne meat dishes

Ovos eggs

Legumes vegetables

Saladas salads

Sobremesa desserts

Queijos cheeses

Main dishes (fish and meat) always include potatoes or rice and vegetables or salad. Ask before ordering extra side dishes or you might end up with too much food.

Porco Assado Roast pork and chips. Main dishes are always served with chips or rice and a salad.

Pão Bread is served at every meal in Portugal along with butter and other spreads. Butter is salted.

quente

Hot

frio

Cold

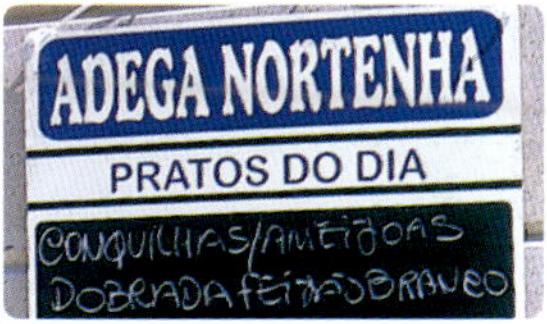

Dishes Of The Day Pratos do dia These are usually served with chips or rice and vegetables and are generally very good value.

Useful Menu Words

no = in
no forno = in the oven (i.e. baked)
com = with. Sometimes abbreviated to **c/** (without is **sem**)
e = and
para = for
P/a = **para** meaning 'for'
p/a criança = for children, i.e. there is a special dish (**prato especial**) for children.

Ementa Turística is a tourist menu. If you want to try traditional dishes, this is the menu to choose. Set-price menus may only be available at lunch.
Ementa do dia is a set-price menu, with 3 courses (starter, meat or fish and dessert). It may also include wine.

Caldo Verde
A traditional Portuguese soup made from shredded kale and potato.

ALMOCOS
Lunches

ANTARES
Dinners (evening)

Bacalhau Assado
Baked salted cod.

Flavours

Azeite Olive oil is used liberally. Many people add a spoonful of olive oil to their soups at the table. Vegetables, poached fish, salt cod and potatoes are also seasoned with lashings of olive oil. A cruet stand (**galheteiro**) is automatically brought to the table for you to use as liberally as you like.

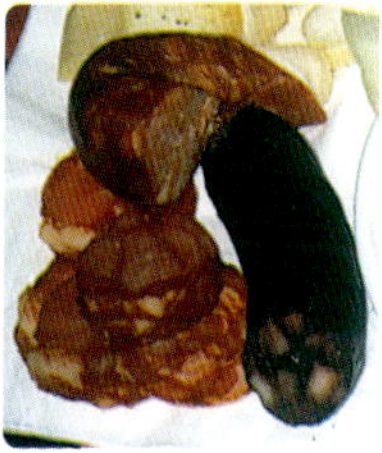

Chouriço Spicy smoked sausage similar to Spanish chorizo. Often baked and sliced to serve as a starter.

Bacalhau (salt cod) Salt cod is eaten all over Portugal. It needs soaking but can be served in many ways.

Pastéis de bacalhau Salt-cod croquettes made with mashed potatoes.

Coentros Coriander is widely used in Portuguese cooking. It is used with garlic to flavour **açordas** – bread-based soups often served with fried or grilled fish. The dish might not look or sound very elegant, but it is comfort food at its best!

Drinks and bill

Wine Douro table wines are normally red, made from the same grapes as Port and by the same producers. They are rich and elegant, smooth and fruity with excellent body and good tannins. They include varieties such as **Quinta do Crasto**, **Poças**, **Cockburns**.

Port Port wines can be white (dry to sweet) – these should be chilled – or red (Ruby, Tawny and Vintage). Tawnys (semi-sweet to sweet) are perhaps the most popular. Grapes for Port (many exclusive to the region) are grown along the slopes of the Douro river, in northern Portugal. This was the very first demarcated wine region in the world, back in 1756, and is also the most difficult to cultivate.

Lista dos vinhos

Wine List

Vinho da casa

House Wine

This is normally very acceptable and good value.

A service charge is generally included in the bill, so tipping is discretionary.

IVA incl. à taxa de 12% (vat at 12% inc.)

Menu reader

...à caçadora hunter-style (poultry or game marinated in wine and garlic)
...à jardineira garden-style with vegetables like green beans and carrots
...à lagareiro baked dish made with lots of olive oil
...à marinheira with white wine, onions and parsley
...à portuguesa Portuguese fashion, i.e. with tomato sauce
abacate avocado
abacaxi pineapple
abóbora pumpkin
sopa de abóbora pumpkin soup
açafrão saffron
acelga swiss chard
acepipes appetisers
acompanhamentos side dishes
açorda typical Portuguese dish with bread
açorda com peixe frito thick bread soup accompanying fried fish
açorda de alho thick bread soup with garlic and beaten egg (generally served with fried fish in traditional restaurants)
açorda de marisco thick bread soup with shellfish and a beaten egg, typical of the Lisbon area
açorda de sável thick bread soup with shad
açorda de Sesimbra thick bread soup with fish, garlic and coriander
açúcar sugar
adocicado slightly sweet
agrião watercress
água water
água mineral com gás sparkling mineral water
água mineral sem gás still mineral water
água tónica tonic water
aguardente brandy **velha** old or **velhíssima** very old
aipo celery
albardado in batter
alcachofra artichoke
fundo de alcachofra artichoke heart
alcaparra caper
alcatra braised beef, typical of the Azores
alecrim rosemary
aletria fine noodles
alface lettuce
alfenim moulded sugar, a speciality of the Azores
alheiras chicken and garlic sausage from Trás-os-Montes
alho garlic
alho francês leek
almoço lunch
almôndegas meatballs
alperces apricots
amargo bitter
amarguinha bitter-almond liqueur made in the Algarve region

amêijoas clams
amêijoas à Bulhão Pato clams with garlic and coriander
amêijoas ao natural steamed clams with herbs and lemon butter
amêijoas na cataplana clams cooked in a 'cataplan' pot, with **chouriço** and herbs
ameixa plum
ameixas de Elvas preserved greengages from Elvas (Alentejo)
ameixa seca prune
amêndoas almonds
amêndoas doces sugared almonds
amendoim peanut
amora blackberry
ananás pineapple
anchovas anchovies
aniz aniseed liqueur
ao in the style of
aperitivo aperitif
areias de Cascais small cookies from Cascais
arenque herring
arjamolho kind of gazpacho soup, typical of the Algarve
arroz branco plain rice
arroz de Cabidela chicken or rabbit highly seasoned risotto
arroz de ervilhas pea rice
arroz de frango chicken with rice
arroz de lampreia lamprey with rice
arroz de lapas limpets with rice (typical of the Azores)
arroz de manteiga rice with butter
arroz de marisco shellfish with rice
arroz de pato rice with duck
arroz de polvo octopus with rice
arroz de tomate tomato rice
arroz doce rice pudding Portuguese-style made on top of the stove with lemon rind, vanilla and topped with cinnamon
arroz no forno rice cooked in the oven
arrufadas de Coimbra sweet buns from Coimbra
assado roasted
assado no espeto spit roasted
assado no forno oven-roasted
atum tuna fish
atum assado braised tuna with onions and tomatoes
atum de cebolada tuna steak with onions and tomato sauce
atum de conserva canned tuna
atum salpresado salted tuna dish often eaten during festivities in Madeira
aveia oats
avelã hazelnut
aves fowl
azeda sorrel
azedas sharp Azorean soups, containing a little vinegar
azedo sour
azeite olive oil
azeitonas olives
preta black
verde green
azevias half-moon shaped cakes

bacalhau salt cod
bacalhau à Brás traditional dish with salt cod, onion and potatoes all bound with scrambled eggs
bacalhau à Gomes de Sá good salt cod dish with layers of potatoes, onions and boiled eggs, laced with olive oil and baked
bacalhau à lagareiro salt cod baked with lots of olive oil
bacalhau assado charcoal-grilled cod
bacalhau com grão poached salt cod with boiled chickpeas, seasonings, olive oil and boiled egg
bacalhau com natas salt cod in cream sauce au gratin
bacalhau com todos salt cod poached with potatoes and vegetables
bacalhau na brasa salt cod grilled on charcoal, served with olive oil
bagaceira brandy similar to eau-de-vie
banana banana
banha lard
barriga de freira a sweet made with yolks and sugar, slightly caramelised
batata potato
batata doce sweet potato
batata doce assada baked sweet potato
batatas a murro potatoes baked in their own skins, crushed, then soaked in olive oil
batatas assadas baked potatoes
batatas cozidas boiled potatoes
batatas fritas chips
batido de fruta fruit milkshake
batido de morango strawberry milkshake
baunilha vanilla
bebida drink
bebida sem álcool/não alcoólica non-alcoholic drink
berbigão cockle
beringela aubergine
besugo sea bream
beterraba beetroot
bica strong small black coffee
bifana pork tenderloin in a roll
bife steak (and chips and perhaps fried egg)
...bem passado well done
...mal passado medium
...muito mal passado rare
bife à café steak in cream sauce topped with a fried egg (with chips)
bife à Portuguesa steak in mustard sauce topped with a fried egg (with chips)
bife com batatas fritas steak and chips
bife do lombo sirloin steak
bifes de atum tuna steaks
bifes de peru turkey steaks
bifinhos de vitela veal fillet served with Madeira sauce
biscoitos cookies
biscoitos de azeite olive oil biscuits
bitoque small steak with fried egg and chips

bola layered bread and cured meat pie
bola de Berlim doughnut
bolachas biscuits
bolachas de água e sal water biscuits (crackers)
boleimas cakes with a bread dough base with olive oil, sugar, eggs and spices
bolinhos de bacalhau cod croquettes
bolo caseiro homemade cake
bolo de chocolate chocolate cake
bolo de mel honey cake
bolo de mel da Madeira Madeira molasses cake made with lots of spices and traditionally eaten at Christmas
bolo de Natal Christmas fruitcake
bolo podre delicious dark cake made with honey, olive oil and spices
bolo rei a cake-ring made with a sweet dough with dried and crystallised fruits, eaten at Epiphany
bolos cakes
bolos de Dom Rodrigo cakes made with egg yolks, sugar, almonds and cinnamon, and sold in little pointed foil parcels to keep the syrup inside
bolos de ovos egg cakes
borracho young pigeon
borrego young (Spring) lamb
branco white
cerveja branca white beer
vinho branco white wine
broa a crusty rustic maize bread
broas de mel small honey cakes eaten at Christmas
broas podres de Natal small spicy cakes eaten at Christmas
brócolos broccoli
Bucelas famous white wine from the Estremadura region
bucho pork haggis
cabrito kid
cabrito à ribatejana marinated roast kid with paprika typical of Ribatejo
cabrito assado roast kid with a spiced marinade
cabrito frito fried kid
cabrito montês roebuck
caça game
cacau cocoa
cachorro hotdog
cachucho small sea bream
café coffee
bica small, strong black coffee (espresso)
carioca small but slightly weaker black coffee
com leite white coffee
duplo large cup of black coffee
frio iced coffee
galão large white coffee served in a tall glass
garoto small white coffee
meia de leite ordinary size cup of half coffee, half milk
sem cafeína decaffeinated

caju cashew nut
caldeirada fish stew
caldeirada à fragateira seafood stew, as prepared by fishermen
caldeirada de enguias eel stew
caldeirada de peixe fish stew
caldo broth
caldo de carne beef broth
caldo de galinha chicken broth
caldo verde green broth, made with shredded kale and potatoes with a little **chouriço** and olive oil
camarões shrimps
caneca medium-sized beer glass
canela cinnamon
canja chicken soup, thickened with rice or small pasta and chicken pieces
capão capon
capilé drink made with iced coffee, lemon rind and sugar
caracóis snails (small, cooked in a tasty broth and served with a toothpick)
caranguejo crab
carapau horse mackerel, served whole, fried or grilled
caril curry
carioca small weak coffee
carioca de limão lemon infusion
carne meat
carne assada roast meat (generally beef, sometimes pork)
carne de porco à alentejana highly seasoned pork dish with clams, typical of the Alentejo
carne de vaca beef
carne de vaca à antiga marinated roast beef, served with new potatoes (speciality from the Azores)
carne de vaca assada roast beef
carne de vinha d'alhos popular festive Madeiran dish, with marinated pork, bread, sweet and new potatoes
carneiro mutton
carnes frias cold meats
carta dos vinhos winelist
casa de chá tea-house
casa de pasto restaurant serving cheap, homely meals
castanha chestnut
castanhas assadas roasted chestnuts
castanhas cozidas boiled chestnuts with aniseed
cataplana meat, fish or shellfish dish cooked with potatoes and a tomato sauce in a cataplana pot
cavala mackerel
cavalas com molho de vilão marinated and fried mackerel, served with a reduced marinade (Madeiran speciality)
cebola onion
cebolada fried onion garnish
cenoura carrot
sopa de puré de cenoura carrot purée soup
cereja cherry
cerveja beer/lager
cerveja à pressão draught beer
cerveja em garrafa bottled beer

cerveja preta dark ale
cervejaria beer house, serving food
chá tea
chá com leite tea with milk
chá com limão tea with lemon
chá de ervas/tisana herb tea
chá forte strong tea
chanfana rich lamb/kid stew
chanfana da Bairrada kid stew
cherne species of grouper with dark skin, a very prized fish normally served grilled
chicória endive
chila or **gila** type of pumpkin (spaghetti squash) made into jam, used as a filling for many cakes and desserts all over Portugal
chispalhada pig's trotters stew
chispe com feijão trotters with beans, cured meats and vegetables
chocolate chocolate
chocolate frio cold chocolate
chocolate quente hot chocolate
chocos com tinta cuttlefish in its own ink
choquinhos squid
choquinhos com tinta squid in its ink
chouriço spicy smoked sausage
chuchu marrow
churrasco barbecued/cooked on charcoal
churrasqueira restaurant specialising in **frango à piri-piri** (chicken with piri-piri)
clarete light red wine
coco coconut
codorniz quail
coelho rabbit
coelho à caçadora hunter's rabbit or hare, cooked in wine and herbs
coentrada with fresh coriander
coentros fresh coriander
cogumelos mushrooms
Colares a famous wine from the Estremadura region
colorau sweet paprika
comidas meals
cominho cumin seed
compota jam or compote
congro conger eel
conhaque cognac
conta bill
copo glass
coração heart
cordeiro (young) lamb
costeletas de porco pork chops
costeletas de porco grelhadas grilled pork chops
couve cabbage
couve-de-bruxelas brussels sprouts
couve-flor cauliflower
couve-lombarda savoy cabbage
couve portuguesa Portuguese cabbage (a large and very tender cabbage), commonly used to accompany poached fish, when in season
couve-roxa red cabbage
covilhetes de leite custard tarts from the Azores
cozido boiled or poached
cozido à Madeirense boiled

Madeira-style pork and vegetables, with pumpkin and couscous
cozido à portuguesa boiled assorted meats, vegetables and rice, served in a large platter
cravinhos cloves
creme custard
creme de leite milk custard
criação fowl
croissants com fiambre ham-filled croissants
croissants recheados filled croissants
croquetes de carne meat croquettes
cru raw
cuba livre rum and coke
damasco apricot
digestivo digestive e.g. brandy
dobrada tripe
dobrada à moda do Porto tripe Oporto fashion in a bean stew
DOC (denominação de origem controlada) denotes a very good wine
doce sweet
doces de amêndoa marzipan sweets
doce de fruta jam
doce de laranja marmalade
dourada sea bream
eirós large eel generally fried and served with an **escabeche** sauce
ementa menu
empadão de batata shepherd's pie
empadas small chicken or veal pies
endívia endive
enguias de caldeirada eel stew, typical of Aveiro
enguias fritas fried eels
ensopado fish or meat stew served on bread slices
ensopado de borrego rich lamb stew served on bread slices
entradas starters
entrecosto entrecôte steak
erva-doce aniseed
ervilhas peas
ervilhas com paio e ovos peas with garlic sausage and poached eggs
escabeche a special sauce containing vinegar, normally served with cold fried fish
escalfado poached
ovo escalfado poached egg
espada the name given in Madeira to **peixe espada** (scabbard fish)
espadarte swordfish
espadarte fumado smoked swordfish
esparguete spaghetti
espargos asparagus
esparregado spinach purée with garlic
especiarias spices
esperanças delicate cakes from the Azores, filled with almonds
espetada kebab
esplanada open-air restaurant/café
espinafre spinach
espumante sparkling wine (champagne type)

estragão tarragon
estufado braised
carne estufada braised meat
esturjão sturgeon
extra-seco extra-dry
farinha flour
farinheira sausage made with flour and pork fat
farófias 'floating islands' made with egg whites and custard sauce
fartes de batata square cakes of sweet potato purée with spices and almonds
fataça grey mullet
fatias de Tomar sponge slices served in a light syrup
fatias douradas slices of bread dipped in egg, fried and covered with sugar and cinnamon
favada à portuguesa broad beans cooked with smoked meats, onions and coriander
favas broad beans
febras thin slices of roast pork
febras de porco à alentejana pork fillet with onions, chouriço and bacon
feijão beans
feijão encarnado red beans
feijão frade black-eyed beans
feijão guisado beans stewed with bacon in a tomato sauce
feijão preto black beans
feijão verde cozido boiled French beans
feijoada bean stew with pork meat and **chouriço**
fiambre ham
fígado liver
fígado de coentrada pork liver with coriander
fígado de galinha chicken liver
fígado de porco de cebolada pork liver with onions
figos figs
figos cheios dried figs stuffed with almonds
figos secos dried figs
filetes de pescada hake fillet in batter
filhós fritters eaten at Christmas
filhós de abóbora pumpkin purée fritters eaten at Christmas
filhoses festive fried cakes sprinkled with sugar and cinnamon or dipped into honey or syrup
fofas do Faial choux-type pastry filled with cream or custard, typical of the Azores
folar a sweet loaf with spices, topped with boiled eggs and eaten at Easter
folhados de carne meat puff-pastries
framboesa raspberry
frango young chicken
frango à piri-piri barbecued tender chicken with chilli
frango assado roast tender chicken
frango no churrasco barbecued tender chicken in a hot sauce (piri-piri)
fresco/a cold or fresh

uma cerveja muito fresca a very cool beer
fressura de porco guisada pork offal casserole
fricassé meat or fish (generally chicken) served with an egg and lemon sauce
frio cold
fritada de peixe deep-fried mixed fish
frito fried
fruta fruit
fruta cristalizada candied fruit
fruta da época fruit in season
fruta em calda fruit in syrup
fumado smoked
salmão fumado smoked salmon
fundo de alcachofra artichoke heart
galheteiro cruet stand
galinha chicken
galinhola woodcock
galinhola à Alentejana Alentejo woodcock, cooked with wine, garlic and seasonings, with a tasty filling
galão milky coffee served in a large glass
gambas large prawns
gambas na chapa large prawns cooked on the hot plate
ganso goose
garoto small white coffee
garoupa grouper
garoupa recheada stuffed and baked grouper, a typical dish from the Azores
garrafa bottle
gasosa soft drink with gas
gaspacho cold soup with finely cut vegetables
gelado ice-cream
geleia jelly
gelo ice
gengibre ginger
gim gin
ginjinha morello-cherry liqueur typical of Portugal
girafa beer glass (equivalent to a pint)
goiaba guava
granizado de café iced coffee
grão chickpeas
gratinado au gratin
grelhado grilled
grelhado misto mixed grill
groselha red currant
guisado stewed
hortaliça generic name given to vegetables
sopa de hortaliça vegetable soup
hortelã mint
chá de hortelã mint tea
hortelã-pimenta peppermint
imperial small beer glass
incluído included
inhame yam, very popular on some of the Azores islands
iscas traditional pork liver dish made with wine and garlic
iscas com elas well-seasoned liver dish served with boiled potatoes, a Lisbon speciality
jantar dinner

jardineira mixed vegetables
jarro carafe
javali wild boar
jeropiga fortified dessert wine
Joaquinzinhos small horse-mackerel fried whole (like white-bait), very popular in some restaurants
lagosta lobster
lagostim-do-rio freshwater crayfish
lagostins king prawns
lampreia lamprey (an eel-like fish)
lampreia de ovos egg lamprey, a rich dessert
lanche afternoon snack consisting of tea and cakes or buttered toast
lapas limpets, popular in Madeira and the Azores
lapas Afonso limpets served with a tasty onion sauce
laranja orange
laranja descascada peeled orange, normally served with a sprinkle of sugar
laranjada fizzy orange
laranjada engarrafada bottled orange juice
lavagante species of lobster
lebre hare
legumes vegetables
leitão assado à moda da Bairrada crisply roasted suckling pig from the Bairrada region
leite milk
leite-creme crème brûlée
leite frio/quente cold/hot milk
lentilha lentil
licor de leite milk liqueur
licor de tangerina mandarin liqueur
lima lime
limão lemon
limonada lemonade
língua tongue
língua estufada braised tongue
linguado sole
linguado frito fried sole
linguado grelhado grilled sole
linguiça pork sausage with paprika
lista dos vinhos wine list
lombinho de porco pork loin
lombo de porco pork fillet
louro bay leaf
lulas squid
lulas à Algarvia squid in garlic, Algarve style
lulas cheias local name in the Algarve for **lulas recheadas** (stuffed squid)
lulas guisadas stewed squid
lulas recheadas small squid stuffed with rice and seasonings
maçã apple
maçã assada large baked russet apple
maçapão marzipan
macarrão macaroni
macedónia de frutas mixed fruit salad
madeira wine from Madeira
maduro mature
maionese mayonnaise
malagueta hot pepper
mal passado rare
mandioca cassava root

manga mango
manjar celeste sweet made with eggs, bread crumbs, almonds and sugar
manjericão basil
manteiga butter
mãozinhas de vitela guisadas stewed calves' trotters
maracujá passion fruit
marinado/a marinated
marisco shellfish
marisqueira a restaurant or bar specialising solely in shellfish
marmelada quince jam – excellent with cheese
marmelo quince, a popular fruit, often baked
massa pasta
medalhão medallion
medronheira strawberry-tree fruit liqueur
meia-dose half-portion
meia garrafa half bottle
meio-doce medium-sweet
meio-seco medium-dry
mel honey
mel de cana molasses
melancia watermelon
melão melon
melão com presunto melon with cured ham slices, a starter
menu turístico budget tourists' menu, good value menu based on local dishes
merenda afternoon snack consisting of tea and cakes or buttered toast
merendinha pastry filled with **chouriço** or **presunto** (ham)
merengue meringue
mero red grouper fish
mexilhões mussels
migas bread cooked with well-seasoned ingredients to form a kind of omelette
migas à alentejana thick bread soup with pork meat and garlic
migas à lagareiro bread cooked with cabbage, salt cod and olive oil
migas de pão de milho thick maize bread soup with olive oil and garlic
mil-folhas millefeuille (custard pastry)
milho corn (maize)
milho doce sweetcorn
milho frito polenta fried in cubes, popular in Madeira
miolos brains
misto mixed
molho sauce
molho béchamel béchamel sauce
molho de caril curry sauce
molho de escabeche a special sauce containing vinegar, normally served with cold fried fish
molho de tomate tomato sauce
molho tártaro piquant mayonnaise with capers, gherkins and olives
morangos strawberries
morcela spicy black pudding
morgado de figo dried pressed figs with spices

moscatel de Setúbal medium-sweet muscat wine
mostarda mustard
mousse de chocolate chocolate mousse
nabiça turnip greens
nabo turnip
...na brasa char-grilled
...na cataplana stewed in cataplana vessel (typical double-wok pot used in the Alentejo and Algarve)
...na frigideira sautéed or fried
nata batida whipped cream
natas cream
natural plain, without dressing or served at room temperature (usually wine or water)
...no espeto kebab/on the spit
...no forno roasted or cooked in the oven
nozes walnuts
nozes de Cascais caramelised walnuts, from Cascais
óleo vegetable oil
omeleta de cogumelos mushroom omelette
omeleta de fiambre ham omelette
omeleta de queijo cheese omelette
omeleta simples plain omelette
ostras oysters
ouriço-do-mar sea-urchin
ovas fish roe
ovos eggs
ovos cozidos boiled eggs
ovos escalfados poached eggs
ovos estrelados fried eggs
ovos mexidos scrambled eggs
ovos moles soft egg sweet
ovos quentes soft-boiled eggs
paio thick smoked sausage made with lean meat
palha de Abrantes sweet made with eggs, looking like straw
panados slices of meat coated in egg and breadcrumbs and fried
pão bread
pão de centeio rye bread
pão de forma sliced bread for toast
pão-de-ló light sponge cake
pão de milho maize bread
pão saloio country-style bread
pãozinho roll
papaia papaya
papas polenta soup
papas de milho doces sweet polenta
papo seco bread roll
papos de anjo small egg cakes with syrup
pargo red bream
parrilhada grilled fish
passas de uva raisins
pastéis tarts, cakes, pasties
pastéis de arroz rice tarts from the Azores
pastéis de bacalhau salt cod cakes
pastéis de carne meat pasties
pastéis de feijão tarts made with beans, eggs and almonds

pastéis de nata/de Belém egg custard tarts from Belém (Lisbon)
pastéis de Santa Clara pastries with a filling of almonds, egg yolk and sugar
pastéis de Tentugal small pastries with an egg filling
pastelaria pâtisserie/pastry shop
pastel de massa tenra meat pasty
pataniscas (de bacalhau) salt cod fritters
paté de fígado liver pâté
pato duck
pato assado com arroz roast duck with rice
pé de porco com feijão pigs' trotters with beans
peito breast
peixe fish
peixe assado/cozido/frito/grelhado baked/poached/fried/grilled fish
peixe e marisco fish and shellfish
peixe espada scabbard fish
peixe espada frito fried scabbard fish
peixe espada grelhado grilled scabbard fish
peixe-galo John Dory
peixinhos da horta French beans fried in batter
pepino cucumber
pequeno almoço breakfast
pêra pear
percebes barnacles, highly prized shellfish
perdiz partridge
perdiz à Montemor Montemor-style partridge, cooked with wine and spices
perdiz com couve lombarda partridge with cabbage
perna leg
perna de porco o forno roast leg of pork
pernil ham
peru turkey
pescada hake
pescada com todos hake poached with potatoes and vegetables
pescadinhas de rabo na boca whole rolled-up small fried hake
pêssego peach
pêssego careca nectarine
petisco savoury or snack
pezinhos de porco de coentrada pork trotters with coriander and garlic
picante spicy
pimenta pepper (spice)
pimentos peppers
pimentos assados grilled peppers
pinhão pine kernel
pinhoada pinenut brittle
pinhões peanuts
piri-piri chilli sauce
polvo octopus
polvo grelhado grilled octopus
polvo guisado stewed octopus
pombo pigeon

porco pork
porco à alentejana traditional dish with pork, clams and herbs
porco assado roast pork
porco preto black pork, only available at certain times of the year and has a completely different taste to ordinary **leitão**, roast suckling pig
posta à mirandesa spit-roasted veal, Miranda-style
pouco picante mild
prato dish
prato do dia dish of the day
prato principal main dish
pratos de carne meat dishes
preço price
pregado turbot
prego steak in a roll
prego com fiambre steak with sliced ham
prego no pão steak roll
prego no prato steak with fried egg and chips served on a plate
presunto cured ham
preta dark
cerveja preta dark beer
pudim Abade de Priscos rich egg pudding flavoured with port and lemon
pudim de bacalhau salt cod loaf served with tomato sauce
pudim da casa restaurant's own dessert (often crème caramel)
pudim de coalhada popular Azorean rich, fresh cheese pudding
pudim de pão bread pudding
pudim de queijo cheese pudding
pudim de requeijão ricotta-type cheese pudding
pudim flan crème caramel
pudim Molotov egg-white pudding with egg sauce or caramel
puré de batata mashed potato
queijadas de Évora cheese tarts made with cheese from ewes' milk
queijadas da Madeira small Madeiran cheese cakes
queijadas de requeijão ricotta-type cheese tarts
queijadas de Sintra little cheese cakes with cinnamon made in Sintra
queijinhos de amêndoa little almond cheeses
queijinhos do céu egg yolk and sugar sweets
queijinhos frescos small, delicious fresh cheeses (cows', ewes' or goats' milk)
queijinhos secos small dried cheeses
queijo cheese
queijo cabreiro goats' cheese
queijo cardiga cheese made from ewes' and goats' milk
queijo fresco fresh cheese
queijo da Ilha cheddar-type cheese from the Azores, also known as **queijo de São Jorge**
queijo da Serra buttery cheese from Estrela Mountain, a soft, runny cheese made with ewes' milk

queijo de Alverca small cheese from Alverca, near Lisbon
queijo de Azeitão hard or soft cheese made with ewes' milk
queijo de cabra goats' cheese
queijo de Évora small ewes' cheese from Évora
queijo de Nisa a rich ewe's cheese from Nisa (Alentejo)
queijo de ovelha small, dried ewes' milk cheeses
queijo saloio small cheese made with ewes' milk or a mixture of goats' and ewes' milk
quente hot
quiabo okra
rabaçal mild cheese from the Coimbra region
rabanada french toast
rabanete radish
raia skate
rancho a substantial soup
recheado com... stuffed/filled with...
recheio stuffing
regiões demarcadas demarcated wine regions
repolho cabbage
requeijão fresh curd cheese resembling ricotta
rim (rins) kidney
rins à Madeira kidneys served in Madeira wine sauce
rins com vinho do Porto kidneys in port wine sauce
rissóis de camarão/peixe shrimp or fish rissoles
robalo sea bass
rojões crisp pieces of marinated pork
romãs pomegranate
sal salt
salada salad
salada de feijão frade black-eyed bean salad, with boiled egg, olive oil and seasonings
salada de fruta fruit salad
salada de polvo a starter with cold octopus, seasoned with olive oil, coriander, onion and vinegar
salada mista mixed salad (tomato, lettuce, cucumber, onion)
salada russa Russian salad
salgados savouries (snacks)
salmão salmon
salmão fumado smoked salmon
salmonetes grelhados grilled red mullet in a butter and lemon sauce
saloio small cheese made from ewes' or goats' milk, often served as a pre-starter to a meal in the Lisbon region
salpicão slices of large **chouriço**
salsa parsley
salsichas sausages
salteado sautéed
salva sage
sandes sandwich
sandes de fiambre cooked ham sandwich
sandes de lombo roast loin of pork sandwich
sandes de presunto cured ham sandwich

sandes de queijo cheese sandwich
sandes mista ham and cheese sandwich
santola spider crab
sapateira crab (generally dressed)
sarapatel a highly seasoned Madeiran dish made with pork blood and liver
sarda mackerel
sardinhas assadas char-grilled sardines
sardinhas na telha oven-baked sardines cooked on a roof tile with olive oil and seasoning
sável shad
seco dry
sericaia baked custard with cinnamon
serpa a type of ewes' milk cheese from the Alentejo region
serra a creamy cheese made from ewes' milk, from the Serra da Estrela region
serviço incluído service included
sidra cider
simples neat (as in 'neat whisky')
sobremesas desserts
solha plaice
sonho doughnut-type small fried cake, dipped in sugar and cinnamon
sopa soup
sopa à alentejana soup Alentejo-style, made with chunks of bread, olive oil, fresh coriander and garlic, topped with poached egg
sopa azeda de feijão bean soup with vegetables and bread, sweet potatoes, cinnamon and a spoonful of vinegar (Azores)
sopa de cabeça de peixe fish head soup, using the head of a large fish, tomatoes, potatoes, stale bread and seasonings (Algarve)
sopa de camarão prawn soup
sopa de castanhas piladas hearty soup made with dried chestnuts, beans and rice
sopa de ervilhas pea soup
sopa de espinafres spinach soup
sopa de feijão bean soup with vegetables
sopa de feijão frade black-eyed bean soup
sopa de feijão verde green bean soup
sopa de funcho fennel soup with beans and bacon fat (Azores)
sopa de grão chickpea soup
sopa de legumes vegetable soup
sopa de marisco shellfish soup
sopa de moganga Madeiran pumpkin soup
sopa de pedra a rich soup with lots of meat, beans and vegetables
sopa de peixe fish soup
sopa de poejos pennyroyal soup with eggs (Alentejo)
sopa de rabo de boi oxtail soup
sopa de tomate tomato soup
sopa do dia soup of the day

sopa do Espírito Santo 'Holy Spirit' soup made with meats, vegetables, bread, herbs and spices (Azores)
sopa dos campinos salt cod and tomato soup
sopa dourada dessert made with egg yolks
sopa e um papo-seco soup and roll
sopa seca thick bread soup with meats
sorvete sorbet
sumo de fruta fruit juice
ananás pineapple
laranja orange
maçã apple
pêra pear
pêssego peach
tomate tomato
uva grape
suspiros meringues
tainha grey mullet
tâmara date
tamboril monkfish
tangerina mandarin
tarte de amêndoa almond tart
tarte de limão lemon tart
tarte de maçã apple tart
tasca small taverna serving cheap food and drink
tasquinha small taverna serving cheap food and drink
tempero seasoning
tenro tender
tibornas slices of freshly baked bread sprinkled with coarse sea salt and olive oil
tigeladas de Abrantes individually baked custards in special cups
tinto red wine
tisana herbal tea
tisana de camomila camomile tea
tisana de Lúcia-Lima vervaine tea
tomate tomato
toranja grapefruit
tornedó prime cut of beef
torradas toast
Torres Vedras red wine from the Estremadura region
torta swiss roll
torta de laranja orange sponge roll
torta de Viana a sponge roll filled with a rich egg sweet
tosta toasted sandwich
tosta de queijo toasted cheese sandwich
tosta mista ham and cheese toasted sandwich
toucinho bacon
toucinho do céu 'bacon from heaven', an egg and almond pudding
tremoços lupin seeds, commonly consumed with beer
tripas à moda do Porto tripe stew with beans and various meats, Oporto-style
trufa truffle
truta trout
trutas à moda do Minho trout cooked in wine and rich seasonings

truta de Barroso traditional northern dish of fried trout stuffed with ham
tutano marrow
uísque whisky
uvas grapes
vaca beef
vagens runner beans
variado assorted
verdelho local Azorean wine
vermute vermouth
vieira scallop
vinagre vinegar
vinha d'alhos marinated in wine and garlic
vinho abafado locally made fortified wine
vinho adamado sweet wine
vinho branco white wine
vinho branco seco dry white wine
vinho branco meio-seco medium-dry white wine
vinho da casa house wine
vinho espumante sparkling wine
vinho generoso fortified wine
vinho Moscatel muscat wine
vinho regional/da região local wine
vinho tinto red wine
vinho tinto encorpado full-bodied red wine, ideal with red meats
vinho tinto meio-encorpado medium-bodied red wine, ideal with salted fish dishes or light meats
vinho tinto velho mature red wine, ideal with red meats
vinho verde dry, sparkling 'green' wine made with slightly unripe grapes from the Minho region
vinhos da Madeira madeira wines
vinhos do Porto port wines
vinhos espumantes sparkling wines
vitela veal
vitela no espeto veal cooked on the spit
xarope syrup
xarope de groselha blackcurrant syrup
xarope de morango strawberry syrup
xerez sherry

Grammar

Nouns

A noun is a word such as 'car', 'horse' or 'Mary', which is used to refer to a person or thing. Portuguese nouns are masculine or feminine, and their gender is shown by the words for 'the' (**o/a**) and 'a' (**um/uma**) used before them (the article):

masculine/plural	feminine/plural
o/um castelo the/a castle	**a/uma mesa** the/a table
os castelos the castles	**as mesas** the tables
(uns) castelos (some) castles	**(umas) mesas** (some) tables

It is usually possible to tell whether a noun is masculine or feminine by its ending: nouns ending in **-o** or **-or** are usually masculine, while those ending in **-a**, **-agem**, **-dade** and **-tude** tend to be feminine. There are exceptions, however, and it's best to learn the noun and the article together.

Plurals

Nouns ending in a vowel form the plural by adding **-s**, while those ending in a consonant usually add **-es**. The exceptions to this are words ending in an **-m** which change to **-ns** in the plural and words ending in **-l** which change to **-is** in the plural: e.g. **hotel - hotéis**.

Note: When used after the words **a** (to), **de** (of), **em** (in) and **por** (by), the articles (and many other words) contract:

a + as = às	ash	to the
de + um = dum	dooñ	of a
em + uma = numa	**noo**-muh	in a
por + os = pelos	**pel**-oosh	by the

This, that, these, those

These depend on the gender and number of the noun they represent:

este rapaz	this boy	**esta rapariga**	this girl
estes rapazes	these boys	**estas raparigas**	these girls
esse rapaz*	that boy	**essa rapariga**	that girl
esses rapazes*	those boys	**essas raparigas**	those girls
aquele rapaz+	that boy	**aquela rapariga**	that girl
aqueles rapazes+	those boys	**aquelas raparigas**	those girls

* 'That/those' when referring to what is near to the person you are addressing.

+ 'That/those' when referring to what is not close to the person you are addressing.

Adjectives

An adjective is a word such as 'small', 'pretty' or 'practical', that describes a person or thing, or gives extra information about them. Adjectives normally follow the nouns they describe in Portuguese, e.g. **a maçã verde** the green apple.

Some exceptions which go before the noun are:

muito much, many	**último** last
pouco little, not much	**bom** good
tanto so much, so many	**nenhum** no, not any
primeiro first	**grande*** great, big

* When before the noun = great; when after = big.

Portuguese adjectives have to reflect the gender of the noun they describe. To make an adjective feminine, **-o** endings change to **-a**, and -**or** and -**ês** change to -**ora** and -**esa**. Otherwise they generally have the same form for both genders. Thus:

masculine	feminine
o livro vermelho	**a saia vermelha**
the red book	the red skirt
o homem falador	**a mulher faladora**
the talkative man	the talkative woman

To make adjectives plural, follow the general rules given for nouns.

My, your, his, her

These words also depend on the gender and number of the following noun and not on the sex of the 'owner'.

	with masc./fem.	with plural nouns
my	**o meu/a minha**	**os meus/as minhas**
his/her/its/your	**o seu/a sua**	**os seus/as suas**
our	**o nosso/a nossa**	**os nossos/as nossas**
their/your (plural)	**o seu/a sua**	**os seus/as suas**

Note: Since **o seu**, **a sua**, etc can mean his, her, your, etc, Portuguese will often replace them with the words for: of him, of her, of you, etc (**dele**, **dela**, **de você**, etc) in order to avoid confusion:

os livros *dela*	her books
os livros *de você*	your books
os livros *deles*	their books

Pronouns

A pronoun is a word that you use to refer to someone or something when you don't need to use a noun, often because the person/thing has been mentioned earlier e.g. 'it', 'she', 'something' and 'myself'.

subject		object	
I	**eu**	me	**me**
you (informal)	**tu**	you (informal)	**te**
you	**você**	you	**o/**
he	**ele**	him	**o**
she	**ela**	her	**a**
it	**ele/ela**	it	**o/a**
we	**nós**	us	**nos**
you	**vós**	you	**vos**
they (masc.)	**eles**	them (masc.)	**os**
they (fem.)	**elas**	them (fem.)	**as**
you (informal)	**vocês**	you (informal)	**os/as**

Notes

1 **YOU** The polite form of addressing someone would be with **o Senhor** or **a Senhora** using the **(s)he** form or the verb and the object pronoun **o/a**. The semi-formal **you** is **você** and the informal **you** is **tu** (like French and Spanish).

2 Subject pronouns are normally not used except for emphasis or to avoid confusion:
_eu_ vou para Lisboa e _ele_ vai para Coimbra
I'm going to Lisbon and he's going to Coimbra'

3 Object pronouns are usually placed after the verb and joined with a hyphen:

vejo-_o_	I see him

However, in sentences beginning with a 'question word' or a 'negative word' the pronoun goes in front of the verb:

quando _o_ viu?	when did you see him?
não _o_ vi	I did not see him

Also, in sentences beginning with 'that' and 'who', etc. (subordinate clauses), the pronoun precedes the verb:

sei que _o_ viu	I know that you saw him
o homem que _o_ viu	the man who saw him

4 **Me** also = to me and **nos** = to us, but **lhe** = to him/to her/to it/ to you (formal), **te** = to you (informal) and **lhes** = to them/to you (plural).

5 When two pronouns are used together they are often shortened. The verb will also change spelling if it ends in **-r**, **-s**, **-z** or a nasal sound:

dá-mo (= dá + me + o)	he gives me it
dê-lho (= dê + lhe + o)	give him it
fá-lo (= faz + o)	he does it
dão-nos(= dão + os or **dão + nos)**	they give them or they give us

6 The pronoun following a preposition has the same form as the subject pronoun, except for **mim** (me), **si** (you – formal), **ti** (you – informal).

Verbs

A verb is a word such as ‘sing’, ‘walk’ or ‘cry’ which is used with a subject to say what someone or something does or what happens to them. Regular verbs follow the same pattern of endings. Irregular verbs do not follow a regular pattern.

There are three main patterns of endings for verbs in Portuguese – those ending **-ar**, **-er** and **-ir** in the dictionary.

Verbs ending in **-ar**

cantar	**to sing**
canto	I sing
cantas	you sing
canta	(s)he/it sings/you sing
cantamos	we sing
cantais	you sing
cantam	they/you sing

Verbs ending in -er

comer	**to eat**
como	I eat
comes	you eat
come	(s)he/it eats/you eat
comemos	we eat
comeis	you eat
comem	they/you eat

Verbs ending in -ir

partir	**to leave**
parto	I leave
partes	you leave
parte	(s)he/it leaves/you leave
partimos	we leave
partis	you leave
partem	they/you leave

Four of the most common verbs are irregular:

ser	**to be**	estar	**to be**
sou	I am	estou	I am
és	you are	estás	you are
é	(s)he/it is/you are	está	(s)he/it is/you are
somos	we are	estamos	we are
sois	you are	estais	you are
são	they/you are	estão	they/you are

ter	**to have**	ir	**to go**
tenho	I have	vou	I go
tens	you have	vais	you go
tem	(s)he/it has/you have	vai	(s)he/it goes/you go
temos	we have	vamos	we go
tendes	you have	ides	you go
têm	they/you have	vão	they/you go

Note: Ser and Estar both mean **to be**.

Ser is used to describe a permanent place or state:

sou inglês	I am English
é uma praia	it is a beach

Estar is used to describe a temporary state or where something is located:

como está?	how are you?
onde está o livro?	where is the book?

Past tense

Verbs ending in **-ar**

cantei	I sang
cantaste	you sang
cantou	(s)he/it/you sang
cantámos	we sang
cantastes	you sang
cantaram	they/you sang

Verbs ending in **-er**

comi	I ate
comeste	you ate
comeu	(s)he/it/you ate
comemos	we ate
comestes	you ate
comeram	they/you ate

Verbs ending in **-ir**

parti	I left
partiste	you left
partiu	(s)he/it/you left
partimos	we left
partistes	you left
partiram	they/you left

Dictionary

A

a um (uma)
abbey a abadia
able: ***to be able (to)*** poder
abortion o aborto
about (roughly) mais ou menos
a book about... um livro sobre...
about ten o'clock por volta das dez
above acima de
abroad adv no estrangeiro
to go abroad ir ao estrangeiro
abscess um abcesso
accelerator o acelerador
accent o acento
(pronunciation) a pronúncia
to accept aceitar
(approve of) aprovar
access o acesso
wheelchair access o acesso para cadeiras de rodas
accident o acidente
accommodation o alojamento
to accompany acompanhar
account (bill) a conta
(in bank) a conta (bancária)
account number o número da conta
accountant o/a contabilista
to ache doer
it aches dói-me
my head aches dói-me a cabeça
acid o ácido
actor/actress o actor/a actriz
to adapt adaptar
adaptor (electrical) o adaptador
adder a cobra
address a morada
what is your address? qual é a sua morada?
address book a agenda
admission charge/fee o preço de entrada
admit: ***to admit to hospital*** ingresar no hospital
adult o/a adulto(a)
for adults para adultos
advance: ***in advance*** antecipadamente
advertisement o anúncio
to advise aconselhar
aerial a antena
aeroplane o avião
aerosol o aerossol
afraid: ***to be afraid of*** ter medo de
after depois
after lunch depois do almoço
afternoon a tarde
in the afternoon à tarde
this afternoon esta tarde
tomorrow afternoon amanhã à tarde
aftershave o aftershave
again outra vez
against prep contra
I am against that sou contra isso
age a idade
old age a idade avançada
agency a agência
ago: ***2 days ago*** há 2 dias
to agree concordar
agreement o acordo
AIDS a SIDA
air bag o airbag
air bed o colchão de ar
air conditioning o ar condicionado
is there air conditioning? tem ar condicionado?
air freshener o purificador do ambiente
airline a linha aérea
airmail a via aérea
airplane o avião
airport o aeroporto
airport bus o autocarro do aeroporto
air ticket o bilhete de avião
aisle (plane, theatre, etc) a coxia
alarm o alarme
alarm clock o despertador
alcohol o álcool
alcohol-free sem álcool

alcoholic *adj* alcoólico(a)
all todo(a), todos(as)
allergic alérgico(a)
I'm allergic to sou alérgico(a) a
allergy a alergia
alley a travessa
to allow permitir
to be allowed ser permitido
all right está bem
are you all right? você está bem?
almond a amêndoa
almost quase
alone sozinho(a)
alphabet o alfabeto
already já
also também
altar o altar
aluminium foil a folha de alumínio
always sempre
a.m. da manhã
amber (light) amarelo(a)
ambulance a ambulância
America os Estados Unidos
American (norte-) americano/a
amount: ***total amount*** o total
anaesthetic a anestesia
general anaesthetic a anestesia geral
local anaesthetic a anestesia local
anchor a âncora
anchovy a anchova
ancient antigo(a)
and e
angel o anjo
angina a angina de peito
angry zangado(a)
animal o animal
aniseed a erva-doce
ankle o tornozelo
anniversary o aniversário
to announce anunciar
announcement o anúncio
annual anual
another um(a) outro(a)
another beer? mais uma cerveja?
answer *n* a resposta
to answer responder
answerphone o gravador de chamadas
ant a formiga
antacid o antiácido
antibiotic o antibiótico
antifreeze o anticongelante
antihistamine o anti-histamínico
anti-inflammatory o anti-inflamatório
antiques as antiguidades
antique shop a loja de antiguidades
antiseptic o antiséptico
any (some) algum(a)
(negative) nenhum(a)
have you any apples? tem maçãs?
I haven't any money não tenho dinheiro
anyone (in questions) alguém
(negative) ninguém
anything (in questions) alguma coisa
(negative) nada
I haven't got anything não tenho nada
anywhere (in any place at all) em qualquer parte
(negative) em nenhuma parte
I haven't seen him anywhere não o vi em nenhuma parte
apartment o apartamento
aperitif o aperitivo
appendicitis a apendicite
apple a maçã
application form o formulário de requerimento
appointment (meeting) o encontro
(doctor) a consulta
(hairdresser) a hora marcada
I have an appointment tenho un encontro marcado
approximately aproximadamente
apricot o damasco
April Abril
architect o/a arquitecto(a)
architecture a arquitectura
arm o braço
armbands (to swim) as braçadeiras
armchair a poltrona
aromatherapy a aromaterapia
to arrange organizar
to arrest prender
arrival a chegada

to arrive chegar
art a arte
art gallery a galeria de arte
arthritis a artrite
artichoke a alcachofra
artificial artificial
artist o/a artista
ashtray o cinzeiro
to ask (question) perguntar
(to ask for something) pedir
asparagus o espargo
asleep: *he/she is asleep* está adormecido(a)
aspirin a aspirina
soluble aspirin aspirina efervescente
asthma a asma
I have asthma tenho asma
at em; a
@ arroba
at 8 o'clock às oito
at home em casa
at once imediatamente
at night à noite
Atlantic Ocean o oceano Atlântico
ATM Multibanco®
to attack atacar
attractive (person) atraente
aubergine a beringela
auction o leilão
audience a platéia
August Agosto
aunt a tia
au pair o/a au pair
Australia a Austrália
Australian australiano(a)
author o/a autor(a)
automatic automático(a)
automatic car o carro automático
autumn o outono
available disponível
avalanche a avalancha
avenue a avenida
average a média; *adj* médio(a)
avocado o abacate
to avoid evitar
awake: *to be awake* estar acordado(a)
awful terrível
axle o eixo

B

baby o bebé
baby food a comida de bebé
baby milk o leite infantil
baby's bottle o biberão
baby seat (in car) o assento do bebé
baby-sitter o/a babysitter
baby-sitting service serviço de baby-sitting
baby wipes as toalhitas
bachelor o solteiro
back (of body) as costas
backache a dor de costas
backpack a mochila
back seat o assento traseiro
bacon o toucinho
bad (weather, news) mau (má)
(fruit, vegetables) podre
badminton o badminton
bag o saco
(handbag) o saco de mão
(case) a mala
baggage a bagagem
baggage allowance o peso limite da bagagem
baggage reclaim a recolha de bagagem
bait (for fishing) a isca
baked assado
baker's a padaria
balcony a varanda
bald (person) calvo(a); careca
(tyre) careca
ball a bola
ballet o ballet
balloon o balão
banana a banana
band (music) a banda musical
bandage a ligadura
bank o banco
(river) a margem
bank account a conta bancária
banknote a nota (bancária)
bankrupt falido(a)

bar o bar
bar of chocolate a barra de chocolate
barbecue o churrasco
to have a barbecue fazer um churrasco
barber o barbeiro
to bark ladrar
barn o celeiro
barrel o barril
basement a cave
basil o manjericão
basket o cesto
basketball o basquete(bol)
basketwork os artigos de vime
bat (animal) o morcego
(for table tennis) a raqueta
bath o banho
to have a bath tomar banho
bathing cap a touca de banho
bathroom a casa de banho
with bathroom com casa de banho
battery (for car) a bateria
(for torch, radio, etc) a pilha
bay a baía
bayleaf a folha de louro
B&B o quarto com pequeno-almoço
(place) a pensão
to be ser; estar
beach a praia
nudist beach a praia naturista
private beach a praia particular
sandy beach a praia arenosa
beach hut a barraca
bean o feijão
broad bean a fava
French/green bean o feijão verde
kidney bean o feijão encarnado
soya bean o feijão de soja
bear (animal) o urso
beard a barba
beautiful belo(a); lindo(a)
beauty salon o salão de beleza
because porque
to become tornar-se
bed a cama
double bed a cama de casal
single bed a cama de solteiro
sofa bed o sofá-cama
twin beds as camas separadas
bedding a roupa de cama
bedclothes a roupa de cama
bedroom o quarto
bee a abelha
beef a carne de vaca; a vitela (veal)
beer a cerveja
bottled beer a cerveja de garrafa
draught beer a imperial; o fino (in North)
beetroot a beterraba
before antes (de)
before breakfast antes do pequeno-almoço
beggar o/a mendigo(a)
to begin começar
behind atrás (de)
behind the bank atrás do banco
beige bege
to believe acreditar
bell (door) a campainha
(church) o sino
to belong to pertencer a
below debaixo (de)
(less than) abaixo (de)
belt o cinto
bend (in road) a curva
berth (in ship) o beliche
beside (next to) ao lado (de)
beside the bank ao lado do banco
best: the best o/a melhor
to bet on apostar em
better (than) melhor (do que)
between entre
bib o babador
bicycle a bicicleta
by bicycle de bicicleta
bicycle lock o cadeado da bicicleta
bicycle repair kit o estojo de ferramentas
bidet o bidé
big grande
bigger (than) maior (do que)
bike (motorbike) a moto
(pushbike) a bicicleta
mountain bike a bicicleta de montanha
bikini o bikini
bill (in hotel, restaurant) a conta

(for work done) a factura
(gas, telephone) a conta
bin o caixote do lixo
bin liner o saco do lixo
binoculars os binóculos
bird o pássaro
biro a esferográfica
birth o nascimento
birth certificate a certidão de nascimento
birthday o aniversário
happy birthday parabéns
my birthday is on... faço anos no...
birthday card o cartão de aniversário
birthday present a prenda de anos
biscuits as bolachas
bit: a bit (of) um bocado (de)
bite (snack) a merenda; o lanche
(of animal) a mordedura
(of insect) a picada
let's have a bite to eat vamos comer algo
to bite (animal) morder
(insect) picar
bitten (by animal) mordido(a)
(by insect) picado(a)
bitter amargo(a)
black preto(a)
blackberry a amora silvestre
blackcurrant a groselha
blank o espaço em branco
blanket o cobertor
bleach a lixívia
to bleed sangrar
blender (for food) o liquificador
blind (person) cego(a)
(for window) a persiana
blister a bolha
block of flats o prédio de apartamentos
blocked (pipe, sink) entupido(a)
(road) cortada ao trânsito
blond (person) louro(a)
blood o sangue
blood group o grupo sanguíneo
blood pressure a tensão arterial
blood test a análise ao sangue
blouse a blusa
blow-dry o brushing
to blow-dry fazer um brushing
blue azul
dark blue azul escuro
light blue azul claro
blunt (knife, etc) embotado(a)
boar o javali
boarding card o cartão de embarque
boarding house a pensão
boat o barco
boat trip a viagem de barco
body o corpo
to boil ferver
boiler a caldeira
boiled cozido(a)
bomb a bomba
bone o osso
fish bone a espinha
bonfire a fogueira
bonnet (of car) a capota
book o livro
book of tickets a caderneta de bilhetes
to book reservar
booking a reserva
booking office a bilheteira
bookshop a livraria
booster seat o banco de segurança para crianças
boot (of car) o porta-bagagem
boots as botas
border a fronteira
boring aborrecido(a)
boss o/a chefe
(employer) o patrão/a patroa
both ambos(as)
bottle a garrafa
a bottle of wine uma garrafa de vinho
a half bottle uma meia-garrafa
bottle opener o abre-garrafas
bowl (for washing) a bacia
(for food) a tigela
bow tie o laço
box a caixa
box office a bilheteira
boxer shorts os boxers
boy o rapaz
boyfriend o namorado

bra o soutien
bracelet a pulseira
brain o cérebro
to brake travar
brake fluid o óleo dos travões
brake light a luz de travagem
brake shoes as sapatas
brakes os travões
branch (of tree) o ramo
(of business, etc) a sucursal
brand (make) a marca
brandy o conhaque
brass o latão
bread o pão
French bread o cacete
sliced bread o pão de forma
wholemeal bread o pão integral
breadcrumbs o pão ralado
bread roll o papo-seco; pãozinho
to break quebrar
breakable frágil
breakdown (car) a avaria
(nervous) o colapso nervoso
breakdown service o pronto-socorro
breakdown van o pronto-socorro
breakfast o pequeno-almoço
breast (chicken) o peito
to breastfeed amamentar
to breathe respirar
brick o tijolo
bride a noiva
bridegroom o noivo
bridge a ponte
(game) o bridge
briefcase a pasta
bright brilhante
Brillo pad® a esponja de aço
brine a salmoura
to bring trazer
Britain a Grã-Bretanha
British britânico(a)
broad largo(a)
broccoli os brócolos
brochure a brochura
broken partido(a)
broken down (car, etc) avariado(a)
bronchitis a bronquite
bronze o bronze
brooch o broche
broom a vassoura
brother o irmão
brother-in-law o cunhado
brown castanho(a)
bruise a nódoa negra
brush a escova
Brussels sprouts as couves-de-Bruxelas
bubble bath a espuma para o banho
bucket o balde
buffet car o vagão restaurante
to build construir
building o edifício
building site o terreno de construção
bulb (light) a lâmpada
bull o touro
bullfight a tourada
bullfighter o toureiro
bullring a praça de touros
bumbag a carteira de cintura
bumper (on car) o pára-choques
bunch (of flowers) o ramo
(of grapes) o cacho
bungee jumping o bungee jumping
bureau de change a casa de câmbio
burger um hambúrguer
burglar o ladrão/a ladra
burglar alarm o alarme de roubo
burglary o roubo
to burn queimar
burnt (food) queimado(a)
burst rebentado(a)
bus o autocarro
bus pass o passe de autocarro
bus station a estação de autocarros
bus stop a paragem de autocarros
bus ticket o bilhete de autocarro
bus tour a excursão de autocarro
business os negócios
on business de negócios
business card o cartão-de-visita
business class a classe executiva
businessman/woman o homem/ a mulher de negócios
business trip a viagem de negócios

busy ocupado(a)
but mas
butcher's o talho
butter a manteiga
button o botão
to buy comprar
by por
(near) perto (de)
(next to) ao lado (de)
by bus de autocarro
by car de carro
by ship de barco
by train de comboio
bypass (road) o desvio

C

cab (taxi) o táxi
cabaret o cabaré
cabbage a couve
cabin (on boat) o camarote
cabin crew os tripulantes de cabine
cable car o teleférico
cable TV a televisão por cabo
café o café
internet café o cibercafé
cafetière a cafeteira
cake o bolo
cake shop a pastelaria
calamine lotion a loção de calamina
calculator a calculadora
calendar o calendário
calf (young cow) o vitelo
to call chamar
call (telephone) uma chamada
a long-distance call uma chamada interurbana
calm calmo(a); tranquilo(a)
camcorder a camcorder
camera a máquina fotográfica
camera case o estojo da máquina fotográfica
to camp acampar
camping gas o gás para campismo
camping stove o fogão portátil; o fogão de campismo
campsite o parque de campismo
can (verb – to be able) poder
can I...? posso...?
can we...? podemos...?
I/we can posso/podemos
I/we cannot não posso/podemos
can a lata
canned goods as conservas
can opener o abre-latas
Canada o Canadá
Canadian canadiano(a)
canal o canal
to cancel cancelar
cancellation o cancelamento
cancer o cancro
candle a vela
canoe a canoa
to go canoeing fazer canoagem
cap (hat) o boné
(diaphragm) o diafragma
capital (city) a capital
cappuccino o capuchino
car o carro
car alarm o alarme do carro
car ferry o barco de passagem
car hire o aluguer de automóveis
car insurance o seguro de automóveis
car keys as chaves do carro
car park o parque de estacionamento
car parts as peças sobressalentes
car radio o rádio do carro
car seat (for children) o assento para crianças
car wash a lavagem automática
carafe a garrafa; o jarro
caravan a caravana
carburettor o carburador
card (business) o cartão (de visita)
(greetings) o cartão
(playing) a carta de jogar
cardboard o cartão
cardigan o casaco de lã
careful cuidadoso(a)
be careful! cuidado!
to be careful ter cuidado
carnation o cravo
carpet a carpete; alcatifa
(rug) o tapete
carriage a carruagem

carrot a cenoura
to carry transportar
carton o pacote
case (suitcase) a mala
cash o dinheiro
to cash (cheque) levantar
cash desk a caixa
cashier o/a caixa
cash machine (ATM) a caixa automática
casino o casino
casserole (dish) o tacho
(meal) o guisado (no forno)
cassette a cassete
cassette player o toca-fitas
castle o castelo
casualty department o Serviço de Urgências
cat o gato
cat food a comida para gatos
catacombs as catacumbas
catalogue o catálogo
to catch (bus, train, etc) apanhar
cathedral a catedral; a sé
Catholic católico(a)
cauliflower a couve-flor
cave a caverna
cavity (in tooth) a cárie dentária
CD o disco compacto; o CD
CD player o leitor de CDs
CD-ROM o CD-ROM
ceiling o tecto
celery o aipo
cellar a cave
cellphone o telefone celular
cemetery o cemitério
centimetre o centímetro
central central
central heating o aquecimento central
central locking o fecho centralizado
cent o cêntimo (i.e. 1/100th of a euro)
centre o centro
century o século
19th century o século dezanove
21st century o século vinte e um
ceramics a cerâmica
cereal (for breakfast) os cereais
certain certo(a)
certificate o certificado
chain a corrente
chair a cadeira
chairlift o teleférico
chalet o chalé
challenge o desafio
chambermaid a empregada de quarto
Champagne o champanhe
change (loose coins) o dinheiro trocado
(money returned) o troco
to change trocar; mudar
to change money trocar dinheiro
to change (clothes) mudar de roupa
(train, etc) mudar
changing room o gabinete de provas
Channel: *the English Channel* o Canal da Mancha
chapel a capela
charcoal o carvão
charge o custo
cover charge o couvert
please charge it to my account por favor ponha na minha conta
charger (for battery) o carregador
charter flight o voo charter
cheap barato(a)
cheaper mais barato(a)
to check verificar
to check in (at airport) fazer o check-in
(at hotel) apresentar-se
check-in desk o balcão do check-in
cheek a bochecha
cheerful alegre
cheers saúde!
cheese o queijo
cheeseburger um hambúrguer com queijo
chef o cozinheiro-chefe/a cozinheira-chefe
chemist's a farmácia
cheque o cheque
chequebook o livro de cheques
cheque card o cartão de cheques
cherry a cereja
chess o xadrez
chest (of body) o peito

chestnut a castanha
chewing gum a pastilha elástica
chicken a galinha; o frango
chicken breast o peito de galinha
chickenpox a varicela
child a criança
child safety seat (car) o banco de segurança para crianças
children as crianças
chilli a malagueta
chimney a chaminé
chin o queixo
china a porcelana
chips as batatas fritas
chocolate o chocolate
chocolates os chocolates
choice a escolha
choir o coro
to choose escolher
chop (meat) a costeleta
chopping board a tábua da cozinha
christening o baptizado
Christian name o nome próprio
Christmas o Natal
merry Christmas! feliz Natal!
Christmas card o cartão de Boas Festas
Christmas Eve a véspera de Natal
Christmas present a prenda de Natal
church a igreja
cider a sidra
cigar o charuto
cigarette o cigarro
cigarette lighter o isqueiro
cigarette papers as mortalhas
cinema o cinema
circle (theatre) o balcão
circuit breaker o disjuntor
circus o circo
cistern a cisterna
citizen o cidadão/a cidadã
city a cidade
city centre o centro (da cidade)
claim *n* a reclamação
to clap bater palmas
class: ***first class*** primeira classe
second class segunda classe
clean limpo(a)
to clean limpar
cleaner (person) o/a empregado(a) de limpeza
(product) produto de limpeza
cleanser o leite de limpeza
clear claro(a)
to click (on) clicar
client o/a cliente
cliff o rochedo
to climb subir
climbing o alpinismo
climbing boots as botas de alpinismo
clingfilm® a película aderente
clinic a clínica
cloakroom o vestiário
clock o relógio
to close fechar
closed fechado(a); encerrado(a)
cloth (fabric) o tecido
(rag) o trapo
clothes as roupas
clothes line o estendal
clothes peg a mola da roupa
clothes shop a loja de roupa
cloudy nublado(a)
clove (spice) o cravinho
club o clube
clutch a embraiagem
coach a camioneta
coach station a rodoviária
coach trip a viagem de camioneta
coal o carvão
coast a costa
coastguard a polícia marítima
coat o casaco
coat hanger o cabide
Coca Cola® a Coca-Cola®
cockroach a barata
cocktail o cocktail
cocoa o cacau
coconut o coco
cod o bacalhau
code o código
coffee o café
decaffeinated coffee o café descafeinado
large white coffee (in a glass) o galão

small black coffee a bica; o café
white coffee o café com leite
coffee shop o café; a pastelaria
coil (contraceptive) o DIU
coin a moeda
Coke® a Coca-Cola®
colander o coador
cold frio(a)
cold water a água fria
I'm cold tenho frio
it's cold está frio(a)
cold (illness) a constipação
I have a cold tenho uma constipação
cold sore a herpes labial
collar (of dress) a gola
(of shirt) o colarinho
collarbone a clavícula
colleague o/a colega
to collect coleccionar
(to collect someone) ir buscar
collection a colecção
colour a cor
colour-blind daltónico(a)
colour film (for camera) o rolo a cores
comb o pente
to come vir
(arrive) chegar
to come back voltar
to come in entrar
come in! entre!
comedy a comédia
comfortable confortável
company (firm) a companhia
compartment o compartimento
compass a bússola
to complain queixar-se (de)
I want to complain of... Quero queixar-me de...
complaint a queixa
complaints book o livro de reclamações
I wish to make a complaint quero fazer uma reclamação
complete completo(a)
to complete completar
composer o/a compositor(a)
compulsory obrigatório(a)
computer o computador
computer disk (floppy) a disquete
computer game o jogo de computador
computer program o programa de computador
computer software o software
computer virus a praga virtual; o vírus
concert o concerto
concert hall a sala de concertos
concession o desconto
concussion o traumatismo craniano
condensed milk o leite condensado
condition (requirement) a condição
(state) o estado
conditioner o amaciador
condom o preservativo
conductor (of orchestra) o maestro/a maestrina
cone o cone
conference a conferência
confession a confissão
to confirm confirmar
please confirm é favor confirmar
confirmation (of booking) a confirmação
confused confuso(a)
congratulations! parabéns!
connection (flight, etc) a ligação
constipated com prisão de ventre
constipation a prisão de ventre
consulate o consulado
to consult consultar
to contact pôr-se em contacto com
contact lens cleaner o líquido para as lentes de contacto
contact lenses as lentes de contacto
to continue continuar
contraception a anticoncepção
contraceptive o preservativo; o anticoncepcional
contract o contrato
convenient: ***is it convenient?*** é conveniente?
convulsions as convulsões
to cook cozinhar
cooked cozinhado(a)
cooker o fogão
cookies os biscoitos

cool fresco(a)
cool box (for picnics) a caixa refrigerada
copper cobre
copy a cópia
to copy copiar
coriander os coentros
cork (in bottle) a rolha
corkscrew o saca-rolhas
corner (inside) o canto;
(street) a esquina
corridor o corredor
cortisone a cortisona
cost o custo
to cost custar
how much does it cost? quanto (é que) custa?
costume o traje
(swimming – men) os calções de banho
(swimming – women) o fato de banho
cot o berço
cottage a casa de campo
cotton o algodão
cotton buds os cotonetes
cotton wool o algodão (***hidrófilo***)
couchette a couchette
to cough tossir
cough a tosse
cough mixture o xarope para a tosse
cough sweets as pastilhas para a tosse
counter (shop, bar etc) o balcão
country o país
countryside o campo
couple (two people) o casal
a couple of... um par de
courgettes as courgetes
courier (tour guide) o guia turístico/ a guia turística
courier service o mensageiro
course (of meal) o prato
(of study) o curso
cousin o/a primo(a)
cover charge o couvert
cow a vaca
crab o caranguejo
crafts o artesanato
craftsman/woman o artesão/ a artesã
cramps as cãibras
crash (car) o choque
to crash colidir
crash helmet o capacete
cream (for face, etc) o creme
(on milk) a nata
soured cream as natas azedas
whipped cream o chantilly
creche a creche
credit card o cartão de crédito
crime o crime
crisps as batatinhas fritas
crop a colheita
croissant o croissant
to cross (road) cruzar; atravessar
cross a cruz
crossed lines as linhas cruzadas
crossing (sea) a travessia
crossroads o cruzamento
crossword puzzle as palavras cruzadas
crowd a multidão
crowded cheio(a) de gente
crown a coroa
cruise o cruzeiro
crutches as muletas
to cry (weep) chorar
crystal o cristal
cucumber o pepino
cufflinks os botões de punho
cul-de-sac o beco sem saída
cumin o cominho
cup a chávena
cupboard o armário
curlers os rolos
currant a passa de corinto
currency a moeda
current a corrente
curtain a cortina
cushion a almofada
custard o leite-creme
custom (tradition) o costume
customer o freguês/a freguesa
customs (at airport etc) a alfândega
customs declaration a declaração alfandegária
customs officer o/a funcionário(a) aduaneiro(a)

to cut cortar
we've been cut off foi interrompida a ligação
cut o corte
cut and blow-dry cortar e secar
cutlery os talheres
cyberspace o ciberespaço
to cycle andar de bicicleta
cycle track a pista para ciclistas
cycling o ciclismo
cyst o cisto
cystitis a cistite

D

daily cada dia
dairy produce os lacticínios
daisy a margarida
dam a barragem
damage os danos
damp húmido(a)
dance o baile
to dance dançar
danger o perigo
dangerous perigoso(a)
dark o escuro; escuro(a) *adj*
after dark depois do anoitecer
date a data
date of birth a data de nascimento
daughter a filha
daughter-in-law a nora
dawn o amanhecer
day o dia
every day todos os dias
per day ao/por dia
dead morto(a)
deaf surdo(a)
dear (on letter) querido(a)
(expensive) caro(a)
death a morte
debt a dívida
decaff o café descafeinado
have you decaff? tem café descafeinado?
decaffeinated coffee o café descafeinado
December Dezembro
deckchair a cadeira de lona
to declare: ***nothing to declare*** nada a declarar
deep fundo(a)
deep freeze o congelador
deer o veado
to defrost descongelar
to de-ice descongelar
delay a demora
how long is the delay? quanto tempo é o atraso?
delayed atrasado(a)
delicatessen a charcutaria
delicious delicioso(a)
demonstration (political) a manifestação
dental floss o fio dental
dentist o/a dentista
dentures a dentadura postiça
deodorant o desodorizante
to depart partir
department o departamento
department store o grande armazém
departure lounge a sala de embarque
departures as partidas
deposit o depósito
to describe descrever
description a descrição
desk a secretária
(in hotel, airport) o balcão
dessert a sobremesa
details os pormenores
detergent o detergente
detour o desvio
to develop desenvolver
diabetes a diabetes
diabetic (person) diabético(a)
(food) comida para diabéticos
I'm diabetic sou diabético(a)
to dial marcar
dialect o dialecto
dialling code o código
dialling tone o sinal
diamond o diamante
diaper a fralda
diaphragm (in body) o diafragma
(contraceptive) o diafragma
diarrhoea a diarreia

diary o diário; a agenda
dice os dados
dictionary o dicionário
to die morrer
diesel o gasóleo
diet a dieta
I'm on a diet estou de dieta
special diet o regime especial
different diferente
difficult difícil
digital camera a câmara digital
digital radio o rádio digital
to dilute diluir
dinghy o bote
dining room a sala de jantar
dinner o jantar
to have dinner jantar
dinner jacket o smoking
diplomat o/a diplomata
direct directo(a)
directions (instructions) instrucções
to ask for directions pedir indicações
directory (phone) a lista telefónica
directory enquiries as informações telefónicas
dirty sujo(a)
disability a incapacidade
disabled deficiente
disabled person o/a deficiente
to disagree discordar
to disappear desaparecer
disappointed desiludido(a)
disaster o desastre
disco a discoteca
discount o desconto
to discover descobrir
disease a doença
dish o prato
dishtowel o pano de cozinha
dishwasher a máquina de lavar louça
dishwasher powder o detergente em pó
disinfectant o desinfectante
disk (computer) o disco
floppy disk a disquete
hard disk o disco duro
to dislocate (joint) deslocar
disposable descartável
distance a distância
distant distante
distilled water a água destilada
district o distrito
to disturb incomodar
to dive mergulhar
diver o/a mergulhador(a)
diversion o desvio
diving o mergulho
divorced divorciado(a)
I'm divorced sou divorciado(a)
DIY shop a loja de bricolage
dizzy tonto(a)
to do fazer
doctor o/a médico(a)
documents os documentos
dog (male) o cão
(female) a cadela
dog food a comida para cães
dog lead a correia
doll a boneca
dollar o dólar
domestic doméstico(a)
domestic flight o voo doméstico
dominoes o dominó
donor card o cartão de doador
donkey o burro
door a porta
doorbell a campainha
double o dobro
double bed a cama de casal
double room o quarto de casal
doughnut a bola de Berlim
down: *to go down* descer
download fazer download/o download
downstairs em baixo
dragonfly a libélula
drain (sewer) o esgoto
draught (of air) a corrente de ar
there's a draught há uma corrente de ar
draught lager a imperial; o fino (North)
drawer a gaveta
drawing o desenho
dress o vestido
to dress (oneself) vestir-se

dressing (for food) o tempero; o molho
(for wound) o penso
dressing gown o roupão
drill (tool) a broca
drink a bebida
to drink beber
drinking chocolate o chocolate
drinking water a água potável
to drive conduzir
driver o/a condutor(a)
driving licence a carta de condução
drizzle o chuvisco
drought a seca
to drown afogar
drug (medicine) o medicamento
(narcotic) a droga
drunk bêbedo(a)
dry seco(a)
to dry secar
dry-cleaner's a limpeza a seco
dryer o secador
duck o pato
due: ***when is it due?*** está previsto para quando?
dummy (for baby) a chupeta
during durante
dust o pó
to dust limpar o pó
duster o pano do pó
dustpan and brush a pá e a vassoura
duty (tax) o imposto
duty-free o duty-free
duvet o edredão
duvet cover o saco do edredão
DVD o DVD
DVD drive a drive de DVD
dye a tinta
dynamo o dínamo

E

each cada
eagle a águia
ear a orelha;
(inner ear) o auvido
earache a dor de ouvidos
I have earache doem-me os ouvidos
earlier mais cedo
early cedo
earphones os auscultadores
earplugs as borrachinhas (de ouvido)
earrings os brincos
earth (planet) a terra
earthquake o terramoto
east o leste
Easter a Páscoa
happy Easter! feliz Páscoa!
easy fácil
to eat comer
ebony o ébano
echo o eco
economy a economia
edge a beira; a borda
eel a enguia
effective eficaz
egg o ovo
fried egg o ovo estrelado
hard-boiled egg o ovo cozido
scrambled eggs os ovos mexidos
soft-boiled egg o ovo quente
egg white a clara de ovo
egg yolk a gema de ovo
either... or... ou... ou...
elastic band o elástico
Elastoplast® o adesivo
elbow o cotovelo
electric eléctrico(a)
electric blanket o cobertor eléctrico
electrician o/a electricista
electricity a electricidade; a luz
electricity meter o contador de electricidade
electric razor a máquina de barbear
electric shock o choque eléctrico
elevator o elevador
elegant elegante
e-mail o correio electrónico; o e-mail
to e-mail someone mandar um e-mail
e-mail address o endereço de e-mail
embarrassing embaraçoso(a)
embassy a embaixada
emergency a emergência
emergency exit a saída de emergência
emery board a lixa de unhas
empty vazio(a)

end o fim
engaged comprometido(a)
(phone, toilet, etc) ocupado(a)
engine o motor
engineer o/a engenheiro(a)
England a Inglaterra
English inglês (inglesa)
(language) o inglês
Englishman o inglês
Englishwoman a inglesa
enjoy oneself divertir-se
enjoy your meal! bom apetite!
enjoy yourself! diverte-te!
I enjoy dancing gosto de dançar
I enjoy swimming gosto de nadar
to enlarge aumentar
enormous enorme
enough bastante
that's enough chega
enquiries as informações
enquiry desk o balcão de informações
to enter entrar (em)
entertainment a diversão
enthusiastic entusiástico(a)
entrance a entrada
entrance fee o bilhete de entrada
envelope o envelope
epileptic epiléptico(a)
epileptic fit o ataque epiléptico
equipment o equipamento
eraser a borracha
error o erro
eruption a erupção
escalator a escada rolante
to escape escapar
escape ladder a escada de salvação
espadrilles as alpercatas
espresso a bica; o café
essential essencial
estate agent o/a agente imobiliário(a)
estate agent's a imobiliária
establish estabelecer
euro o euro
euro cent o cêntimo
Europe a Europa
European europeu (européia)
European Union a União Européia
eve a véspera
Christmas eve a véspera de Natal
New Year's eve a véspera de Ano Novo
even (number) par
evening a noite
in the evening à noite
this evening esta noite
tomorrow evening amanhã à noite
evening dress o traje de cerimónia
evening meal o jantar
every cada
everyone toda a gente; todos
everything todas as coisas; tudo
everywhere por todo o lado
examination o exame
example: ***for example*** por exemplo
excellent excelente
except excepto
excess baggage/luggage o excesso de bagagem
to exchange trocar
exchange rate o câmbio
exciting emocionante
excursion a excursão
excuse a desculpa
excuse me! desculpe!
exercise (physical) o exercício
exercise book o caderno
exhaust pipe o tubo de escape
exhibition a exposição
exit a saída
expenses as despesas
expensive caro(a)
expert o/a perito(a)
to expire (ticket, etc) caducar
expiry date o vencimento
to explain explicar
explosion a explosão
to export exportar
express (train) o expresso
express: ***to send a letter express*** mandar uma carta por correio expresso
extension (electrical) a extensão
extra extra
an extra bed uma cama adicional
to extinguish apagar
eye o olho

eyebrows as sobrancelhas
eyedrops as gotas para os olhos
eyelashes as pestanas
eyeliner o lápis para os olhos
eyeshadow a sombra para os olhos

F

fabric o tecido
face a cara; o rosto
face cloth a toalha de rosto
facial a limpeza facial
facilities as facilidades; instalações
factory a fábrica
to fail fracassar
(engine, brakes) falhar
to faint desmaiar
fainted desmaiado(a)
fair (hair) louro(a)
fair (just) justo(a)
fair (funfair) o parque de diversões
(trade) a feira
fairway (golf) o fairway
fake falso(a)
fall (autumn) o Outono
to fall cair
he/she has fallen ele/ela caiu
false teeth os dentes postiços
family a família
famous famoso(a)
fan (hand-held) o leque
(electric) a ventoínha
(football, jazz) o/a fã
fan belt a correia da ventoínha
fancy dress o traje de fantasia
far longe
how far is it to...? a que distância fica...?
is it far? é longe?
fare (train, bus, etc) o preço (da passagem)
farm a quinta
farmer o/a agricultor(a)
farmhouse a casa da quinta
fashionable de moda
fast rápido(a)
too fast rápido demais
to fasten (seatbelt) apertar
fat gordo(a)
saturated fats gorduras saturadas
unsaturated fats gorduras insaturadas
father o pai
father-in-law o sogro
fault (defect) o defeito
it's not my fault a culpa não é minha
favour o favor
favourite favorito(a)
fax o fax
by fax por fax
to fax mandar por fax
fax number o número de fax
feather a pena
February Fevereiro
to feed alimentar
to feel apalpar; sentir
I don't feel well sinto-me mal-disposto(a)
I feel sick tenho náuseas
feet os pés
fellow o companheiro
felt-tip pen a caneta de feltro
female a mulher
ferry o ferry-boat
festival o festival
to fetch (to bring) trazer
(to go and get) ir buscar
fever a febre
few poucos(as)
a few alguns (algumas)
fiancé(e) o/a noivo(a)
field o campo
fig o figo
fight a briga
to fight brigar
file (computer) o ficheiro
(nail) a lima
(folder) a pasta
filigree a filigrana
to fill encher
fill it up! encha o depósito!
to fill in (form) preencher
fillet o filete
filling (in tooth) a obturação
filling station a estação de serviço
film (at cinema) o filme
(for camera) o rolo de filme

black and white film o rolo a preto e branco
colour film o rolo a cores
Filofax® a agenda
filter o filtro
to find achar
fine (to be paid) a multa
fine fino(a)
fine arts as belas-artes
finger o dedo
to finish acabar
finished acabado(a)
fire o fogo
fire alarm o alarme contra incêndios
fire brigade os bombeiros
fire engine o carro dos bombeiros
fire escape a saída de incêndios
fire extinguisher o extintor
fireplace a lareira
fireworks os fogos de artifício
firm (company) a firma
first o/a primeiro(a)
first aid os primeiros socorros
first aid kit o estojo de primeiros socorros
first class a primeira classe
first-class de primeira classe
first floor o primeiro andar
first name o nome próprio
fish o peixe
to fish pescar
to go fishing ir pescar
fisherman o pescador
fisherwoman a pescadora
fishing permit a licença de pesca
fishing rod a cana de pesca
fishmonger's a peixaria
to fit: ***it doesn't fit me*** não me serve
fit o ataque
he had a fit ele teve um ataque
to fix reparar; consertar
can you fix it? pode arranjá-lo(la)?
fizzy gasoso(a)
flag a bandeira
flame a chama
flash (for camera) o flash
flashlight a lanterna
flask o termo
flat (apartment) o apartamento
flat plano(a)
(battery) descarregado(a)
this drink is flat esta bebida já perdeu o gás
flat tyre o furo
flavour o sabor
which flavour? de que sabor?
flaw a falha
fleas as pulgas
fleece (material) de fibra polar
flesh a carne
flex o cabo eléctrico
flight o voo
flip flops os chinelos
flippers as barbatanas
flood a inundação
flash flood a inundação repentina
floor o chão
(storey) o andar
which floor? qual é o andar?
ground floor o rés-do-chão
first floor o primeiro andar
second floor o segundo andar
floorcloth o pano do chão
floppy disk a disquete
florist's shop a florista
flour a farinha
flower a flor
flu a gripe
fly a mosca
to fly voar
fly sheet o duplo-tecto
fog o nevoeiro
foggy nevoento
foil (silver) o papel de alumínio
to follow seguir
food a comida
food poisoning a intoxicação alimentar
fool tonto(a)
foot o pé
on foot a pé
football o futebol
football match o jogo de futebol
football pitch o campo de futebol

football player o jogador de futebol
footpath o caminho
for para
for me para mim
for you para si
for him/her/us para ele/ela/nós
for them para eles (elas)
forbidden proibido(a)
forecast a previsão
weather forecast a previsão do tempo
forehead a testa
foreign estrangeiro(a)
foreigner o/a estrangeiro(a)
forest a floresta
forever para sempre
to forget esquecer-se de
to forgive perdoar
fork (for eating) o garfo
(in road) a bifurcação
form (document) o formulário
formal dress o traje de cerimónia
fortnight a quinzena
fortress a fortaleza
forward(s) para a frente
foul (in football) a falta
fountain a fonte
four-wheel drive o quatro-vezes-quatro (= 4x4)
fox a raposa
fracture a fractura
fragile frágil
fragrance a fragrância
frame (picture) a moldura
France a França
free (not occupied) livre
(costing nothing) grátis
freezer o congelador
French francês (francesa)
(language) o francês
French beans o feijão-verde
French fries as batatas fritas
frequent frequente
fresh fresco(a)
fresh water a água doce
Friday a sexta-feira
fridge o frigorífico
fried frito(a)
friend o/a amigo(a)
friendly simpático(a)
frog a rã
from de
from England da Inglaterra
from Scotland da Escócia
front a frente
in front of em frente de
front door a porta da frente
frost a geada
frozen congelado(a)
fruit a fruta
dried fruit os frutos secos
fruit juice o sumo de frutas
fruit salad a salada de frutas
to fry fritar
frying pan a frigideira
fuel (petrol) a gasolina
fuel gauge o medidor de gasolina
fuel pump a bomba de gasolina
fuel tank o depósito
full cheio(a)
full board a pensão completa
fumes (of car) os fumos de escape
fun a diversão
funeral o funeral
funfair o parque de diversões
funny engraçado(a)
(strange) estranho(a)
fur a pele
furnished mobilado(a)
furniture a mobília; os móveis
fuse o fusível
fuse box a caixa de fusíveis
futon o futon
future o futuro

G

gallery (art) a galeria de arte
gallon = approx. 4.5 litres
game o jogo
(animal) a caça
garage (private) a garagem
(for repairs) a oficina (de reparos)
(for petrol) a estação de serviço
garden o jardim
gardener o/a jardineiro(a)

garlic o alho
to garnish guarnecer
gas o gás
gas cooker o fogão a gás
gas cylinder a botija de gás
gastritis a gastrite
gate (airport) a porta;
(home) o portãs
gay (person) gay
gear a velocidade
first gear a primeira velocidade
second gear a segunda velocidade
third gear a terceira velocidade
fourth gear a quarta velocidade
fifth gear a quinta velocidade
neutral o ponto morto
reverse a marcha atrás
gearbox a caixa de velocidades
gear lever a alavanca das velocidades
generous generoso(a)
gents' (toilet) Homens
where is the gents'? onde é o lavabo de homens?

genuine (leather, antique etc) autêntico(a)
German alemão (alemã)
(language) o alemão
German measles a rubéola
Germany a Alemanha
to get (to obtain) obter
(to receive) receber
(to fetch) ir buscar
to get in (vehicle) subir em
to get into entrar em
to get off descer de
to get on (vehicle) subir para
gift o presente; a prenda
gift shop a loja de lembranças
gigabyte o gigabyte
gigahertz o gigahertz
gin and tonic um gim tónico
ginger o gengibre
girl a rapariga
girlfriend a namorada
to give dar
to give back devolver
glacier o glaciar
glass (substance) o vidro; o cristal
(to drink out of) o copo
a glass of water um copo de água
glasses os óculos
glasses case a caixa dos óculos
gloss o brilho
gloves as luvas
glue a cola
to go ir
I'm going to... vou para...
we're going to... vamos para...
to go back voltar
to go down descer
to go in entrar (em)
to go out saír
goat a cabra
God o Deus
godchild o/a afilhado(a)
goggles os óculos protectores
gold o ouro
golf o golfe
golf ball a bola de golfe
golf clubs os tacos de golfe
golf course o campo de golfe
good bom (boa)
very good muito bom
good afternoon boa tarde
goodbye adeus
good evening boa noite
good morning bom dia
good night boa noite
goose o ganso
gooseberry a groselha branca
Gothic gótico(a)
graduate o/a licenciado(a)
gram o grama
grandchild o/a neto(a)
granddaughter a neta
grandfather o avô
great grandfather o bisavô
grandmother a avó
great grandmother a bisavó
grandparents os avós
grandson o neto
grapefruit a toranja
grapefruit juice o sumo de toranja
grapes as uvas

black grapes as uvas pretas
green grapes as uvas brancas
grass a erva
grated (cheese, etc) ralado(a)
grater (for cheese, etc) o ralador
greasy oleoso(a); gorduroso(a)
great (big) grande
(wonderful) óptimo(a)
Great Britain a Grã-Bretanha
green verde
green card (car insurance) o cartão verde
greengrocer's a frutaria
greetings card o cartão de felicitações
grey cinzento(a)
grill a grelha
to grill grelhar
grilled grelhado(a)
grocer's a mercearia
ground (earth) a terra
(floor) o chão
ground floor o rés-do-chão
on the ground floor... no rés-do-chão...
groundsheet a cobertura impermeável
group o grupo
to grow crescer
guarantee a garantia
guard o/a guarda
guest o/a convidado(a)
(in hotel) o/a hóspede
guesthouse a pensão
guide o/a guia
to guide guiar
guidebook a guia
guided tour a excursão guiada
guitar a guitarra; o violão
gun a pistola
gym o ginásio
gym shoes os ténis

H

haberdasher's a retrosaria
haddock o eglefim
haemorrhoids as hemorróidas
hail o granizo
hair o cabelo
hairbrush a escova de cabelo
haircut o corte de cabelo
hairdresser o/a cabeleireiro(a)
hairdryer o secador de cabelo
hair dye a tinta para o cabelo
hair gel o gel para o cabelo
hairgrip o gancho de cabelo
hair mousse a espuma para o cabelo
hairspray a laca
hake a pescada
half a metade
a half bottle of meia garrafa de
half an hour meia hora
half board a meia pensão
half fare meio-bilhete
half-price pela metade do preço
ham (boiled) o fiambre
(smoked) o presunto
hamburger o hambúrguer
hammer o martelo
hand a mão
handbag a bolsa
handbrake o travão de mão
handicapped (person) deficiente
handkerchief o lenço
handle (of cup) a asa
(of door) a maçaneta
handlebars os guiadores
hand luggage a bagagem de mão
hand-made feito(a) à mão
hands-free phone o kit de mãos livres
handsome bonito(a), giro(a)
to hang up (phone) desligar
hanger o cabide
hang gliding a asa-delta
hangover a ressaca
to happen acontecer
what happened? o que aconteceu?
happy feliz; contente
happy birthday! feliz aniversário!; parabéns!
harbour o porto
hard duro(a)
(difficult) difícil
hard disk o disco duro
hard drive o disco rígido
hardware shop a loja de ferragens
hare a lebre
harm o mal; o dano

harvest a colheita
hat o chapéu
to have ter
do you have...? tem...?
I have... eu tenho...
I don't have... eu não tenho...
we have... nós temos...
we don't have... nós não temos...
to have to ter que; ter de
hay fever a febre dos fenos
hazelnut a avelã
he ele
head a cabeça
headache a dor de cabeça
I have a headache dói-me a cabeça
headlights os faróis
headphones os auscultadores
head waiter o chefe de mesa
health a saúde
health food shop a loja de produtos dietéticos
healthy saudável
to hear ouvir
hearing aid o aparelho auditivo
heart o coração
heart attack o ataque de coração
heartburn a azia
to heat up aquecer
heater o aquecedor
heating o aquecimento
heatstroke a insolação
heaven o Céu
heavy pesado(a)
heel (of foot) o calcanhar
(of shoe) o salto
heel bar o sapateiro
height a altura
helicopter o helicóptero
hello olá
(on phone) está?
helmet o capacete
help a ajuda
help! socorro!
to help ajudar
can you help me? pode-me ajudar?
hem a bainha
hen a galinha
hepatitis a hepatite
herb a erva aromática
herbal tea a tisana
here aqui
here is... aqui está...
here is my passport aqui está o meu passaporte
hernia a hérnia
hi! olá!
to hide (something) esconder
(oneself) esconder-se
high (price, speed, building) alto(a)
(number) grande
high blood pressure a tensão alta
highchair a cadeira de bebé
high tide a maré alta
hill a colina
hill-walking o alpinismo
him (direct object) o
(indirect object) lhe
(after preposition) ele
hip a anca
hip replacement a prótese de anca
hire o aluguer
bike hire o aluguer de bicicletas
boat hire o aluguer de barcos
car hire o aluguer de carros
ski hire o aluguer de esquis
to hire alugar
historic histórico(a)
history a história
to hit bater
to hitchhike andar à boleia
HIV o vírus da SIDA
HIV positive seropositivo(a)
hobby o passatempo
to hold (to contain) conter
hold-up (traffic) o engarrafamento
hole o buraco
holiday as férias
(public holiday) o feriado
on holiday de férias
holiday rep o/a representante da agência de viagens
hollow oco(a)
holy santo(a)
home a casa

at home em casa
to go home voltar para casa
homeopath o/a homeopata
homeopathic homeopático(a)
homeopathy a homeopatia
homepage a homepage *f*
homesick: *to be homesick* ter saudades de casa
I'm homesick tenho saudades de casa
homosexual homossexual
honest honesto(a)
honey o mel
honeymoon a lua-de-mel
hood (of jacket) o capuz
(of car) a capota
hook (for fishing) o anzol
to hope esperar
I hope so/not espero que sim/não
horn (of car) a buzina
hors d'œuvre a entrada
horse o cavalo
horse racing as corridas de cavalo
horse riding: *to go horse riding* montar a cavalo
hosepipe a mangueira
hospital o hospital
hostel a pousada (de juventude)
hot quente
I'm hot tenho calor
it's hot está quente
it's hot (weather) faz/está calor
hot chocolate o chocolate quente
hotel o hotel
hot water a água quente
hot-water bottle o saco de água quente
hour a hora
half an hour meia hora
1 hour uma hora
2 hours duas horas
house a casa
housewife/husband a/o dona(o) de casa
house wine o vinho da casa
housework o trabalho doméstico
hovercraft o hovercraft
how como
how are you? como está?
how many? quantos(as)?
how much? quanto(a)?
hundred cem;
(101+) cento
five hundred quinhentos(as)
hungry: *I am hungry* tenho fome
hunt a caça
to hunt caçar
hunting permit a licença de caça
hurry: *I'm in a hurry* tenho pressa
to hurt doer
my back hurts tenho dor de costas
that hurts isso dói
husband o marido
hut a cabana
hydrofoil o hidrofólio
hyperlinks as hiperligacões
hypodermic needle a agulha hipodérmica

I

I eu
ice o gelo
(cube) o cubo de gelo
with ice com gelo
without ice sem gelo
ice box o frigorífico
ice cream o gelado
iced coffee o café gelado
iced tea o chá gelado
ice lolly o gelado; picolé
ice rink o rinque de patinagem
to ice-skate patinar sobre o gelo
ice skates os patins de lâmina
idea a idéia
identity card o bilhete de identidade
if se
ignition a ignição
ignition key a chave de ignição
ill doente
I'm ill estou doente
illness a doença
immediately imediatamente
immersion heater o esquentador de imersão
immigration a imigração
immunisation a imunização

to import importar
important importante
impossible impossível
to improve melhorar
in em
(within) dentro de
in London em Londres
in 10 minutes dentro de dez minutos
in front of em frente de
included incluído(a)
inconvenient inconveniente
to increase aumentar
indicator (on car) o pisca-pisca
indigestion a indigestão
indigestion tablets os comprimidos para indigestão
indoors em casa
inefficient ineficiente
infection a infecção
infectious contagioso(a)
informal (person) sem formalidades
(costume) informal
information a informação
information desk o balcão de informações
information office o departamento de informações
ingredient o ingrediente
inhaler (for medication) o inalador
injection a injecção
to injure lesionar; ferir
injured ferido(a)
injury a lesão
ink a tinta
inn a estalagem
inner tube a câmara-de-ar
inquiries as informações
inquiry desk o balcão de informações
insect o insecto
insect bite a picada de insecto
insect repellent o repelente contra insectos
inside dentro
instalment a prestação
instant coffee o café instantâneo
instead of em vez de
instructor o/a instrutor(a)
insulin a insulina
insurance o seguro
insurance certificate a apólice de seguro
to insure pôr no seguro
insured: ***to be insured*** estar no seguro
intelligent inteligente
to intend to do tencionar fazer
interesting interessante
internet a internet
internet café o cibercafé
internet connection a ligação à internet
international internacional
interpreter o/a intérprete
interval o intervalo
interview a entrevista
into em; a; para
into the centre ao centro
to introduce someone to someone apresentar alguém a alguém
invitation o convite
to invite convidar
invoice a factura
Ireland a Irlanda
Irish irlandês (irlandesa)
iron (metal) o ferro
(for clothes) o ferro de engomar
to iron passar a ferro
ironing board a tábua de engomar
ironmonger's a loja de ferragens
island a ilha
Italian italiano(a)
(language) o italiano
Italy a Itália
itch a comichão
to itch fazer comichão
it itches faz comichão; irrita
item o artigo
itemized bill a factura detalhada
ivory o marfim

J

jack (for car) o macaco
jacket o casaco
waterproof jacket o casaco impermeável

jackpot o prémio (de lotaria, rifa)
jacuzzi® o jacuzzi
jam a compota
jammed (stuck) bloqueado(a)
January Janeiro
jar o jarro
jaundice a icterícia
jaw o maxilar
jazz o jazz
jealous ciumento(a)
jeans as jeans; calças de ganga
jelly a geleia
jellyfish a medusa; a alforreca
jet ski a motonáutica
jetty o quebra-mar
jewel a jóia
jewellery a joalharia
Jewish judeu (judia)
job o emprego
to jog ir fazer jogging
to join (club) associarse a
joint (of body) a articulação
joke a piada; a anedota
to joke brincar
journalist o/a jornalista
journey a viagem
judge o juiz (a juíza)
jug o jarro
juice o sumo
a carton of juice um pacote de sumo
apple juice o sumo de maçã
orange juice o sumo de laranja
tomato juice o sumo de tomate
July Julho
to jump saltar
jump leads os cabos para ligar a bateria
junction o cruzamento
June Junho
just: ***just two*** apenas dois
I've just arrived acabo de chegar

K

karaoke o karaokê
to keep guardar
(retain) ficar com
keep the change! fique com o troco!
kennel a casota
kettle a chaleira
key a chave
card key a chave-cartão
keyboard o teclado
keyring o porta-chaves
to kick (person) dar um pontapé em
(ball) chutar
kid (young goat) o cabrito
(child) a criança
kidneys os rins
to kill matar
kilo o quilo
a kilo of apples um quilo de maçãs
2 kilos dois quilos
kilogram o quilograma
kilometre o quilómetro
kind (person) amável
kind (sort) a espécie
king o rei
kiosk o quiosque
kiss o beijo
to kiss beijar
kitchen a cozinha
kitchen paper o papel de cozinha
kite o papagaio
kitten o/a gatinho(a)
knee o joelho
knickers as cuecas
knife a faca
to knit fazer malha
to knock (on door) bater
to knock down (with car) atropelar
to knock over (vase, glass) derrubar
knot o nó
to know (have knowledge of) saber
(person, place) conhecer
I don't know não sei
to know how to do something
saber fazer alguma coisa
to know how to swim saber nadar
kosher kosher

L

label a etiqueta
lace a renda
laces (for shoes) os atacadores
ladder a escada

ladies' (toilet) Senhoras
lady a senhora
lager a cerveja
bottled lager a cerveja de garrafa
draught lager a imperial;
(in North) o fino
lake o lago
lamb o cordeiro
lame coxo(a)
lamp a lâmpada
lamppost o poste de iluminação
lampshade o abajur
land a terra
(country) o país
to land aterrar
landing (of plane) a aterragem
landlady a senhoria
landlord o senhorio
landslide o desabamento
lane (on motorway) a faixa
language a língua
language school a Escola de Línguas
laptop o computador portátil
large grande
last último(a)
last night ontem à noite
last week a semana passada
last year o ano passado
the last bus o último autocarro
the last time a última vez
the last train o último comboio
late tarde
sorry we are late desculpe o atraso
the train is late o comboio está atrasado
later mais tarde
to laugh rir
launderette a lavandaria automática
laundry service o serviço de lavandaria
lavatory o lavabo
lavender a alfazema
law a lei
lawn o relvado
lawyer o/a advogado(a)
laxative o laxante
layby a berma
lazy preguiçoso(a)
lead (electrical) o cabo
(for dog) a correia
lead (metal) o chumbo
lead-free sem chumbo
leaf a folha
leak (of gas, liquid) o escape; o derrame
to leak: *it's leaking* (pipe) está a verter
(gas) o escape de gás
(roof) o infiltração
to learn aprender
lease o arrendamento
least: *at least* pelo menos
leather o couro; o cabedal
leather goods os cabedais
to leave (leave behind) deixar
(train, bus etc) partir
when does it leave? a que horas parte?
when does the bus leave? a que horas parte o autocarro?
when does the train leave? a que horas parte o comboio?
leek o alho francês
left: *on/to the left* à esquerda
left-handed canhoto(a)
left luggage (office) o depósito de bagagens
left luggage locker o cacifo
leg a perna
legal legal
lemon o limão
lemonade a limonada
lemon tea o chá de limão
to lend emprestar
length o comprimento
lens (of glasses) a lente
(of camera) a objectiva
lenses (contact lenses) as lentes de contacto
lesbian a lésbica
less menos
less than menos do que
lesson a lição
let (allow) deixar
(lease) alugar
letter a carta
(of alphabet) a letra
letterbox o marco do correio

lettuce a alface
level crossing a passagem de nível
library a biblioteca
licence a licença
(driving) a carta de condução
lid a tampa
lie (untruth) a mentira
to lie down deitar-se
life a vida
lifebelt o cinto salva-vidas
lifeboat o salva-vidas
lifeguard o/a guarda salva-vidas
life insurance o seguro de vida
life jacket o colete de salvação
life raft a bolsa salva-vidas
lift (elevator) o elevador
(in car) a boleia
light a luz
have you a light? tem lume?
light (not heavy) leve
(colour) claro(a)
light bulb a lâmpada
lighter o isqueiro
lighthouse o farol
lightning os relâmpagos
lights out luzes apagadas
like como
it's like this é assim
to like gostar de
I like coffee gosto de café
I don't like... não gosto de...
I'd like to... gostava de...
we'd like to... gostávamos de...
lilo o colchão de ar
lime a lima
line (row, queue) a fila
(phone) a linha
linen (cloth) o linho
(bed linen) a roupa de cama
lingerie a roupa interior
lion o leão
lip reading a leitura de lábios
lips os lábios
lip salve a manteiga de cacau
lipstick o batom
liqueur o licor
list a lista
to listen to ouvir
litre o litro
a litre of milk um litro de leite
litter (rubbish) o lixo
little pequeno(a)
a little... um pouco de...
to live viver; morar
I live in Edinburgh moro em Edimburgo
he lives in London ele vive em Londres
he lives in a flat ele vive num apartamento; ele mora num apartamento
liver o fígado
living room a sala de estar
lizard o lagarto
loaf (of bread) o pão
lobster a lagosta
local local
to lock fechar com chave
lock a fechadura
the lock is broken a fechadura está quebrada
bike lock o cadeado da bicicleta
locker (luggage) o cacifo de bagagem
locksmith o/a serralheiro(a)
log o tronco
log book (for car) a documentação do carro
lollipop o chupa-chupa
London Londres
in London em Londres
to London a Londres
long comprido(a); longo(a)
for a long time durante muito tempo
long-sighted presbíope
to look after cuidar de
to look at olhar para
to look for procurar
loose solto(a)
it's come loose soltou-se
lorry o camião
to lose perder
lost perdido(a)
I have lost my wallet perdi a minha carteira
I am lost estou perdido(a)

lost property office a secção de perdidos e achados
lot: ***a lot*** (much) muito(a)
(many) muitos(as)
lotion a loção
lottery a lotaria
loud (noisy) ruidoso(a); barulhento(a)
(volume) alto(a)
lounge (in hotel) a sala de estar
(in house) a sala de estar
(in airport) o salão
to love amar
I love swimming gosto muito de nadar
I love you amo-te
lovely encantador(a)
low baixo(a)
low-fat magro(a)
low tide a maré baixa
luck a sorte
lucky: ***to be lucky*** ter sorte
luggage a bagagem
luggage rack o porta-bagagens
luggage tag a etiqueta de bagagem
luggage trolley o carrinho
lump (swelling) o inchaço
(on head) o galo
lunch o almoço
lunch break a hora do almoço
lung o pulmão
luxury o luxo

M

machine a máquina
mad (insane) louco(a)
(angry) furioso(a)
madam a senhora
magazine a revista
maggot a larva
magnet o íman
magnifying glass a lupa
magpie a pega
maid a empregada
maiden name o nome de solteira
mail o correio
by mail pelo correio
main principal
main course (of meal) o prato principal
main road a estrada principal
mains (electrical) a rede eléctrica
to make (generally) fazer
(meal) preparar
make-up a maquilhagem
male masculino(a)
mallet o maço
man o homem
to manage (cope) arranjar-se
manager o/a gerente
managing director o/a director(a) geral
manual manual
many muitos(as)
map o mapa
marathon a maratona
marble o mármore
March Março
margarine a margarina
marina a marina
marinated marinado(a)
marjoram o orégão
mark (stain) a nódoa
market o mercado
when is the market? quando é que há mercado?
where is the market? onde é que fica o mercado?
marketplace o mercado
marmalade o doce de laranja
married casado(a)
are you married? é casado(a)?
I'm married sou casado(a)
marry: ***to get married*** casar(-se)
marsh o pântano
marzipan o maçapão
mascara o rímel®
mashed potato o puré de batata
Mass (church service) a missa
mast o mastro
masterpiece a obra-prima
match (game) o jogo; a partida
matches os fósforos
material o material
(cloth) o tecido
to matter: ***it doesn't matter*** não tem importância

what is the matter? o que é que se passa?
mattress o colchão
maximum o máximo
May Maio
mayonnaise a maionese
mayor o presidente do município/ da Câmara
me me
(after preposition) mim
meadow o prado
meal a refeição
to mean significar
what does this mean? o que é que quer dizer isto?
measles o sarampo
to measure medir
meat a carne
I don't eat meat não como carne
red meat as carnes vermelhas
white meat as carnes brancas
mechanic o/a mecânico(a)
medical insurance o seguro de doença
medicine o medicamento
medieval medieval
Mediterranean o Mediterrâneo
medium médio(a)
medium rare (meat) ao ponto
to meet (by chance) encontrar; dar com
(by arrangement) encontrar-se com
pleased to meet you prazer em conhecê-lo(a)
meeting a reunião
meeting point o ponto de encontro
megahertz o megahertz
melon o melão
to melt derreter
member (of club, etc) o/a sócio(a)
membership card o cartão de sócio(a)
memory a memória
(thing remembered) a lembrança
memory card (for digital camera) o cartão memória
men os homens
to mend arranjar; consertar
meningitis a meningite
menu a ementa
à la carte menu a ementa a la carte
set menu a ementa fixa
meringue o merengue
message a mensagem; o recado
metal o metal
meter o contador
metre o metro
microwave oven o micro-ondas
midday o meio-dia
at midday ao meio-dia
middle o meio
middle-aged de meia-idade
midge o mosquito
midnight a meia-noite
at midnight à meia-noite
migraine a enxaqueca
I've a migraine tenho uma enxaqueca
mild (climate) temperado(a)
(taste) suave
mile a milha
milk o leite
fresh milk o leite fresco
full-cream milk o leite gordo
hot milk o leite quente
long-life milk o leite ultrapasteurizado
powdered milk o leite em pó
semi-skimmed milk o leite meio-gordo
skimmed milk o leite magro
soya milk o leite de soja
with milk com leite
without milk sem leite
milkshake o batido de leite
millennium o milénio
millimetre o milímetro
million o milhão
mince (meat) a carne picada
mind a mente
to mind (take care of) ocupar-se de
(object to) objectar
do you mind if...? importa-se...?
I don't mind não me importo
mineral water a água mineral
minibar o minibar
minimum o mínimo
minister (political) o ministro
(church) o pastor

mink o vison; a manta
minor road a estrada secundária
mint (herb) a hortelã
(sweet) o rebuçado de mentol
minute o minuto
mirror o espelho
to misbehave comportar-se mal
miscarriage o aborto (espontâneo)
Miss... a Menina...
to miss (plane, train, etc) perder
missing (lost) perdido(a)
my son is missing o meu filho desapareceu
mistake o erro
misty: *it's misty* há nevoeiro
misunderstanding o mal-entendido
to mix misturar
mixer a batedeira
mobile phone o telemóvel
mobile phone charger o carregador de telemóvel
modem o modem
modern moderno(a)
moisturizer o creme hidratante
mole (on skin) o sinal
moment: *just a moment* um momento
monastery o mosteiro
Monday a segunda-feira
money o dinheiro
I've no money não tenho dinheiro
money order o vale postal
monkey o macaco
month o mês
last month o mês passado
next month o mês que vem
this month este mês
monthly mensalmente
monument o monumento
moon a lua
mooring o atracadouro
mop a esfregona
moped a motocicleta
more mais
more bread mais pão
more than 3 mais de três
more wine mais vinho
morning a manhã
in the morning de manhã
this morning esta manhã
tomorrow morning amanhã de manhã
morning-after pill a pílula abortiva
mosque a mesquita
mosquito o mosquito
mosquito net o mosquiteiro
mosquito repellent o repelente contra mosquitos
most: *most of* a maioria de
moth a mariposa
(clothes) a traça
mother a mãe
mother-in-law a sogra
motor o motor
motorbike a moto
motorboat o barco a motor
motorcycle a motocicleta
motorway a auto-estrada
mould (mildew) o bolor
mountain a montanha
mountain bike a bicicleta de montanha
mountain biking o ciclismo de montanha
mountain rescue o socorro para alpinistas
mountaineering o alpinismo
mouse o rato
mousse (food) a mousse
(hair) a espuma
moustache o bigode
mouth a boca
mouthwash o desinfectante para a boca
to move mexer; mover
it isn't moving não se mexe; não se move
movie o filme
to mow cortar
Mr o Senhor
Mrs a Senhora
Ms a Senhora
much muito(a)
too much demais; demasiado
mud a lama
muddy (road) lamacento(a)
(clothes) enlameado(a)

mugging o assalto
mumps a papeira
muscle o músculo
museum o museu
mushroom o cogumelo
music a música
musical o musical
mussel o mexilhão
must (to have to) dever
I must devo
we must devemos
I mustn't não devo
we mustn't não devemos
mustard a mostarda
mutton o carneiro
my o meu (a minha)

N

nail (metal) o prego
(on finger) a unha
nailbrush a escova das unhas
nail clippers o corta-unhas
nail file a lima para as unhas
nail polish o verniz das unhas
nail polish remover a acetona
nail scissors as tesouras para as unhas
name o nome
my name is... o meu nome é...
what's your name? como é que te chamas?
nanny a ama
napkin o guardanapo
nappy a fralda
narrow estreito(a)
national nacional
national park o parque nacional
nationality a nacionalidade
natural natural
nature a natureza
nature reserve a reserva natural
navy blue azul-marinho(a)
near perto
is it near? fica perto?
near the bank perto do banco
necessary necessário(a)
neck o pescoço
necklace o colar
nectarine a nectarina
to need precisar de
I need... preciso de
we need... precisamos de
I need to go tenho que ir
needle a agulha
a needle and thread uma agulha e a linha
negative (photo) o negativo
neighbour o/a vizinho(a)
nephew o sobrinho
nest o ninho
net a rede
nettle a urtiga
neutral (car) o ponto-morto
never nunca
I never drink wine nunca bebo vinho
new novo(a)
news a notícia
(on television) o noticiário; telejornal
newsagent a tabacaria
newspaper o jornal
newsstand o quiosque
New Year o Ano Novo
happy New Year! Feliz Ano Novo!
New Year's Eve a véspera de Ano Novo
New Zealand a Nova Zelândia
next próximo(a)
next to ao lado de
next week a semana que vem
the next bus o próximo autocarro
the next stop a próxima paragem
the next train o próximo comboio
nice (person, holiday) agradável
(place) bonito(a)
niece a sobrinha
night a noite
at night à noite
last night ontem à noite
per night por noite
tomorrow night amanhã à noite
nightclub a boîte
nightdress a camisa de noite
night porter o porteiro da noite
no não
no entry entrada proibida
no ice sem gelo

no smoking proibido fumar
no sugar sem açúcar
no thanks não, obrigado(a)
(without) sem
nobody ninguém
noise o barulho
noisy barulhento(a); ruidoso(a)
it's very noisy há muito barulho
non-alcoholic não-alcoólico(a)
none nenhum(a)
there's none left não sobrou nada
non-smoker o/a não-fumador(a)
non-smoking não-fumador(a)
north o norte
Northern Ireland a Irlanda do Norte
North Sea o Mar do Norte
nose o nariz
not não
note (banknote) a nota
(letter) a nota
note pad o bloco-notas
nothing nada
nothing else mais nada
notice o aviso
noticeboard o quadro de avisos
novel o romance
November Novembro
now agora
nowhere (be) em nenhum lugar
(go) a lugar nenhum
nuclear nuclear
nudist beach a praia para nudistas
number o número
numberplate (car) a matrícula
nurse o/a enfermeiro(a)
nursery (creche) a creche
nursery slope a rampa para principiantes
nut (to eat) a noz
(for bolt) a porca
nutmeg a noz moscada

O

oak o carvalho
oar o remo
oats a aveia
to obtain obter
obvious óbvio(a)
occasionally às vezes
occupation (work) a ocupação
ocean o oceano
October Outubro
octopus o polvo
odd (number) ímpar
of de
a bottle of water uma garrafa de água
a glass of wine um copo de vinho
made of... feito(a) de...
off (radio, engine, etc) desligado(a)
(milk, food, etc) estragado(a)
this meat is off esta carne está estragada
to offer oferecer
office o escritório
often muitas vezes
how often? quantas vezes?
oil o óleo
oil filter o filtro do óleo
oil gauge o indicador do óleo
ointment a pomada
OK está bem
old velho(a)
how old are you? quantos anos tem?
I'm ... years old tenho ... anos
olive a azeitona
olive oil o azeite
omelette a omeleta
on (light, TV) aceso(a)
(engine) a trabalhar
on em
on the table na mesa
on time a horas
once uma vez
at once imediatamente
one um (uma)
one-way de sentido único
onion a cebola
only somente; só; único(a)
open aberto(a)
to open abrir
opera a ópera
opera house o teatro da ópera
operation (surgical) a operação
operator (phone) o/a telefonista

opposite: ***opposite (to)*** em frente de
opposite the hotel em frente do hotel
optician's o oculista
or ou
tea or coffee? chá ou café?
orange adj cor-de-laranja
orange (fruit) a laranja
orange juice o sumo de laranja
orchestra a orquestra
order: ***out of order*** fora de serviço; avariado(a)
to order (in restaurant) pedir
can I order? posso pedir?
oregano o orégão
organic biológico(a)
to organize organizar
original original
ornament o ornamento
other: ***the other one*** o/a outro(a)
have you any others? tem outros(as)?
ounce = approx. 30 g
our o(a) nosso(a)
out fora
he's gone out ele saiu
he's out não está
out of order fora de serviço; avariado(a)
outdoor ao ar livre
outside: ***it's outside*** está lá fora
oven o forno
oven gloves as luvas de cozinha
ovenproof refratário(a)
over (on top of) sobre
to be overbooked ter mais reservas que lugares
to overcharge cobrar demais
overcoat o sobretudo
overdone (food) cozido(a) demais
overdose a dose excessiva
to overheat aquecer demasiado
to overload sobrecarregar
to oversleep dormir além da hora
to overtake (in car) ultrapassar
to owe dever
I owe you... devo-lhe...
you owe me... deve-me...
owl o mocho
owner o/a dono(a)
oxygen o oxigénio
oyster a ostra

P

pace o passo
pacemaker o pacemaker
to pack bags fazer as malas
package o embrulho
package tour a viagem organizada
packet o pacote
padded envelope o envelope almofadado
paddling pool a piscina para crianças
padlock o cadeado
page a página
paid pago(a)
pain a dor
painful doloroso(a)
painkiller o analgésico
to paint pintar
paintbrush o pincel
painting a pintura
(picture) o quadro
pair o par
palace o palácio
pale pálido(a)
pan (frying) a frigideira
(saucepan) o tacho
pancake a panqueca
panniers (for bike) as bolsas para a bicicleta
pants (briefs) as cuecas
panty liners os pensos higiénicos
paper o papel
(newspaper) o jornal
paper hankies os lenços de papel
paper napkins os guardanapos de papel
papoose (for carrying baby) a mochila para levar o bebé
paracetamol o paracetamol
paraffin o óleo de parafina
paragliding o para-pente
paralysed paralisado(a)
parcel a encomenda
pardon desculpe?

I beg your pardon! desculpe-me!
parents os pais
park o parque
to park estacionar
parking disk o disco de estacionamento
parking meter o parquímetro
parking ticket a multa (por estacionamento em lugar proibido)
parsley a salsa
parsnip a cherivia
part a parte
partner (business) o/a sócio(a)
(friend) o/a companheiro(a)
party (celebration) a festa
(political) o partido
pass (mountain) o desfiladeiro
(train, bus) o passe
passenger o/a passageiro(a)
passport o passaporte
passport control o controle de passaportes
pasta as massas
pastry (dough) a massa
(cake) o bolo
pâté o paté
path o caminho
patient o/a paciente *adj*; o/a doente
pavement o passeio
to pay pagar
I'd like to pay queria pagar
I've paid já paguei
where do I pay? onde é que se paga?
payment o pagamento
payphone o telefone público
peace a paz
peach o pêssego
peak rate a taxa alta
peanut o amendoim
peanut allergy a alergia a amendoins
peanut butter a manteiga de amendoim
pear a pêra
pearls as pérolas
peas as ervilhas
pedal o pedal
pedal boat o barco de pedáis
pedestrian o/a peão
pedestrian crossing a passadeira para peões
to peel (fruit) descascar
peg (clothes) a mola
(tent) a estaca
pen a caneta
pencil o lápis
penfriend o/a correspondente
penicillin a penicilina
penis o pénis
penknife o canivete
pension a pensão
pensioner o/a reformado(a); o/a idoso(a)
people as pessoas
pepper (spice) a pimenta
(vegetable) o pimento
per por
per day por dia
per hour por hora
per week por semana
per person por pessoa
50 km per hour 50 km por hora
perch (fish) a perca
perfect perfeito(a)
performance a representação
the next performance a próxima representação
perfume o perfume
perhaps talvez
period (menstruation) a menstruação
perm a permanente
permit a licença
person a pessoa
per person por pessoa
personal organizer a agenda
personal stereo o Walkman®
pet o animal de estimação
pet food a comida para animais domésticos
pet shop a loja para animais domésticos
petrol a gasolina
4-star petrol a gasolina super
unleaded petrol a gasolina sem chumbo
petrol cap a tampa do depósito de gasolina
petrol pump a bomba de gasolina

petrol station a estação de serviço
petrol tank o depósito da gasolina
pewter o estanho
pharmacy a farmácia
pheasant o faisão
phone o telefone
mobile telephone o telemóvel
to phone telefonar
phonebook a lista telefónica
phonebox a cabine telefónica
phonecard o credifone
photocopy a fotocópia
I need a photocopy preciso duma fotocópia
photograph a fotografia
to take a photograph tirar uma fotografia
phrase book o guia de conversação
piano o piano
to pick (fruit, flowers) colher
(to choose) escolher
pickled de conserva
pickpocket o/a carteirista
picnic o piquenique
to have a picnic fazer um piquenique
picnic area a zona de piqueniques
picnic hamper o cesto para piqueniques
picnic rug a manta
picnic table a mesa para piqueniques
picture (painting) o quadro
(photo) a foto
pie (savoury) a empada
(sweet) a torta
piece o bocado; o pedaço
pier o cais
pig o porco
pill o comprimido
to be on the Pill tomar a pílula
pillow a almofada
pillowcase a fronha
pilot o/a piloto(a)
pin o alfinete
safety pin o alfinete de segurança
PIN number o PIN (pessoal)
pineapple o ananás
pink cor-de-rosa
pint = approx. 0.5 litre
a pint of beer uma caneca de cerveja
pipe (for smoking) o cachimbo
(drain, etc) o tubo; o cano
pity: ***what a pity!*** que pena!
pizza a pizza
place o lugar
place of birth o lugar de nascimento
plain (yoghurt, etc) natural
(obvious) claro(a)
plait a trança
plan o plano
to plan planear
plane o avião
plant a planta
plaster (sticking) o adesivo
(for broken limb) o gesso
plastic o plástico
plastic bag o saco de plástico
plate o prato
platform (railway) a linha; a plataforma
which platform? qual é a linha?
play (at theatre) a peça
to play (sport) jogar
(musical instrument) tocar
(general play) brincar
playground o pátio de recreio
play park o parque infantil
playroom o quarto de brinquedos
pleasant agradável
please por favor; (se) faz favor
pleased: ***pleased to meet you*** prazer em conhecê-lo(a)
plenty: ***plenty of*** (much) muito(a)
(many) muitos(as)
pliers o alicate
plug (electric) a ficha; a tomada
(for sink) a válvula
to plug in ligar
plum a ameixa
plumber o canalizador
plumbing (pipes) a canalização
plunger (for sink) o desentupidor
p.m. (afternoon/evening) de tarde
(night) de noite
poached (fish) cozido(a)
poached egg o ovo escalfado

pocket o bolso
points (in car) os platinados
poison o veneno
poisonous venenoso(a)
police (force) a polícia
police officer o/a polícia
police station a esquadra
polish (for shoes) a pomada para o calçado
(for furniture) a cera
pollen o pólen
polluted poluído(a)
pollution a poluição
pony o pónei
pony trekking o passeio a cavalo
pool a piscina
pool attendant o/a empregado(a) da piscina
poor pobre
poorly: ***he feels poorly*** ele não se sente bem
pope o papa
poppy a papoila
popular popular
pork a carne de porco
port (wine) o vinho do porto
(seaport) o porto
portal o portal
porter (for door) o porteiro
(for luggage) o carregador
portion a porção
Portugal Portugal
Portuguese português (portuguesa)
(language) o português
possible possível
post: ***by post*** pelo correio
to post pôr no correio
postbox o marco do correio
postcard o postal
postcode o código postal
poster o póster
(advertising) o cartaz
postman/woman o/a carteiro(a)
post office os correios
to postpone adiar
pot (for cooking) a panela
potato a batata
baked potato a batata assada
boiled potatoes as batatas cozidas
fried potatoes as batatas fritas
mashed potatoes o puré de batata
roast potatoes as batatas assadas
sautéed potatoes as batatas salteadas
potato masher o passe-vite
potato peeler o descascador de batatas
potato salad a salada de batata
pothole o buraco
pottery a cerâmica
pound (money) a libra
(weight) = approx. 0.5 kilo
to pour deitar
powdered: ***in powdered form*** em pó
powdered milk o leite em pó
power o poder
power cut o corte de energia
pram o carrinho do bebé
prawn o lagostim
to pray rezar
prayer a oração
to prefer preferir
pregnant grávida
I'm pregnant estou grávida
to prepare preparar
to prescribe receitar
prescription a receita médica
present (gift) o presente; a oferta; a prenda
preservative o preservativo
president o/a presidente
press (newspapers) a imprensa
pressure a pressão
blood pressure a tensão arterial
tyre pressure a pressão dos pneus
pretty bonito(a)
price o preço
price list a lista de preços
priest o padre
prince o príncipe
princess a princesa
print (photo) a cópia
printer a impressora
to print out imprimir
prison a prisão
private privado(a)

prize o prémio
probably provavelmente
problem o problema
no problem não tem problema
programme o programa
professor o/a professor(a) catedrático(a)
prohibited proibido(a)
promise a promessa
to promise prometer
pronounce pronunciar
how is this pronounced? como se pronuncia isto?
protein a proteína
Protestant protestante
to provide fornecer
prune a ameixa seca
public público(a)
public holiday o feriado
publisher o/a editor(a)
pudding o pudim;
(dessert) a sobremesa
to pull puxar
I've pulled a muscle distendi o músculo
to pull over (car) encostar
pullover o pulóver
pump a bomba
pumpkin a abóbora
puncture o furo
puncture repair kit o estojo de ferramentas
puppet o fantoche
puppet show o teatro de marionetas; os fantoches
puppy o cachorro
purple roxo(a)
purpose: *on purpose* de propósito
purse o porta-moedas
to push empurrar
pushchair o carrinho
to put pôr
to put back repor
pyjamas o pijama

Q

quail a codorniz
quality a qualidade
quantity a quantidade
quarantine a quarentena
to quarrel discutir
quarter o quarto
quay o cais
queen a rainha
query a pergunta
question a pergunta
queue a fila; a bicha
to queue fazer fila
quick rápido(a)
quickly depressa
quiet (place) sossegado(a)
a quiet room um quarto tranquilo
quilt o edredão
quite: *it's quite good* é bastante bom
quite expensive é muito caro
quiz o concurso
quiz show (TV) o concurso televisivo

R

rabbit o coelho
rabies a raiva
race (sport) a corrida
(human) a raça
race course o hipódromo
rack (luggage) o porta-bagagens
racket a raqueta
radiator (car) o radiador
(heater) o radiador
radio o rádio
radish o rabanete
raffle a rifa
rag o trapo
railcard o passe do comboio
railway o caminho de ferro
railway station a estação de comboio; caminho de ferro
rain a chuva
to rain: *it's raining* está a chover
rainbow o arco-íris
raincoat o impermeável; a gabardina
raisin a passa de uva
rake o ancinho
rape a violação
to rape violar
raped: *I've been raped* fui violado(a)

rare (unique) raro(a)
(steak) mal passado(a)
rash (skin) a urticária
raspberries as framboesas
rat a ratazana
rate (price) a taxa
rate of exchange o câmbio
raw cru(a)
razor a máquina de barbear
razorblades as lâminas de barbear
to read ler
ready pronto(a)
to get ready preparar-se
real real
to realize perceber
rearview mirror o retrovisor
reason a razão
receipt o recibo
receiver (phone) o auscultador
recently recentemente
reception (desk) a recepção
receptionist o/a recepcionista
to recharge recargar
recipe a receita
to recognize reconhecer
to recommend recomendar
record (music) o disco
to record (facts) registar
(music) gravar
to recover (from illness) recuperar
to recycle reciclar
red vermelho(a); encarnado(a)
redcurrants as groselhas
to reduce reduzir
reduction o desconto
reel (fishing) o carretel
to refer to referir-se a
referee o/a árbitro(a)
refill (pen, lighter) a recarga
refund o reembolso
to refuse recusar
regarding com relação a
region a região
to register (at hotel) preencher o registo
registered (letter) registado(a)
registration form a folha de registo

regulations os regulamentos
to reimburse reembolsar
relation (family) o/a parente
relationship (personal) as relações
(family) o parentesco
relative (family) o/a parente
to relax repousar; relaxar; descansar
reliable de confiança
to remain ficar
to remember lembrar-se de
I don't remember não me lembro
remote control o comando
removal firm a companhia de mudanças
to remove retirar
rent (house) a renda; o aluguer
(car) o aluguer
to rent (house, car) alugar;
(house) arrendar
rental o aluguer;
(house) o arrendamento
repair a reparação
to repair reparar; consertar
to repeat repetir
to reply responder
report o relatório
to report (crime, person) comunicar
request o pedido
to request pedir
to require precisar de
to rescue salvar
reservation a reserva
to reserve reservar
reserved reservado(a)
resident (at hotel) o/a hóspede
resort a estância
rest (repose) o descanso
(remainder) o resto
the rest of the wine o resto do vinho
to rest descansar
restaurant o restaurante
restaurant car o vagão restaurante
to retire reformar-se
retired reformado(a)
I'm retired estou reformado(a)
to return (to go back) voltar
(to give something back) devolver

return ticket o bilhete de ida e volta
to reverse fazer marcha atrás
to reverse the charges fazer uma chamada pagável no destino
reverse-charge call a chamada pagável no destino
reverse gear a marcha atrás
rheumatism o reumatismo
rhubarb o ruibarbo
rib a costela
ribbon a fita
rice o arroz
rich (person) rico(a)
(food) suculento(a)
to ride (horse) montar a cavalo
(in a car, bus, etc) viajar
right (correct) certo(a)
to be right ter razão
right: *on/to the right* à direita
right-handed destro(a)
right of way a prioridade
ring (for finger) o anel
to ring (bell) tocar
(phone) telefonar
it's ringing está a tocar
ring road a circunvalação
ripe maduro(a)
river o rio
road a estrada
road map o mapa das estradas
road sign o sinal de trânsito
roadworks as obras na estrada
roast assado(a)
robber o ladrão (a ladra)
robin o pintarroxo
roll (bread) o pãozinho; o papo-seco
rollerblades os patins em linha
rollers os rolos
roller skates os patins de rodas
rolling pin o rolo da massa
romance (novel) o romance
Romanesque românico(a)
romantic romântico(a)
roof o telhado
roof rack o porta-bagagens
room (in house, hotel) o quarto
(space) o espaço
double room o quarto de casal
family room o quarto de família
single room o quarto individual
room number o número do quarto
room service o serviço de quarto
root a raíz
rope a corda
rose a rosa
rosemary o alecrim
rosé wine o vinho rosé
rotten (fruit, etc) podre; estragado(a)
rough (surface) áspero(a)
(sea) agitado(a)
round (shape) redondo(a)
roundabout (traffic) a rotunda
route a rota
row (line) a fila
to row (boat) remar
rowing (sport) o remo
rowing boat o barco a remos
royal real
rubber (eraser) a borracha
(material) a borracha
rubber band o elástico
rubber gloves as luvas de borracha
rubbish o lixo
rubella a rubéola
rucksack a mochila
rudder o leme
rug o tapete
ruins as ruínas
ruler (for measuring) a régua
rum o rum
to run correr
rush hour a hora de ponta
rusty ferrugento(a)
rye o centeio

S

saccharin a sacarina
sad triste
saddle (bike) o selim
(horse) a sela
safe (for valuables) o cofre
safe seguro(a)
is it safe? é seguro?
safety belt o cinto de segurança

safety pin o alfinete de segurança
sage (herb) a salva
to sail (sport, leisure) velejar
sailboard a prancha
sail(ing) a vela
sailing boat o barco a vela
saint o/a santo(a)
salad a salada
green salad a salada verde
mixed salad a salada mista
potato salad a salada de batatas
tomato salad a salada de tomates
salad dressing o tempero da salada
salami o salame
salary o salário
sale(s) o saldo
salesman/woman o/a vendedor(a)
sales rep o/a representante de vendas
salmon o salmão
smoked salmon o salmão fumado
salt o sal
salt water a água salgada
salty salgado(a)
same mesmo(a)
sample a amostra
sand a areia
sandals as sandálias
sandwich a sandes; sanduíche
toasted sandwich a tosta
sanitary towel o penso higiénico
sardine a sardinha
satellite dish a antena parabólica
satellite TV a televisão via satélite
Saturday o sábado
sauce o molho
tomato sauce o molho de tomate
saucepan a caçarola
saucer o pires
sauna a sauna
sausage a salsicha
to save (life) salvar
(money) poupar
savoury saboroso(a)
savouries os salgados
saw a serra
to say dizer
scales (weighing) a balança
scallops as vieiras
scampi as gambas panadas
scan o scan *n*
to scan fazer um scan
scanner o scanner
scarf (woollen) o cachecol
(headscarf) o lenço (de pescoço)
scenery a paisagem
schedule o programa
school a escola
primary school a escola primária
secondary school o colégio
scissors a tesoura
score (of match) o resultado
to score marcar
Scot o/a escocês (escocesa)
Scotland a Escócia
Scottish escocês (escocesa)
scouring pad a palha de aço
screen (computer, TV) o ecrã
screenwash o detergente para o pára-brisas
screw o parafuso
screwdriver a chave de parafusos
phillips screwdriver® a chave phillips®
scuba diving mergulhar; o mergulho
sculpture a escultura
sea o mar
seafood os mariscos
seagull a gaivota
seal a foca
seam (of dress) a costura
to search (internet) pesquisar
to search for procurar
seasick enjoado(a)
I get seasick fico enjoado(a)
seasickness o enjoo
seaside a praia
at the seaside na praia
season (of year) a estação
(holiday) a temporada
in season da época
season ticket o passe
seasoning o tempero
seat (chair) a cadeira
(on bus, train, etc) o lugar

seatbelt o cinto de segurança
seaweed a alga marinha
second segundo(a)
second class a segunda classe; *adj* de segunda classe
second-hand em segunda mão; usado(a)
secretary o/a secretário(a)
security a segurança
security guard o guarda de segurança
sedative o sedativo
to see ver
seed a semente
to seize agarrar
self-catering com cozinha
self-employed que trabalha por conta própria
self-service o auto-serviço
to sell vender
do you sell...? vende...?
sell-by date... usar antes de...
Sellotape® a fita-cola
semi-skimmed milk o leite meio-gordo
to send mandar; enviar
senior citizen o/a reformado(a)
sensible sensato(a)
separated separado(a)
separately: *to pay separately* pagar separadamente
September Setembro
septic tank a fossa séptica
sequel (film, book) a continuação; a sequela
serious sério(a)
(illness) grave
to serve servir
server (internet) o servidor
service (in church) o serviço religioso
(in restaurant) o serviço
is service included? o serviço está incluído?
service charge o serviço
service station a estação de serviço
serviette o guardanapo
set menu a ementa fixa
settee o sofá
several vários(as)
to sew coser
sewer o esgoto
sex (gender) o sexo
(intercourse) o sexocf
shade a sombra
in the shade à sombra
to shake (bottle) sacudir
shallow pouco profundo(a)
shampoo o champô
shampoo and set a lavagem e mise
to share dividir
to share out distribuir
sharp (razor, knife) afiado(a)
to shave fazer a barba
shaving cream o creme de barbear
shawl o xaile
she ela
sheep a ovelha
sheet (for bed) o lençol
shelf a prateleira
shell (seashell) a concha
(egg, nut) a casca
shellfish o marisco
sheltered abrigado(a)
shepherd o pastor
sherry o xerez
to shine brilhar
shingles (illness) o herpes zóster
ship o barco
shirt a camisa
shock absorber o amortecedor
shoe o sapato
shoelaces os atacadores
shoe polish a graxa
shoe repairer's o sapateiro
shoe shop a sapataria
shop a loja
shop assistant o/a vendedor(a)
shop window a montra
shopping: *to go shopping* ir às compras
shopping centre o centro comercial
shore a costa
short curto(a)
short circuit o curto-circuito
short cut o atalho

shortage a escassez
shorts os calções
short-sighted míope
shoulder o ombro
to shout gritar
show o espectáculo
to show mostrar
shower o duche; o chuveiro
to have a shower tomar um duche
(rain) o chuveiro; o aguaceiro
shower cap a touca de banho
shower curtain a cortina do chuveiro
shower gel o gel para banho
shrimps os camarões
to shrink encolher
shrub o arbusto
shut (closed) fechado(a); encerrado(a)
to shut fechar; encerrar
shutters as persianas; as venezianas
shuttle service o serviço de ligação
shy tímido(a)
sick (ill) doente
I feel sick sinto-me mal-disposto(a)
side o lado
side dish o acompanhamento
sidelight o farolim
sidewalk o passeio
sieve (for liquids) o coador
(for flour) a peneira
to sightsee fazer turismo
sightseeing o turismo
to go sightseeing fazer turismo
sightseeing tour a excursão
sign (road-, notice, etc) o sinal
to sign assinar
signal: *there's no signal* não há sinal; pulso
signature a assinatura
signpost a sinalização
silk a seda
silver a prata
similar: *similar to* semelhante a
simple simples
since (time) desde (que)
(because) porque
since Saturday desde sábado
to sing cantar
single (not married) solteiro(a)
(not double) simples; individual
single bed a cama de solteiro
single room o quarto individual
single ticket o bilhete de ida; simples
sink o lava-louça
sir senhor
sister a irmã
sister-in-law a cunhada
to sit sentar-se
please, sit down faça o favor de se sentar
size (clothes) o tamanho
(shoes) o número
to skate patinar
skates (ice) os patins de lâmina
(roller) os patins de rodas
skating rink o rinque de patinagem
ski o esqui
skis os esquis
to ski esquiar
skimmed milk o leite magro
skin a pele
skindiving mergulhar; o mergulho
skirt a saia
sky o céu
slang o calão
sledge o trenó
to sleep dormir
to sleep in dormir até tarde
sleeper (on train) a carruagem-cama
sleeping bag o saco cama
sleeping car a carruagem-cama
sleeping pill o comprimido para dormir
slice a fatia
slide (photograph) o diapositivo
to slip escorregar
slippers os chinelos
slow lento(a)
small pequeno(a)
smaller mais pequeno(a)
smell o cheiro
smile o sorriso
to smile sorrir
smoke o fumo
to smoke fumar
can I smoke? posso fumar?

I don't smoke não fumo
smoke alarm o alarme contra incêndios
smoked fumado(a)
smokers os fumadores
smoking: *no smoking* proibido fumar
smooth liso(a); macio(a)
snack o lanche
to have a snack comer qualquer coisa
snack bar o snack-bar; o café
snake a cobra
snake bite a mordedura de cobra
to sneeze espirrar
to snore ressonar
snorkel o tubo de ar
snorkelling o mergulho
snow a neve
to snow nevar
it's snowing está a nevar
so tão
so much tanto(a)
so then portanto; então
soap o sabão
soap powder o sabão em pó
sober sóbrio(a)
socket (electrical) a tomada
socks as peúgas
soda water a água com gás
sofa o sofá
sofa bed o sofá-cama
soft macio(a)
soft drink o refrigerante
software o software
soldier o soldado
sole (fish) o linguado
(of shoe) a sola
soluble solúvel
some alguns (algumas)
someone alguém
something alguma coisa
sometimes às vezes
son o filho
son-in-law o genro
song a canção
soon em breve
as soon as possible o mais antes possível
sore magoado(a)
sore throat: *I have a sore throat* dói-me a garganta
sorry: *I'm sorry!* lamento; desculpe!
sort: *what sort of cheese?* que tipo de queijo?
sound o som
soup a sopa
sour azedo(a)
soured cream as natas azedas
south o sul
souvenir a recordação
spa as termas
space o espaço
spade a enxada
Spain a Espanha
Spanish espanhol(a)
(language) o espanhol
spanner a chave inglesa
spare parts as peças sobressalentes
spare room o quarto de hóspedes
spare tyre o pneu sobressalente
spare wheel a roda sobressalente
sparkling espumoso(a)
sparkling water a água com gás
sparkling wine o espumante
spark plug a vela
to speak falar
do you speak English? fala inglês?
I don't speak Portuguese não falo português
special especial
specialist o/a especialista
speciality a especialidade
speech a fala
(address) o discurso
speed a velocidade
speedboat a lancha
speeding o excesso de velocidade
speeding ticket a multa por excesso de velocidade
speed limit o limite de velocidade
to exceed the speed limit ultrapassar o limite de velocidade
speedometer o conta-quilómetros
spell: *how do you spell it?* como se escreve?

to spend (money) gastar
spices as especiarias
spicy picante
spider a aranha
to spill entornar
spinach o espinafre
spin-dryer a secadora
spine a coluna
spirits as bebidas alcoólicas
splinter a lasca
spoke (wheel) o raio
sponge a esponja
spoon a colher
sport o desporto
sports centre o centro de desportos; centro desportivo
sports shop a loja de artigos desportivos
spot (pimple) a borbulha
to sprain: *to sprain one's ankle* torcer o tornozelo
spring (season) a primavera
(coil) a mola
spring onion a cebolinha
square (in town) a praça
squash (drink) o sumo
(game) o squash
to squeeze apertar
squid as lulas
stadium o estádio
staff o pessoal
stage o palco; a cena
stain a nódoa
stained glass o vitral
stain remover o tira-nódoas
stairs a escada
stale (bread) duro(a)
stalls (in theatre) a plateia
stamp (postage) o selo
to stand estar em pé
to stand up levantar-se
star (in sky, in films) a estrela
starfish a estrela-do-mar
to start começar
starter (in meal) a entrada
(in car) o motor de arranque
station a estação
stationer's a papelaria
statue a estátua
stay a estadia; a visita
enjoy your stay! desfrute a sua visita!
to stay ficar
I'm staying at a hotel fico num hotel
steak o bife
medium steak o bife ao ponto
rare steak o bife malpassado
well-done steak o bife bem-passado
to steal roubar
to steam cozer a vapor
steamed cozido(a) a vapor
steel o aço
steep: *is it steep?* custa a subir?
steeple o campanário
steering wheel o volante
step (stair) o degrau
stepdaughter a enteada
stepfather o padrasto
stepmother a madrasta
stepson o enteado
stereo o estéreo
personal stereo o Walkman®
sterling (pounds) esterlino(a)
stew o guisado
steward (on plane) o comissário de bordo
stewardess (on plane) a hospedeira de bordo
to stick (with glue) colar
sticking plaster o adesivo
still (not moving) imóvel
(not sparkling) sem gás
(yet) ainda
sting a picada
to sting picar
stitches (surgical) os pontos
stock cube o cubo de caldo
stockings as meias
stolen roubado(a)
stomach o estômago
stomach upset o mal-estar de estômago
stone a pedra
(weight) = approx. 6.5 kg
to stop (come to a halt) parar

(stop doing something) deixar de fazer alguma coisa
stop sign o sinal de paragem
store (shop) a loja
storey o andar
storm a tempestade
story a história
straightaway imediatamente
straight on sempre em frente
strainer o coador
strange estranho(a)
straw (for drinking) o canudo
strawberry o morango
stream o riacho
street a rua
street map o mapa das ruas
strength a força
stress o stress
strike (of workers) a greve
to be on strike estar em greve
string o cordel
striped às riscas
stroke (medical) a trombose
to have a stroke ter uma trombose
strong forte
strong coffee o café forte
strong tea o chá forte
stuck: ***it's stuck*** está preso(a)
student o/a estudante
student discount o desconto para estudantes
stuffed recheado(a)
stung picado(a)
stupid estúpido(a)
subscription a assinatura
subtitles as legendas
subway (underpass) a passagem subterrânea
suddenly de repente
suede a camurça
sugar o açúcar
icing sugar o açúcar em pó
sugar-free sem açúcar
to suggest sugerir
suit (men's and women's) o fato; o conjunto
suitcase a mala
sum a soma
summer o verão
summer holidays as férias de verão
summit o cume
sun o sol
to sunbathe tomar banhos de sol
sunblock o protector solar
sunburn a queimadura de sol
Sunday o domingo
sunflower o girassol
sunflower oil o óleo de girassol
sunglasses os óculos de sol
sunny: ***it's sunny*** está sol
sunrise o nascer do sol
sunroof o tecto de abrir
sunscreen o filtro solar
sunset o pôr do sol
sunshade o guarda-sol; o toldo
sunstroke a insolação
suntan o bronzeado
suntan lotion a loção de bronzear
supermarket o supermercado
supper a ceia
supplement o suplemento
to supply abastecer
surcharge a sobretaxa
sure seguro(a)
I'm sure estou seguro(a); tenho a certeza
to surf fazer surf
to surf the Net navegar a Internet
surfboard a prancha de surf
surgery (operation) a cirurgia
(building) o consultório
surname o apelido
my surname is... o meu apelido é...
surprise a surpresa
surrounded by rodeado(a) por
suspension a suspensão
to survive sobreviver
to swallow engolir
swan o cisne
to swear (bad language) blasfemar; praguejar
(in court) jurar
to sweat suar
sweater o pulóver

sweatshirt a sweatshirt
sweet (not savoury) doce
sweet (dessert) a sobremesa
sweetener o adoçante
sweets os rebuçados
to swell (injury etc) inchar
to swim nadar
swimming pool a piscina
swimsuit o fato de banho
swing (for children) o baloiço
Swiss suíço(a)
switch o interruptor
to switch off apagar; desligar
to switch on acender; ligar
Switzerland a Suíça
swollen (finger, ankle, etc) inchado(a)
swordfish o espadarte
synagogue a sinagoga
syringe a seringa

T

table a mesa
tablecloth a toalha de mesa
tablespoon a colher de sopa
tablet (pill) o comprimido
table tennis o ping-pong
table wine o vinho de mesa
tail o rabo; a cauda
tailor's a alfaiataria
take (carry) levar; transportar
(to grab, seize) agarrar
(medicine etc) tomar
(to take someone to) levar
how long does it take? quanto tempo demora?
take-away (food) para levar
to take off levantar voo
to take out (of bag etc) tirar
talc o talco
to talk to conversar com
tall alto(a)
tame (animal) manso(a)
tampons os tampões
tangerine a tangerina
tank (car) o depósito
(fish) o aquário
tap a torneira
tap water a água da torneira
tape (video) a cassette de vídeo
tape measure a fita métrica
tape recorder o gravador
target o alvo
tarragon o estragão
tart a tarte
tartar sauce o molho tártaro
taste o sabor
to taste provar
can I taste it? posso provar?
tax o imposto
taxi o táxi
taxi driver o/a taxista
taxi rank a praça de táxis
tea o chá
herbal tea a tisana
lemon tea o chá de limão
strong tea o chá forte
tea with milk o chá com leite
teabag o saquinho de chá
teapot o bule (de chá)
to teach ensinar
teacher o/a professor(a)
team a equipa
tear (in eye) a lágrima
(in material) o rasgão
teaspoon a colher de chá
teat (on baby's bottle) o tetina
tea towel o pano de cozinha
teenager o/a adolescente
teeshirt a 'T-shirt'; camiseta
teeth os dentes
teething a dentição
telegram o telegrama
telephone o telefone
mobile telephone o telemóvel
to telephone telefonar
telephone box a cabine telefónica
telephone call a chamada
telephone card o cartão telefónico; credifone
telephone directory a lista telefónica
telephone number o número de telefone
television a televisão
television set o televisor

telex o telex
to tell dizer
temperature a temperatura
to have a temperature ter febre
temple o templo
temporary temporário(a)
tenant o/a inquilino(a)
tendon o tendão
tennis o ténis
tennis ball a bola de ténis
tennis court o campo de ténis
tennis racket a raqueta de ténis
tent a tenda
tent peg a estaca
terminal (airport) o terminal
terrace a esplanada
terracotta a terracota; o barro
terrorist o/a terrorista
to test (try out) testar
testicles os testículos
tetanus o tétano
text message o SMS
than que
better than melhor do que
more than five mais de cinco
more than you mais do que tu
to thank agradecer
thank you/thanks obrigado(a)
no thanks não, obrigado(a)
thank you very much muito obrigado(a)
that (one) aquele (aquela) (= over there); esse (essa) (= near person addressed)
the (sing) o (a)
(plural) os (as)
theatre o teatro
theft o roubo
their o seu (a sua)
them (direct object) os (as)
(indirect object) lhes
(after preposition) eles (elas)
then então; depois
there (over there) ali
there is/there are há
thermometer o termómetro
these estes (estas)
these ones estes (estas)
they eles (elas)
thick grosso(a)
thief o ladrão (a ladra)
thigh a coxa
thin magro(a)
thing a coisa
my things as minhas coisas
to think pensar
(to be of opinion) achar
third terceiro(a)
thirsty: *I'm thirsty* tenho sede
this este (esta)
this one este (esta)
thorn o espinho
those aqueles (aquelas)
those ones aqueles (aquelas)
thousand mil
thread a linha
thriller (film) o filme de suspense
(book) o livro de suspense
throat a garganta
throat lozenges as pastilhas para a garganta
through através de; por
to throw away deitar fora; descartar
thrush (candida) a candidíase vaginal
thumb o polegar
thunder o trovão
thunderstorm o temporal; a tempestade
Thursday a quinta-feira
thyme o tomilho
ticket (bus, train, etc) o bilhete
(for cinema, theatre etc) a entrada
a book of tickets uma caderneta de bilhetes
a return ticket um bilhete de ida e volta
a single ticket um bilhete de ida
a tourist ticket um bilhete de turista
ticket collector o/a revisor(a)
ticket inspector o/a inspector(a) de bilhetes
ticket office a bilheteira
tide (sea) a maré
high tide a maré alta

low tide a maré baixa
tidy arrumado(a)
to tidy up arrumar
tie a gravata
tight apertado(a)
tights os collants
tile (floor) o ladrilho
(wall) o azulejo
till (cash desk) a caixa
(until) até
till 2 o'clock até às duas
time o tempo
(clock) as horas
this time esta vez
what time is it? que horas são?
timetable o horário
tin (can) a lata
tinfoil a folha de alumínio
tin-opener o abre-latas
tip a gorjeta
to tip dar uma gorjeta
tipped (cigarette) com filtro
Tippex® o fluido corrector
tired cansado(a)
tissues os lenços de papel
to a; para
to London para Londres
to the airport ao aeroporto
toadstool o cogumelo venenoso
toast (to eat) a torrada
(raising glass) o brinde
tobacco o tabaco
tobacconist's a tabacaria
today hoje
toddler a criança pequena
toe o dedo
together juntos(as)
toilet a casa de banho; o lavabo
disabled toilets a casa de banho para deficientes
toilet brush a escova da sanita
toilet paper o papel higiénico
toiletries os artigos de toilette
token (for bus) o bilhete; a senha
toll (motorway) a portagem
tomato o tomate
tinned tomatoes os tomates em lata
tomato juice o sumo de tomate
tomato purée o concentrado de tomate
tomato sauce o molho de tomate
tomato soup a sopa de tomate
tomorrow amanhã
tomorrow morning amanhã de manhã
tomorrow afternoon amanhã à tarde
tomorrow evening amanhã ao fim da tarde/à noite
tomorrow night amanhã à noite
tongue a língua
tonic water a água tónica
tonight esta noite
tonsillitis a amigdalite
too (also) também
too big grande demais
too hot (food) quente demais
too noisy demasiado barulhento(a)
too small pequeno(a) demais
tool a ferramenta
toolkit o jogo de ferramentas
tooth o dente
toothache a dor de dentes
toothbrush a escova de dentes
toothpaste a pasta dentífrica
toothpick o palito
top: *the top floor* o último andar
top (of hill) a parte de cima; o topo
on top of... em cima de...
topless: *to go topless* fazer topless
torch (flashlight) a lanterna
torn rasgado(a)
total (amount) o total
to touch tocar
tough (meat) duro(a)
tour (trip) a excursão
(of museum etc) a visita
guided tour a visita guiada
tour guide o/a guia turístico(a)
tour operator a empresa de viagens
tourist o/a turista
tourist information a informação turística
tourist office o posto de turismo
tourist route a rota turística

tourist ticket o bilhete turístico
to tow rebocar
towbar o gancho de reboque
towel o toalha
tower a torre
town a cidade
town centre o centro da cidade
town hall a Câmara Municipal
town plan o mapa da cidade
towrope o cabo de reboque
toxic tóxico(a)
toy o brinquedo
toy shop a loja de brinquedos
tracksuit o fato de treino
traditional tradicional
traffic o trânsito
traffic jam o engarrafamento
traffic lights o semáforo
traffic warden o/a guarda de trânsito
trailer o reboque
train o comboio
by train de comboio
the first train o primeiro comboio
the last train o último comboio
the next train o próximo comboio
trainers os ténis; as sapatilhas
tram o eléctrico
tranquillizer o calmante
to transfer transferir
to translate traduzir
translation a tradução
to travel viajar
travel agent o agente de viagens
travel documents os documentos de viagem
travel guide o/a guia turístico(a)
travel insurance o seguro de viagem
travel sickness o enjoo
traveller's cheque o cheque de viagem
tray o tabuleiro; a bandeja
tree a árvore
trip a viagem
trolley (luggage, shopping) o carrinho
trouble os problemas
to be in trouble estar em dificuldades
trousers as calças
trout a truta
truck o camião
true verdadeiro(a)
trunk (luggage) o baú; a mala grande
trunks (swimming) os calções de banho
truth a verdade
to try (attempt) tentar
to try on (clothes, shoes) provar; experimentar
T-shirt a T-shirt; camiseta
Tuesday a terça-feira
tulip a túlipa
tumble dryer a máquina de secar roupa
tuna o atum
tunnel o túnel
turkey o peru
to turn voltar; girar; virar
to turn around voltar-se
to turn off (light etc) apagar
(engine) desligar
(tap) fechar
to turn on (light etc) acender
(engine) ligar
(tap) abrir
turnip o nabo
turquoise (colour) turquesa
tweezers a pinça
24-hour *adj* 24-horas; permanente
twice duas vezes
twin-bedded room o quarto com duas camas
twins os(as) gémeos(as)
identical twins os(as) gémeos(as) idênticos(as)
to type escrever à máquina; dactilografar
typical típico(a)
tyre o pneu
tyre pressure a pressão dos pneus

U

ugly feio(a)
ulcer a úlcera
umbrella o guarda-chuva; a sombrinha
(sunshade) o guarda-sol

uncle o tio
uncomfortable incómodo(a)
unconscious inconsciente
under debaixo de
undercooked mal cozido(a)
underground (metro) o metropolitano
underpants as cuecas
underpass a passagem subterrânea
to understand compreender; perceber
do you understand? percebe?
I don't understand não percebo
underwear a roupa interior
underwater debaixo da água
undo desfazer
to undress despir-se
unemployed desempregado(a)
to unfasten desatar
unhappy triste; infeliz
to be unhappy with... não estar satisfeito(a) com...
United Kingdom o Reino Unido
United States os Estados Unidos
university a universidade
unleaded petrol a gasolina sem chumbo
unlikely improvável
to unlock destrancar
unlucky infeliz; sem sorte
to unpack (suitcases) desfazer as malas
unpleasant desagradável
(person) antipático(a)
to unplug desligar
to unscrew desaparafusar
until até
until 2 o'clock até às duas
unusual insólito(a)
up: ***to get up*** levantar-se
upside down invertido(a)
upstairs em cima
urgent urgente
urine a urina
us nos
(after preposition) nós
USA os EUA
USB port a porta USB
to use utilizar
useful útil
usual habitual
usually geralmente
U-turn a meia-volta

V

vacancies (in hotel etc) os quartos vagos
(jobs) as vagas
vacant livre
(hotel room) o quarto vago
vacation as férias
on vacation de férias
vaccination a vacinação
vacuum cleaner o aspirador
vagina a vagina
valid válido(a)
valley o vale
valuable valioso(a)
valuables os objetos de valor
value o valor
valve a válvula
van a carrinha
vanilla a baunilha
vase (for flowers) a jarra
VAT o IVA
veal a carne de vitela
vegan vegetalista
I'm vegan sou vegetalista
vegetables os legumes; os vegetais
vegetarian vegetariano(a)
I'm vegetarian sou vegetariano(a)
vehicle o veículo
vein a veia
Velcro® o Velcro®
velvet o veludo
vending machine a máquina de venda automática
venereal disease a doença venérea
venison a carne de veado
ventilator o ventilador
very muito
vest a camisola interior
vet o/a veterinário(a)
via por
video o vídeo

to video (from TV) gravar
video camera a câmara de vídeo
video cassette a videocassete
video game o jogo de vídeo
video phone o videofone
video recorder o gravador de vídeo
view a vista
village a aldeia
vinaigrette a vinagreta
vinegar o vinagre
vineyard a vinha
violet (flower) a violeta
viper a víbora
virus o vírus
visa o visto
visit a visita
to visit visitar
visiting hours (hospital) as horas de visita
visitor a visita
vitamin a vitamina
vodka a vodka
voice a voz
volcano o vulcão
volleyball o voleibol
voltage a voltagem
volts os volts
to vomit vomitar
voucher o vale; o recibo

W

wage o salário
waist a cintura
waistcoat o colete
to wait for esperar por
waiter o empregado de mesa
waiting room a sala de espera
waitress a empregada de mesa
to wake up acordar
Wales o País de Gales
to walk andar
walk o passeio
Walkman® o Walkman®
walking boots as botas de montanha
walking stick a bengala
wall (inside) a parede
(outside) o muro
wallet a carteira
walnut a noz
to want querer
I want... quero...
we want... queremos...
war a guerra
ward (in hospital) a enfermaria
wardrobe o guarda-fatos; guarda-roupa
warehouse o armazém
warm quente
I'm warm estou com calor
it's warm (weather) está calor
to warm up aquecer
warning triangle o triângulo de sinalização
wash: *to have a wash* lavar-se
to wash lavar
wash and blow-dry lavar e secar
washbasin o lavatório
washing machine a máquina de lavar roupa
washing powder o detergente para a roupa
washing-up bowl a bacia
washing-up liquid o detergente para a louça
wasp a vespa
waste bin o balde do lixo
watch o relógio
to watch ver; observar
watchstrap a pulseira de relógio
water a água
bottled water a água mineral (engarrafada)
cold water a água fria
drinking water a água potável
fresh water a água corrente
hot water a água quente
mineral water a água mineral
salt water a água salgada
sparkling water a água com gás
still water a água sem gás
watercress o agrião
waterfall a queda de água
water heater o esquentador
watermelon a melancia

waterproof impermeável
to waterski fazer esqui aquático
water-skiing o esqui aquático
waterwings as braçadeiras
waves as ondas
wax a cera
waxing (hair removal) a depilação com cera
way (path) o caminho
(manner) a maneira
way in (entrance) a entrada
way out (exit) a saída
we nós
weak fraco(a)
(tea, etc) aguado(a)
to wear vestir
weather o tempo
weather forecast a previsão do tempo
website o website
wedding o casamento
wedding anniversary o aniversário de casamento
wedding cake o bolo de noiva
wedding dress o vestido de noiva
wedding present a prenda de casamento
wedding ring a aliança de casamento
Wednesday a quarta-feira
week a semana
during the week durante a semana
last week a semana passada
next week a semana que vem
per week por semana
this week esta semana
weekday o dia útil
weekend o fim-de-semana
next weekend o próximo fim-de-semana
this weekend este fim-de-semana
weekly por semana; semanal
weekly ticket o bilhete semanal
to weigh pesar
weight o peso
welcome bem-vindo(a)
well bem
he's not well ele não se sente bem
well (for water) o poço
well-done (steak) bem-passado(a)
wellington boots as galoshas
Welsh galês (galesa)
(language) o galês
west o oeste
wet molhado(a)
(weather) chuvoso(a)
wetsuit o fato de mergulhador
what que
what is it? o que é?
wheat o trigo
wheel a roda
wheelchair a cadeira de rodas
wheel clamp o imobilizador
when? quando?
where? onde?
which: ***which is it?*** qual é?
while enquanto
in a while dentro de pouco
whipped cream o chantilly
whisky o uísque
white branco(a)
who: ***who is it?*** quem é?
whole inteiro(a)
wholemeal bread o pão integral
whose: ***whose is it?*** de quem é?
why? porquê?
wide largo(a)
widow a viúva
widower o viúvo
width a largura
wife a mulher; a esposa
wi-fi o wi-fi
wig a peruca
to win ganhar
wind o vento
windbreak o guarda-vento
windmill o moínho
window a janela
(shop) a montra
windscreen o pára-brisas
windscreen wipers o limpa-pára-brisas
to windsurf fazer windsurf
windsurfing o wind-surf
windy: ***it's windy*** está vento

wine o vinho
dry wine o vinho seco
house wine o vinho da casa
red wine o vinho tinto
rosé wine o vinho rosé
sparkling wine o vinho espumante
sweet wine o vinho doce
table wine o vinho de mesa
white wine o vinho branco
wine list a lista de vinhos
wing a asa
wing mirror o retrovisor exterior
winter o inverno
wire a arame
(electric) o fio (eléctrico)
wireless sem fio
with com
with ice com gelo
with milk com leite
with sugar com açúcar
without sem
without milk sem leite
without sugar sem açúcar
witness a testemunha
wolf o lobo
woman a mulher
wonderful maravilhoso(a)
wood (substance) a madeira
woods a floresta
wool a lã
word a palavra
to work (person) trabalhar
(machine) funcionar
it doesn't work não está a funcionar; não funciona
work permit a autorização de trabalho
world o mundo
worldwide no mundo inteiro
worried preocupado(a)
worse pior
worth: ***it's worth...*** vale...
to wrap (parcel, etc) embrulhar
wrapping paper o papel de embrulho
wrinkles as rugas
wrist o pulso
to write escrever
please write it down escreve-o, por favor
writing paper o papel de carta
wrong errado(a)
wrought iron o ferro forjado
www. www ponto

X

x-ray a radiografia
to x-ray radiografar

Y

yacht o iate
year o ano
last year o ano passado
next year o ano que vem
this year este ano
yearly: ***twice yearly*** duas vezes por ano
yellow amarelo(a)
Yellow Pages as Páginas Amarelas
yes sim
yesterday ontem
yet: not yet ainda não
yoghurt o iogurte
plain yoghurt o iogurte natural
yolk a gema
you see Grammar section
young novo(a)
(person) o/a jovem
your (o) teu (a tua)
youth hostel o albergue da juventude

Z

zebra crossing a passadeira para peões
zero o zero
zip o fecho éclair
zone a zona
zoo o jardim zoológico
zoom lens o zoom

A

a to; the *(feminine)*
abadia *f* abbey
abaixo down; below
aberto(a) open
aberto todo o ano open all year round
abre-garrafas *m* bottle-opener
abre-latas *m* tin/can-opener
Abril *m* April
abrir to open; to unlock *(door)*
acabar to end; to finish
acampar to camp
aceder à Internet to access the Internet
aceitar to accept
acelerador *m* accelerator
acender to switch/turn on; to light *(fire, cigarette)*
acenda as luzes switch on the lights
acepipe *m* titbit
acepipes starters; hors d'œuvres
aceso(a) on *(light, etc)*
acesso *m* access
achar to think; to find
acha bem? do you think it's all right?
acidente *m* accident
acima above
aço *m* steel
aço inoxidável stainless steel
açorda *f* bread-based dish
acordo *m* agreement
Açores *mpl* the Azores archipelago
actual present(-day)
actualizar to modernize; to update
açúcar *m* sugar
adega *f* wine cellar
adesivo *m* plaster *(for cut)*
adeus goodbye
adiantado(a) fast *(watch)*; early *(train, etc)*
adulto(a) adult
advogado(a) *m/f* lawyer
aéreo(a): ***a linha aérea*** airline
via aérea air mail
aeroporto *m* airport
agência *f* agency
agência de viagens travel agents
agente *m/f* agent
agora now
Agosto *m* August
agradável pleasant
agradecer to thank
água *f* water
água com gás fizzy water
água potável drinking water
água mineral mineral water
água sem gás still water
aguardente *f* spirit brandy
agudo(a) sharp *(pain)*
ajuda *f* help
ajudar to help
alavanca das velocidades *f* gear lever
albergue *m* hostel
albergue da juventude youth hostel
alcoólico(a) alcoholic
aldeia *f* small village
alegre jolly
Alemanha *f* Germany
alemão (alemã) German
alérgico(a) a allergic to
alface *f* lettuce
alfaiate *m* tailor
alfândega *f* customs
alfinete *m* pin
alforreca *f* jellyfish
algodão *m* cotton
algum(a) some; any
alguns (algumas) a few; some
mais alguma coisa? anything else?
alho *m* garlic
alhos-porros *mpl* leeks
ali there
alimentação *f* food
alívio *m* relief
almoço *m* lunch
pequeno-almoço breakfast
almofada *f* pillow; cushion
alojamento *m* accommodation

alpinismo *m* climbing
alto! stop!
alto(a) high; tall; loud
a estação alta high season
altura *f* height
alugar to hire; to rent
aluga-se to rent
alugam-se quartos rooms to let
aluguer *m* rental
amanhã tomorrow
amarelo(a) yellow
amargo(a) bitter
ambulância *f* ambulance
amêijoa *f* clam; cockle
ameixa *f* plum
ameixa seca prune
amêndoa *f* almond
amêndoa amarga bitter almond liqueur
amendoim *m* peanut
amigo(a) *m/f* friend
amora *f* blackberry; mulberry
amortecedor *m* shock absorber
amostra *f* sample
analgésico *m* painkiller
ananás *m* pineapple
anchovas *fpl* anchovies
andar to walk
andar *m* floor; storey
o primeiro andar first floor
anel *m* ring
anis *m* aniseed liqueur
aniversário *m* anniversary; birthday
ano *m* year
Ano Novo New Year
antena *f* aerial; antenna
antena parabolica satellite dish
antes (de) before
antiguidades *fpl* antiques
apagado(a) off *(radio, etc)*; out *(light, etc)*
apagar to switch/turn off *(light, etc)*
aparelho *m* gadget; machine; apparatus
aparelho para a surdez hearing aid
apartamento *m* apartment; flat
apelido *m* surname
apelido de solteira maiden name
apenas only
apertado(a) tight
apetite *m* appetite
bom apetite! enjoy your meal!
apólice de seguro *f* insurance certificate
aquecedor *m* heater; electric fire
aquecimento *m* heating
aqui here
ar *m* air; choke *(car)*
ar condicionado air conditioning
arder to burn
areia *f* sand
arenque *m* herring
armário *m* cupboard; closet
armazém *m* warehouse
grande armazém department store
arrendar to let
arroz *m* rice
arroz doce rice pudding
artesanato *m* handicrafts
artigo *m* item
artigos de ménage household goods
artigos de vime wickerwork
árvore *f* tree
ascensor *m* lift
assado(a) roast; baked
assinar to sign
assinatura *f* signature
assistência *f* audience; assistance
atacadores *mpl* laces
até until; as far as
aterrar to land
atrás behind
atrasado(a) late; delayed *(for appointment)*
atrasar to delay
atraso *m* delay
atravessar to cross
atum *m* tuna (fish)
autocarro *m* bus; coach
a paragem de autocarro bus stop
auto-estrada *f* motorway
automobilista *m/f* driver
automóvel *m* car
autorização *f* licence; permit
avaria *f* breakdown
avariado(a) out of order *(machine)*; broken down *(car)*
ave *f* bird
avelã *f* hazelnut

avenida *f* avenue
avião *m* plane
aviso *m* warning
avô *m* grandfather
avó *f* grandmother
azedo(a) sour
azeite *m* olive oil
azeitona *f* olive
azul blue
azulejo *m* ornamental tile

B

bacalhau *m* dried salt cod
bagaceira *f* eau de vie *(firewater)*
bagaço *m* eau de vie
bagagem *f* luggage; baggage
Bairrada region producing full-bodied red and aromatic white wines
bairro *m* quarter; district
Baixa *f* commercial centre of Lisbon
baixar to lower
baixo: ***em baixo*** below
balança *f* scales *(weighing machine)*

balcão *m* shop counter; circle in theatre
banco *m* bank; seat *(in car, etc)*
bandeira *f* flag; banner
bandeja *f* tray; salver
bandido *m* gangster; robber
banheira *f* bath-tub
banheiro *m* lifeguard
banho *m* bath
a casa de banho bathroom
tomar banho to have a bath; to bathe
banquete *m* banquet; sumptuous dinner
barato(a) cheap
barba *f* beard
fazer a barba to shave
barbeiro *m* barber
barco *m* boat; ship
barco a remos rowing boat
barco a vela sailing boat
barraca *f* hut *(shed)*; beach hut
barreira *f* trench; obstacle; barrier
barriga *f* belly
barro *m* pottery; terracotta
barulho *m* noise
bastante enough
batata *f* potato
batatas fritas chips; crisps
bater to beat; to knock
bata à porta please knock
bateria *f* battery *(for car)*
batido de leite *m* milk shake
baunilha *f* vanilla
bebé *m* baby
beber to drink
bebida *f* drink
beco *m* alley
belo(a) beautiful
bem well
bem passado(a) well done *(steak)*
está bem OK
bem-vindo(a) welcome
bengaleiro *m* cloakroom *(at theatre)*; hat and umbrella stand
benzer to bless
beringela *f* aubergine
berma *f* hard shoulder
bermas baixas steep verge – no hard shoulder
berço *m* crib; cradle; cot
besugo *m* sea bream
beterraba *f* beetroot
bexiga *f* bladder
bica *f* espresso coffee
bicha *f* queue
fazer bicha to queue
bicicleta *f* bicycle
bife *m* steak
bifurcação *f* junction
bilhar *m* billiards
bilhete *m* ticket; fare
bilhete de entrada admission ticket
bilhete de identidade identity card
bilheteira *f* ticket office
binóculos *mpl* binoculars
boa *see* bom
boca *f* mouth
bocado: ***um bocado*** a bit; a portion
boîte *f* nightclub
bola *f* ball
bola de Berlim doughnut
bolacha *f* biscuit
bolo *m* cake

bolsa *f* stock exchange; handbag
bom (boa) good; fine *(weather)*; kind
bom dia good morning
boa tarde good afternoon
boa noite good evening; good night
bomba *f* bomb; pump *(petrol)*
bombeiros *mpl* fire brigade
bondade *f* kindness
boneco(a) doll; puppet toy
bonito(a) pretty
borbulha *f* spot; pimple
bordados *mpl* embroidered items
borrego *m* lamb
bosque *m* small forest; woodland
bota *f* boot *(to wear)*
botão *m* button; bud
braço *m* arm
branco(a) white
vinho branco white wine
breve brief
em breve soon
brigada de trânsito *f* traffic police
brincos *mpl* earrings
brinquedo *m* toy
britânico(a) British
broa *f* corn (maize) bread
broas corn (maize) cakes
bronzeador *m* suntan oil
brushing *m* blow-dry
bugigangas *fpl* bric-à-brac
burro(a) *m/f* ass; donkey; stupid person
buscar to look for
bússola *f* compass
buzinar to toot *(car horn)*

C

cá here; in this place
cabana *f* shack; hut
cabeça *f* head
cabedais *mpl* leather goods
cabeleireiro(a) *m/f* hairdresser
cabelo *m* hair
cabide *m* coat hanger; peg *(for clothes)*
cabine *f* cabin; booth
cabine telefónica phone box
cabo *m* knife handle; electric lead
cabos de emergência jump leads
cabo de reboque tow rope
cabra *f* goat
queijo de cabra goat's cheese
cabrito *m* kid (goat)
caça *f* game *(to eat)*; hunting
caçador *m* hunter
cachorro *m* hot dog; puppy
cada each; every
cadeado *m* padlock
cadeia *f* jail; chain
cadeira *f* chair
cadeira de bebé high chair; push chair
cadeira de lona deck chair
cadeira de rodas wheelchair
cadela *f* female dog
café *m* (black) coffee; café; coffee-shop
cãibra *f* cramp
cair to fall; to fall over
cais *m* quay
caixa *f* cash desk
caixa automática cash machine
caixa do correio letterbox
caixão *m* coffin
caixote *m* bin; wooden box; container 179
calar to stop talking; to keep silent
calçado *m* footwear
calças *fpl* trousers
calções *mpl* shorts
calções de banho swimming trunks
calços para travões *mpl* brake pads
calcular to estimate; to calculate
caldeirada *f* fish stew
caldo *m* stock *(for soup)*
caldo verde cabbage (kale) soup
calor *m* heat
cama *f* bed
a roupa de cama bedding
cama de bebé cot
cama de casal double bed
cama de criança child's bed
cama de solteiro single bed
câmara de ar *f* inner tube
câmara digital *f* digital camera
câmara municipal *f* town hall
camarão *m* shrimp
camarote *m* cabin; box *(theatre)*
cambiar to exchange; to change money

câmbio *m* exchange rate
casa de câmbios *f* money exchange shop
camião *m* lorry
caminho *m* path; way; route
camioneta *f* coach
camisa *f* shirt
camisa de noite nightdress
camomila *f* camomile *(tea)*
campaínha *f* bell *(on door)*
campismo *m* camping
campo *m* field; countryside
campo de golfe *m* golf course
camurça *f* suede
cancelar to cancel
canela *f* cinnamon
caneta *f* pen
cano de esgoto *m* drain
canoagem *f* canoeing
cansaço *m* fatigue
cansado(a) tired
cantar to sing
cantina *f* canteen

canto *m* corner *(inside)*
cão *m* dog
capacete *m* crash helmet
capela *f* chapel
capitão *m* captain
capota *f* bonnet *(of car)*
capuchino *m* cappuccino
cara *f* face
caracóis *mpl* snails; curls *(hair)*
caramelos *mpl* toffees
caranguejo *m* crab
carapau *m* horse mackerel
caravana *f* caravan
carburador *m* carburettor
carga *f* refill; load
caril *m* curry
carioca *m* weak coffee
carioca de limão lemon infusion
carne *f* meat
carne de borrego spring lamb
carne de porco pork
carne picada mince
carne de vaca beef
carne de vitela veal
carnes frias cold meats
carneiro *m* mutton; lamb
caro(a) expensive
caro(a) amigo(a) dear friend
caroço *m* kernel; pip
caregador de telemóvel *m* mobile phone charger
carregamento *m* cargo; load
carrinha *f* van
carrinho *m* trolley
carrinho de bebé pram; carry cot
carro *m* car
carruagem *f* carriage *(railway)*
carruagem-cama sleeper *(railway)*
carruagem-restaurante *f* restaurant car
carta *f* letter
cartão *m* card; business card
cartão bancário cheque card
cartão de crédito credit card
cartão de embarque boarding card
cartão de felicitações greetings card
cartão garantia cheque card
cartaz *m* poster; billboard
carteira *f* wallet
carteirista *m* pickpocket
carteiro *m* postman
carvalho *m* oak tree
carvão *m* coal
casa *f* home; house
casa de banho toilet; bathroom
casaco *m* jacket; coat
casado(a) married
casal *m* couple
casamento *m* wedding
caso *m* case
em caso de... in case of...
castanha *f* chestnut
castanhas assadas roast chestnuts
castanhas piladas dried chestnuts
castanho(a) brown
castelo *m* castle
catedral *f* cathedral
causa *f* cause
por causa de because of
cautela take care
cavala *f* mackerel
cavalheiro *m* gentleman

cavalo *m* horse
cave *f* cellar
CD-ROM *m* CD-ROM
cebola *f* onion
cedo early
cego(a) *adj* blind *m/f* blind man/woman
ceia *f* supper
célebre famous
cem one hundred
cemitério *m* cemetery
cenoura *f* carrot
centígrado *m* centigrade
centímetro *m* centimetre
cêntimo *m* cent
cento: *por cento* per cent
centro *m* centre
centro da cidade city centre
centro comercial shopping centre
centro de saúde health centre
cera *f* wax
cerâmica *f* pottery
cérebro *m* brain
cereja *f* cherry
certeza *f* certainty
ter a certeza to be sure
certificado *m* certificate
certo(a) right *(correct, accurate)*; certain
cerveja *f* beer; lager
cerveja preta bitter *(beer)*
cervejaria *f* beer house
cesto *m* basket
céu *m* sky
chá *f* tea
chá de limão lemon tea
chamada *f* telephone call
chamada gratuita free call
chamada internacional international call
chamada pagável no destino reverse charge call
chamar to call
champô *m* shampoo
chão *m* floor
chapa de matrícula *f* number plate
chapéu *m* hat
chapéu de sol sunhat; sunshade
charcutaria *f* delicatessen
chave *f* key
fechar à chave to lock up
chávena *f* cup
chefe *m/f* boss
chefe de cozinha chef
chega! that's enough!
chegadas *fpl* arrivals
chegar to arrive
cheio(a) full
cheirar to smell
cheiro *m* smell
mau cheiro bad smell
cheque *m* cheque
cheque de viagem traveller's cheque
levantar um cheque to cash a cheque
cherne *m* black jewfish or grouper
chispe *m* pig's trotters
chocos *mpl* cuttlefish
chouriço *m* spicy sausage
churrascaria *f* barbecue restaurant
churrasco *m* barbecue
no churrasco barbecued
chuva *f* rain
chuveiro *m* shower *(bath)*
Cia. *see* companhia
ciberespaço *m* cyberspace
ciclismo de montanha *m* mountain biking
cidadão (cidadã) *m/f* citizen
cidade *f* town; city
cigarro *m* cigarette
cima: *em cima de* on (top of)
cinco five
cinto *m* belt
cinto de salvação lifebelt
cinto de segurança seat belt
cinzento(a) grey
circuito *m* circuit
cirurgia *f* surgery *(operation)*
claro(a) light *(colour)*; bright
classe *f* class
clicar to click (on)
cliente *m/f* client
clínica *f* clinic
clube *m* club
cobertor *m* blanket
cobrar to cash; charge

cobrir to cover
código *m* code; dialling code
código postal postcode
codorniz *f* quail
coelho *m* rabbit
coentro *m* coriander
cofre *m* safe
cogumelo *m* mushroom
coisa *f* thing
cola *f* glue
colar *n* necklace
colar *vb* to stick
colcha *f* bedspread
colchão *m* mattress
colecção *f* collection *(of stamps etc)*
colégio *m* (secondary) school
colete de salvação *m* life jacket
colher *f* spoon
colina *f* hill
collants *mpl* tights
colorau *m* paprika
coluna *f* pillar
coluna vertebral spine
com with
comando *m* TV remote control
comandos *mpl* controls
comboio *m* train
combustível *m* fuel
começar to begin; to start
comer to eat
comida *f* food
comissário de bordo *m* steward; purser
como as; how
como disse? I beg your pardon?
como está? how are you?
comodidade *f* comfort
companheiro(a) *m/f* live-in partner
companhia (Cia.) *f* company
compartimento *m* compartment
completar to complete
completo no vacancies *(sign in hotel etc)*
compota *f* jam
compra *f* purchase
ir às compras to go shopping
comprar to buy
compreender to understand
comprido(a) long
comprimento *m* length
comprimido *m* pill; tablet
computador *m* computer
concelho *m* council
concordar to agree
concorrente *m/f* candidate
concurso *m* competition
condução *f* driving
a carta de condução driving licence
condutor *m* driver; chauffeur
conduzir to drive
conferência *f* conference
conferir to check
congelado(a) frozen *(food)*
congelar to freeze
não congelar do not freeze
conhaque *m* cognac; brandy
conhecer to know *(person, place)*
conselho *m* advice
consertos *mpl* repairs
conservar to keep; to preserve
conservar no frio store in a cold place
constipação *f* cold *(illness)*
consulado *m* consulate
consulta *f* consultation; appointment
consultório *m* surgery
consumir antes de... best before... *(label on food)*
conta *f* account; bill
contador *m* meter *(electricity, water)*
conter to contain
não contem... does not contain...
contra against
contraceptivo *m* contraceptive
contrato *m* contract
convidado(a) *m/f* guest
convidar to invite; to ask *(invite)*
convite *m* invitation
copo *m* glass *(container)*
cor *f* colour
coração *m* heart
cordeiro *m* lamb
cor-de-laranja orange *(colour)*
cor-de-rosa pink
corpo *m* body
correia *f* strap
correia de ventoinha fan belt

correio *m* post office
correio electrónico e-mail
pelo correio by post
corrente *f* chain; current
correr to flow; to run *(person)*
correspondência *f* mail
corrida *f* race
corrida de touros bullfight
corridas de cavalos races
cortar to cut; to cut off
cortar e fazer brushing cut & blow-dry
corte *m* cut
cortiça *f* cork
costa *f* shore; coastline
costela *f* rib
costeleta *f* chop *(meat)*; cutlet
cotovelo *m* elbow
couro *m* leather
couve *f* cabbage
couves-de-Bruxelas Brussels sprouts
couve-flor *f* cauliflower
couvert *m* cover charge
coxia *f* aisle
cozer to boil
cozido(a) boiled
mal cozido(a) underdone
cozinha *f* kitchen
cozinhar to cook
cozinheiro(a) *m/f* cook
cravinhos *mpl* cloves
cravo *m* carnation
creche *f* creche
creme *m* custard
creme de barbear shaving cream
creme de limpeza cleansing cream
creme hidratante moisturizer
creme para bronzear suntan cream
criança *f* child
cru(a) raw
cruz *f* cross
cruzamento *m* junction *(crossroads)*
cruzar to cross
cruzeiro *m* cruise
cuecas *fpl* briefs; pants
cuidado *m* care *(caution)*
cuidado! watch out/take care!
cumprimento *m* greeting
cumprimentos regards
cunhado(a) *m/f* brother/sister-in-law
curso *m* course
curto(a) short
curva *f* bend; turning; curve
curva perigosa dangerous bend
custar to cost
custo *m* charge; cost

D

damasco *m* apricot
dança *f* dance
dano *m* damage
Dão fruity red and white wine from north Portugal
dar to give
dar prioridade to give way
data *f* date
data de nascimento date of birth
de of; from
debaixo de under
decidir to decide
dedo *m* finger
dedo do pé *m* toe
defeito *m* flaw
deficiente disabled
degrau *m* step *(stair)*
deitar-se to lie down
deixar to let *(allow)*; to leave behind
delito *m* crime
demais too much; too many
demasia *f* change *(money)*; excess
demorado(a) late
demorar to delay
dente *m* tooth
dentes *mpl* teeth
dentes postiços *mpl* false teeth
dentista *m/f* dentist
dentro inside
depois after(wards)
depósito *m* deposit *(in bank)*
depósito de bagagens left-luggage
depósito da gasolina petrol tank
depressa quickly
desafio *m* match; game *(sport)*; challenge
desaparecido(a) missing
desapertar to loosen

descafeinado *m* decaffeinated
descansar to rest
descartável throw-away; disposable
descer to go down
descoberta *f* discovery
descongelar to defrost *(food)*; to de-ice
desconhecido(a) *m/f* stranger
desconhecido(a) *adj* unknown
desconto *m* discount; reduction
desculpe excuse me; sorry
desejar to desire; to wish
desembarcar to disembark
desempregado(a) unemployed
desenho *m* design; drawing
desinchar to go down *(swelling)*
desinfectante *m* disinfectant
desligado(a) off *(engine, gas)*
desligar to hang up *(phone)*; to switch off *(engine, radio)*
desligue o motor switch off your engine
desmaiar to faint
desodorizante *m* deodorant
despachante *m* shipper; (transport) agent

despesa *f* expense
desporto *m* sport
destinatário *m* addressee
desvio *m* bypass; detour; diversion
detergente *m* detergent
detergente para a louça washing-up liquid
detergente para a roupa washing powder
devagar slowly; slow down *(sign)*
dever: ***eu devo*** I must
deve-me... you owe me...
devolver to give back; to return
Dezembro *m* December
dia *m* day
dias da semana weekdays
dia útil working day
dia de anos birthday
diabético(a) diabetic
diante de in front of *(place)*
diário(a) daily
diarreia *f* diarrhoea
dieta *f* diet; special diet
diferença *f* difference
difícil difficult
digestão *f* digestion
diluir to dilute
diminuir to reduce
dínamo *m* dynamo
dinheiro *m* money; cash
direcção *f* direction; address; steering
directo(a) direct
direita *f* right(-hand side)
à direita on the right
para a direita to the right
direito(a) straight; right(-hand)
Dto. on right-hand side *(address)*
direitos *mpl* duty *(tax)*; rights
dirigir to direct
disco *m* record *(music, etc)*
disco de estacionamento parking disk
disco rigido hard drive
disponível available
dissolver to dissolve
distância *f* distance
distrito *m* district
divã-cama *m* bed settee
diversões *fpl* entertainment
divertir-se to enjoy oneself; to have fun
dívida *f* debt
divisas *fpl* foreign currency
dizer to say
dobrada *f* tripe
dobrado(a) bent
dobro *m* double
doce *adj* sweet *(taste)*
doce *m* dessert; jam
documentos *mpl* documents
doente ill; sick
doer to ache; to hurt
dólar *m* dollar
domicílio *m* residence
domingo *m* Sunday
dono(a) *m/f* owner
dona de casa housewife
dor *f* ache; pain
dormir to sleep
Douro region producing port
download *m* download
Dto. *see* direito(a)
duche *m* shower

duplo(a) double
durante during
durar to last
duro(a) hard; stiff; tough *(meat)*
dúzia *f* dozen
DVD *m* DVD
a drive de DVD DVD drive

E

e and
é he/she/it is; you are
economizar to save
ecrã *m* screen
edifício *m* building
edredão *m* duvet; quilt
educado(a) polite
eixo de roda *m* axle
ela she; her; it
elas they; them *(feminine)*
elástico *m* elastic band
ele he; him; it
eles they *(masculine)*
electricista *m/f* electrician
eléctrico *m* tram
electrodomésticos *mpl* electrical appliances
elevador *m* lift
em at; in *(with towns, countries)*; into
embaixada *f* embassy
embarcar to board *(ship, plane)*
embarque *m* embarkation; time of sailing
embraiagem *f* clutch
ementa *f* menu
ementa fixa set menu
emergência *f* emergency
empregado(a) *m/f* waiter(ess); maid; attendant *(at petrol station)*; assistant *(in shop)*; office worker
emprego *m* job; employment
empurrar to push
empurre push *(sign)*
EN *see* estrada
encaracolado(a) curly
encarnado(a) red
encerrado(a) closed
encher to fill up; to pump up *(tyre)*
enchidos *mpl* processed meats; sausages
encomenda *f* parcel
encontrar to meet; to find
encontro *m* date; meeting
encosta *f* hill *(slope)*
endereço *m* address
energia *f* energy
o corte de energia power cut
enfermeiro(a) *m/f* nurse
enganar-se to make a mistake
engano *m* mistake
engolir to swallow
não engolir do not swallow
engraxar to polish *(shoes)*
enguia *f* eel
enjoar to be sick
ensinar to teach
ensopado *m* stew served on slice of bread
enorme big; huge
entender to understand
entorse *f* sprain
entrada *f* entrance; starter *(in meal)*
entrada livre admission free
entrar to go in; to come in; to get into
entre among; between
entregar to deliver; hand in; hand over
entrevista *f* interview
enviar to send
enxaqueca *f* migraine
época *f* period *(time in history)*
equipamento *m* equipment
equitação *f* horse riding
erro *m* mistake
erva *f* grass; herb
ervilhas *fpl* peas
esc. *see* escudo
escada *f* ladder; stairs
escada rolante escalator
escalfado(a) poached *(egg)*
escape *m* exhaust
escocês (escocesa) Scottish
Escócia *f* Scotland
escola *f* school
escova *f* brush
escova de dentes toothbrush
escrever to write
escrito: *por escrito* in writing

escritório *m* office
escuro(a) dark *(colour)*
escutar to listen to
esferográfica *f* ballpoint pen
esgotado(a) sold out *(tickets)*; exhausted
esgoto *m* drain
esmalte *m* enamel
espaço *m* space
espadarte *m* swordfish
espalhar to scatter
Espanha *f* Spain
espanhol *m* Spanish *(language)*
espanhol(a) Spanish
espargo *m* asparagus
esparguete *m* spaghetti
esparregado *m* puréed spinach
especialidade *f* speciality
especiarias *fpl* spices
espectáculo *m* show *(in theatre etc)*
espelho *m* mirror
espelho retrovisor driving mirror
esperar to expect; to hope
esperar por to wait for

espetada *f* kebab
espinafre *m* spinach
esplanada *f* terrace
esposa *f* wife
espumante *m* sparkling wine
espumoso(a) sparkling *(wine)*
Esq. *see* esquerda
esquadra *f* police station
esquentador *m* water heater
esquerda *f* left(-hand side)
à esquerda onto the left
Esq. on left(-hand) side *(address)*
esqui *m* ski
esquina *f* corner *(outside)*
está he/she/it is; you are
estação *f* station
estação alta high season
estação baixa low season
estação de autocarros bus station
estação de serviço service station
estação de comboios train station
estação do ano season
estacionamento *m* parking
estacionar to park *(car)*
estádio *m* stadium
estado *m* state
estado civil marital status
Estados Unidos (EUA) *mpl* United States
estalagem *f* inn
estância termal *f* spa
estar to be
este/esta *m/f* this
estes/estas *m/f* these
estômago *m* stomach
o mal-estar de estômago stomach upset
estores *mpl* blinds
estrada *f* road
estrada em mau estado uneven road surface
estrada nacional (EN) major road; national highway
estrada secundária minor road
estrada sem saída no through road
estrangeiro(a) *m/f* foreigner
estranho(a) strange
estreito(a) narrow
estudante *m/f* student
estufado(a) braised
etiqueta *f* ticket; label; etiquette
eu I
EUA *see* Estados Unidos
euro *m* euro
europeu (europeia) European
evitar to avoid
excepto except
excepto aos domingos except Sundays
excesso de bagagem *m* excess luggage; excess baggage
excursão *f* excursion; tour
excursão guiada guided tour
exemplo *m* example
por exemplo for example
expirar to expire
explicar to explain
exportação *f* exportation
exportar to export
exposição *f* exhibition
extintor *m* fire extinguisher
extremidade *f* edge; extremity

F

fábrica *f* factory
fabricado(a) em... made in...
faca *f* knife
fácil easy
facilidade *f* facility; ease
factura *f* invoice
fado *m* traditional Portuguese song
faiança *f* pottery
faisão *m* pheasant
faixa *f* lane *(in road)*
falar to speak
falecido(a) deceased
falésias *fpl* cliffs
falta *f* lack
falta de corrente power cut
família *f* family
farinha *f* flour
farinheira *f* sausage made with pork fat and flour
farmácia *f* chemist's
farmácia permanente duty chemist
farmácias de serviço emergency chemists'
faróis *mpl* headlights
farol *m* headlight; lighthouse
farolim *m* sidelight
fatia *f* slice
fato *m* suit *(man's)*
fato de banho swimsuit
fato de treino tracksuit
favas *fpl* broad beans
favor *m* favour
(se) faz favor please
por favor please
fazer to do; to make
fazer download download
febras de porco *fpl* slices of roast pork
febre *f* fever
febre dos fenos hay fever
ter febre to have a temperature
fechado(a) closed
fechado Domingos e Feriados closed Sundays and Bank holidays
fechar to shut; to close
feijão *m* beans
feijão-verde *m* French beans
feio(a) awful; ugly
feira *f* fair *(commercial)*; market
feito(a) à mão handmade
feliz happy
feriado *m* public holiday
feriado nacional bank holiday
férias *fpl* holidays
ferido(a) injured
ferragens *fpl* ironware
ferro *m* iron
ferro de engomar iron *(for clothes)*
ferver to boil
festa *f* party *(celebration)*
Fevereiro *m* February
fiambre *m* ham *(boiled)*
ficar to stay; to be; to remain
ficar bem to suit
ficha *f* plug *(electrical)*; registration card *(in hotel, clinic)*
ficha dupla/tripla adaptor *(electrical)*
ficheiro *m* file
fígado *m* liver
figo *m* fig
figos secos dried figs
fila *f* row *(line)*; queue
filete *m* fillet steak; tenderloin
filha *f* daughter
filho *m* son
filial *f* branch *(of bank, etc)*
filigranas *fpl* filigree work
fim *m* end
fim-de-semana weekend
fio *m* wire
sem fio wireless *(adj)*
fita *f* tape; ribbon
fita métrica tape measure
flor *f* flower
floresta *f* forest
florista *f* florist
fogão *m* cooker
fogo *m* fire
fogos de artifício fireworks
folha *f* leaf
folha de alumínio aluminium foil
folha de estanho tinfoil
folhados *mpl* puff pastries
folheto *m* leaflet

fome *f* hunger
tenho fome I'm hungry
fonte *f* fountain; source
fora out; outside
força *f* power *(strength)*; force
formiga *f* ant
fornecer to supply
forno *m* oven
fortaleza *f* fortress
forte strong
forte *m* fortress
fósforo *m* match
fotografia *f* photograph; print
fraco(a) weak
fralda *f* nappy
framboesa *f* raspberry
França *f* France
francês *m* French *(language)*
francês (francesa) French
frango *m* chicken *(young and tender)*
frango assado roast chicken
frase *f* sentence
freguês (freguesa) *m/f* customer

frente *f* front
em frente de in front of; opposite
fresco(a) fresh; cool; crisp
sirva fresco serve cool
frigorífico *m* fridge
frio(a) cold
fritar to fry
frito(a) fried
fronha *f* pillow case
fronteira *f* border *(frontier)*
fruta *f* fruit
frutaria *f* fruit shop
fruto *m* fruit
fuga *f* leak; escape
fugir to run away
fumadores *mpl* smokers
para não fumadores non-smoking *(compartment, etc)*
fumar to smoke
não fumar no smoking
fumo *m* smoke
funcionar to work *(machine)*
não funciona out of order *(sign)*
funcionário(a) *m/f* employee; civil servant
fundo *m* bottom
fundo(a) deep
furar to pierce
furnas *fpl* caverns
furto *m* theft
fusível *m* fuse
futebol *m* football

G

gabinete de provas *m* changing room
gado *m* cattle
gado bravo beware – unfenced bulls
gaivota *f* seagull; pedal boat
galão *m* large white coffee; gallon
galeria *f* gallery
Gales: *o País de Gales* Wales
galês (galesa) Welsh
galinha *f* hen; chicken
gamba *f* prawn
ganhar to earn; to win
ganso *m* goose
garagem *f* garage *(house)*
garantia *f* guarantee
gare *f* platform
garfo *m* fork
garganta *f* throat
garoto *m* boy; small white coffee
garrafa *f* bottle
garrafão *m* two or five-litre bottle
gás *m* gas
a botija de gás gas cylinder
gasóleo *m* diesel
gasolina *f* petrol
gasosa *f* fizzy sweetened water
gastar to spend
gaveta *f* drawer
gelado *m* ice cream; ice lolly
gelar to freeze
gelataria *f* ice cream parlour
geleia *f* jelly
gelo *m* ice
gémeo(a) *m/f* twin
género *m* kind; type
o meu género de filme my kind of film
gengibre *m* ginger
gengivas *fpl* gums

genro *m* son-in-law
gente *f* people
toda a gente everybody
geral *f* gallery *(in theatre)*
geral *adj* general
em geral generally
geralmente usually
gerente *m/f* manager
gigabyte *m* gigabyte
gigahertz *m* gigahertz
ginjinha *f* morello cherry liqueur
gira-discos *m* record player
girassol *m* sunflower
gola *f* collar
golfe *m* golf
o taco de golfe golf club *(stick)*
gordo(a) fat
gorjeta *f* tip *(to waiter, etc)*
gostar de to like
gosto *m* taste
governo *m* government
Grã-Bretanha *f* Britain
grama *m* gramme
grande big; large; great
grão *m* chickpeas
grátis free *(costing nothing)*
gravador *m* tape recorder
gravata *f* tie
grávida pregnant
gravura *f* print *(picture)*
grelhado(a) grilled
greve *f* strike *(industrial)*
em greve on strike
gripe *f* flu
groselha *f* (red)currant
grosso(a) thick
grupo *m* group; party *(group)*
grupo sanguíneo blood group
grutas *fpl* caves
guarda *m/f* police officer
guarda-chuva *m* umbrella
guarda-lamas *m* mudguard
guardanapo *m* napkin
guardar to keep; to watch over
guarda-sol *m* sunshade
guia *m/f* guide
guiché *m* window *(at post office, bank)*
guisado *m* stew
guitarra *f* guitar

H

há there is; there are
habitação *f* residence; home
habitar to reside
hiperligações *fpl* hyperlinks
história *f* history; story
hoje today
homem *m* man
o wc dos Homens gents' toilet
homepage *f* homepage
hora *f* hour; time *(by the clock)*
hora de chegada time of arrival
hora de partida departure time
hora de ponta rush hour
horário *m* timetable
hortelã *f* mint *(herb)*
hortelã-pimenta *f* peppermint
hóspede *m/f* guest
hospedeira *f* hostess
hospedeira de bordo flight attendant

I

iate *m* yacht
icterícia *f* jaundice
ida *f* visit; trip; single trip
ida e volta return trip
idade *f* age
identificação *f* identification
idosos *mpl* the elderly; old people
ignição *f* ignition; starter *(in car)*
igreja *f* church
igual equal; the same as
ilha *f* island
impedir to prevent
impedido(a) engaged *(phone)*
imperial *m* draught beer
impermeável *m* raincoat; *adj* waterproof
importação *f* importation
importância *f* importance; amount *(money)*
importante important
imposto *m* tax; duty
impostos duty; tax
impressão digital *f* fingerprint

impresso *m* form *(to fill in)*
imprevisto(a) unexpected
imprimir to print out
impulso *m* unit of charge *(for phone)*; impulse
incêndio *m* fire
inchado(a) swollen
incluído(a) included
incomodar to disturb
não incomodar do not disturb
indicativo *m* dialling code
indigestão *f* indigestion
infecção *f* infection
infeccioso(a) infectious *(illness)*
inflamação *f* inflammation
informação *f* information
infracção *f* offence
Inglaterra *f* England
inglês *m* English *(language)*
inglês (inglesa) English
iniciais *fpl* initials
iniciar to begin
início *m* beginning
inquilino *m* tenant
inscrever to register
insecto *m* insect
insolação *f* heatstroke; sunstroke
instalações *fpl* facilities
instituto *m* institute
insuflável inflatable
inteiro(a) whole
interdito(a) forbidden
interessante interesting
interior inside
internet *f* internet
interno(a) internal
intérprete *m/f* interpreter
interruptor *m* switch
intervalo *m* interval *(in theatre)*
intestinos *mpl* bowels
intoxicação *f* food poisoning
introduzir to introduce; insert
inundação *f* flood
inverno *m* winter
iogurte *m* yoghurt
ir to go
Irlanda *f* Ireland
a Irlanda do Norte Northern Ireland
irlandês (irlandesa) Irish
irmã *f* sister
irmão *m* brother
iscas *fpl* marinated pig's liver with potatoes
isqueiro *m* lighter
isso that *(thing)*
isto this *(thing)*
Itália *f* Italy
ialiano *m* Italian *(language)*
italiano(a) Italian
itinerário *m* route; itinerary
IVA *m* VAT

J

já already; now
jamais never
Janeiro *m* January
janela *f* window
jantar *m* dinner; evening meal
jardim *m* garden
joalharia *f* jeweller's; jewellery
joelho *m* knee
jogar to play *(sport)*
jogo *m* match; game; play
jóia *f* jewel
jornal *m* newspaper
jovem young
judeu (judia) *m/f* Jew; Jewish
juiz(a) *m/f* judge
julgamento *m* verdict; sentence
Julho *m* July
Junho *m* June
juntar to join
junto near
justiça *f* justice
juventude *f* youth

K

kg. *see* quilo(grama)

L

lã *f* wool
lábio *m* lip
laço *m* bow *(ribbon, string)*; bow-tie
lado *m* side

ao lado de next to
ladrão (ladra) *m/f* thief
lagarto *m* lizard
lago *m* lake
lagosta *f* lobster
lagostim *m* king prawn
lâminas de barbear *fpl* razor blades
lâmpada *f* light bulb
lampreia *f* lamprey
lançar to throw
lanchar to go for a snack
lanche *m* light mid-afternoon snack
lápis *m* pencil
lápis de cera crayons *(wax)*
lar *m* home
laranja *f* orange
o doce de laranja marmalade
largo *m* small square
largo(a) broad; loose *(clothes)*; wide
largura *f* width
lata *f* tin; can *(of food)*
latão *m* brass
lavabo *m* lavatory; toilet
lava-louça *m* sink
lavandaria *f* laundry
lavandaria automática launderette
lavandaria a seco dry-cleaner's
lavar to wash *(clothes, etc)*
lavar a louça to wash up
lavar à mão to handwash
lavável washable
lebre *f* hare
legumes *mpl* vegetables
lei *f* law
leilão *m* auction
leitão *m* sucking pig
leite *m* milk
com leite white *(coffee)*
leite desnatado skimmed milk
leite evaporado evaporated milk
leite gordo full-cream milk
leite magro skimmed milk
leite meio-gordo semi-skimmed milk
lembranças *fpl* souvenirs
lembrar-se to remember
leme *m* rudder; helm
lenço *m* handkerchief; tissue
lençol *m* sheet
lente *f* lens
lentes de contacto contact lenses
lento(a) slow
leque *m* fan *(hand-held)*
ler to read
leste *m* east
letra *f* letter *(of alphabet)*
letra maiúscula capital letter
levantar to draw *(money)*; to lift
levantar-se to stand up; get up *(from bed)*
levar to take; to carry
leve light *(not heavy)*
libra *f* pound
libras esterlinas pounds sterling
lição *f* lesson
licença *f* permit
liceu *m* secondary school
licor *m* liqueur
ligação *f* connection *(trains, etc)*
ligação à internet internet connection
ligado(a) on *(engine, gas, etc)*
ligar to plug in; to phone
ligeiro(a) light
lima *f* lime *(fruit)*
lima *f* file
lima das unhas nail file
limão *m* lemon
limite *m* limit
limite de velocidade speed limit
limonada *f* lemonade
limpar to wipe; to clean
limpeza *f* cleaning
limpeza a seco dry-cleaning
limpo(a) clean
língua *f* language; tongue
linguado *m* sole *(fish)*
linguiça *f* narrow spicy pork sausage
linha *f* line; thread; platform *(railway)*
linho *m* linen
liquidação *f* (clearance) sale
Lisboa (Lx) Lisbon
liso(a) smooth; straight
lista *f* list
lista de preços price list
lista telefónica telephone directory

litro *m* litre
livraria *f* bookshop
livre free; vacant; for hire
livro *m* book
lixívia *f* bleach
lixo *m* rubbish
loção *f* lotion
loja *f* shop
lombo *m* loin *(cut of meat)*
Londres London
longe far
é longe? is it far?
longo(a) long
lotaria *f* lottery
louça *f* dishes; crockery
louro(a) fair *(hair)*
louro *m* bay leaf *(herb)*
lua *f* moon
lua-de-mel *f* honeymoon
lugar *m* seat *(theatre)*; place
lulas *fpl* squid
luvas *fpl* gloves
luxo *m* luxury

luz *f* light
luzes de perigo hazard lights
luzes de presença sidelights
Lx *see* Lisboa

M

M. underground *(metro)*
má *see* mau
maçã *f* apple
macho *m* male *(animal)*
macio(a) soft; smooth
maço *m* packet *(of cigarettes)*
Madeira *f* Madeira
madeira *f* wood
Madeira *m* Madeira wine
madrugada *f* early morning
maduro(a) ripe
mãe *f* mother
magro(a) thin
Maio *m* May
maior larger
a maior parte de the majority of
mais more
o/a mais the most
mal wrong; evil
mala *f* suitcase; bag; trunk
malagueta *f* chilli
mal-entendido *m* misunderstanding
mal-estar *m* discomfort
mancha *f* stain
mandar to send; to order
maneira *f* way *(method)*
manga *f* sleeve; mango
manhã *f* morning
manteiga *f* butter
manter to keep; to maintain
mão *f* hand
mapa *m* map
mapa das estradas road map
mapa das ruas street plan
máquina *f* machine
máquina fotográfica camera
mar *m* sea
maracujá *m* passion fruit
marca *f* brand; mark
marcação *f* booking; dialling
marcar to dial *(phone)*; to mark
marcha-atrás *f* reverse *(gear)*
Março *m* March
marco do correio *m* post box
maré *f* tide
maré alta high tide
maré baixa low tide
marfim *m* ivory
marido *m* husband
marisco *m* seafood; shellfish
marmelada *f* quince jam
marmelo *m* quince
mármore *m* marble *(substance)*
Marrocos Morocco
marroquinaria *f* leather goods
mas but
massa *f* dough
massas pasta
massa folhada puff pastry
matrícula *f* number plate
mau (má) bad; evil
máximo(a) maximum
mazagrã *m* iced coffee and lemon
me me
mecânico *m* mechanic

média *f* average
medicamento *m* medicine
médico(a) *m/f* doctor
medida *f* measure; size
médio(a) medium
medusa *f* jellyfish
megahertz *m* megahertz
meia *f* stocking; half
meia-hora *f* half-hour
meia-noite *f* midnight
meio *m* middle
no meio de in the middle of
meio(a) half
meia de leite cup of milky coffee *(half milk, half coffee)*
meia garrafa a half bottle
meia pensão half board
meio-dia *m* midday; noon
meio-seco medium sweet *(wine)*
mel *m* honey
melancia *f* watermelon
melão *m* melon
melhor better
o/a melhor the best
meloa *f* small round melon
menina *f* Miss; girl
menino *m* boy
menor smaller; minor *(underage)*
menos least; less
mensagem *f* message
mensal monthly
menstruação *f* period *(menstruation)*
mercado *m* market
mercearia *f* grocer's
merengue *m* meringue
mergulho *m* diving; snorkelling
mês *m* month
mesa *f* table
mesmo(a) same
mesquita *f* mosque
metade *f* half
pela metade do preço half-price
meter to put in
metro *m* metre; underground *(rail)*
metropolitano *m* tube *(underground)*
(o) meu (a minha) my; mine
mexer to move
não mexer do not touch
mexilhão *m* mussel
migas à alentejana *fpl* bread dish with pork meats
mil thousand
milhão *m* million
milho *m* maize; corn
mim me
minha *see* meu
mínimo(a) minimum
minúsculo(a) tiny
missa *f* Mass *(church service)*
mobília *f* furniture
mochila *f* backpack; rucksack
moda *f* fashion
modem *m* modem
moeda *f* coin; currency
moído(a) ground *(coffee, etc)*
moinho *m* windmill
moinho de café coffee grinder
mola *f* peg; spring *(coiled metal)*
molhado(a) wet
molho *m* sauce; gravy
momento *m* moment
montanha *f* mountain
montante *m* amount *(total)*
montra *f* shop window
morada *f* address
moradia *f* villa
morango *m* strawberry
morar to live; to reside
morcela *f* black pudding
mordedura *f* bite *(animal)*
morder to bite
fui mordido(a) por um cão I was bitten by a dog
moreno(a) tanned; dark-skinned
morrer to die
mortadela *f* cold meat *(salami)*
mosaicos *mpl* mosaic tiles
mosca *f* fly *(insect)*
mostarda *f* mustard
mosteiro *m* monastery
mostrador *m* dial; glass counter
mostrar to show
motocicleta *f* motorbike
motor *m* engine; motor

motor de arranque starter motor
motorista *m/f* driver
motorizada *f* motorbike
muçulmano(a) *m/f* Muslim
mudar to change
mudar-se to move house
muito very; much; quite *(rather)*
muitos(as) a lot (of); many; plenty (of)
mulher *f* female; woman; wife
multa *f* fine
multidão *f* crowd
mundial worldwide
mundo *m* world
muralhas *fpl* ramparts
muro *m* wall
museu *m* museum
música *f* music

N

nabo *m* turnip
nacional national
nacionalidade *f* nationality; citizenship
nada nothing

nada a declarar nothing to declare
nadar to swim
namorada *f* girlfriend
namorado *m* boyfriend
não no; not
nariz *m* nose
nascer to be born
nascimento *m* birth
nata *f* cream
natação *f* swimming
Natal *m* Christmas
natureza *f* nature
navegar to surf *(internet)*
navio *m* ship
neblina *f* mist
negar to refuse
negativo(a) negative
negócios *mpl* business
negro(a) black
nem: ***nem... nem...*** neither... nor...
nenhum(a) none
neta *f* granddaughter
neto *m* grandson
neve *f* snow
nevoeiro *m* fog
ninguém nobody
nível *m* level
nó *m* knot
No. *see* número
nocivo(a) harmful
nódoa *f* stain
noite *f* evening; night
à noite in the evening/at night
boa noite good evening/night
noivo(a) *adj* engaged (to be married) *m/f* bride/groom; fiancé(e)
nome *m* name
nome próprio first name
nora *f* daughter-in-law
nordeste *m* north-east
normalmente usually
noroeste *m* north-west
norte *m* north
nós we; us
(o/a) nosso(a) our
nota *f* note; banknote
notar to notice
notícia *f* piece of news
Nova Zelândia *f* New Zealand
Novembro *m* November
novo(a) new; young; recent
noz *f* nut; walnut
noz-moscada *f* nutmeg
nu(a) naked
nublado(a) dull *(weather)*; cloudy
número (No.) *m* number; size *(shoes etc.)*
nunca never
nuvem *f* cloud

O

o the *(masculine)*
objeto *m* object
objetos perdidos lost property
obra-prima *f* masterpiece
obras *fpl* roadworks; repairs
obrigado(a) thank you
oceano *m* ocean
ocidental western
oculista *m/f* optician
óculos *mpl* glasses
óculos de sol sunglasses

ocupado(a) engaged *(phone, toilet)*
oeste *m* west
oferecer to offer; to give something
ofereço este livro I give this book
oferta *f* offer; gift
olá hello
olaria *f* pottery
óleo *m* oil
óleo dos travões brake fluid
oleoso(a) greasy; oily
olhar para/por to look at/after
olho *m* eye
onda *f* wave *(on sea)*
onde where
ontem yesterday
óptimo(a) excellent
ora now; well now
orçamento *m* budget
ordem *f* order
ordenado *m* wage
orelha *f* ear *(outer)*
organizado(a) organized
orquídea *f* orchid
osso *m* bone
ostra *f* oyster
ou or
ou... ou... either... or...
ourivesaria e joalharia *f* goldsmith's and jeweller's
ouro *m* gold
de ouro gold *(made of gold)*
outono *m* autumn
outro(a) other
outra vez again
Outubro *m* October
ouvido *m* ear *(inner)*
ouvir to hear; to listen (to)
ovelha *f* sheep
ovo *m* egg
oxigénio *m* oxygen

P

padaria *f* baker's
pagamento *m* payment
pagamento a pronto cash payment
pagar to pay
página *f* page
página pessoal personal page *(internet)*
páginas amarelas Yellow Pages
pago(a) paid
pai *m* father
pais parents
país *m* country
palácio *m* palace
palavra *f* word
pálido(a) pale
palito *m* toothpick
panado(a) fried in egg and breadcrumbs
pane *f* breakdown
panela *f* pan; pot
pano *m* cloth
pão *m* bread; loaf
pão de centeio rye bread
pão de ló sponge cake
pão de milho maize bread
pão de trigo wheat bread
pão integral wholemeal bread
pão torrado toasted bread
papel *m* paper
papel de carta writing paper
papel de embrulho wrapping paper
papel higiénico toilet paper
papelaria *f* stationer's
papo-seco *m* roll *(of bread)*
par *m* pair; couple
para for; towards; to
parabéns *mpl* congratulations; happy birthday
pára-brisas *f* windscreen
pára-choques *m* bumper
parafuso *m* screw
paragem *f* stop *(for bus, etc)*
parar to stop
pare stop *(sign)*
pare ao sinal vermelho stop when lights are red
parede *f* wall
parente *m/f* relation *(family)*
pargo *m* sea bream
parque *m* park
parquímetro *m* parking meter
parte *f* part
parte de frente front
parte de trás back

particular private
partidas *fpl* departures
partir to break; to leave
a partir de... from...
Páscoa *f* Easter
passa *f* raisin
passadeira *f* zebra crossing
passado *m* the past
passado(a): *mal passado(a)* rare *(steak)*
bem passado(a) well done *(steak)*
passageiro *m* passenger
passagem *f* fare; crossing
passagem de nível level-crossing
passagem de peões pedestrian crossing
passagem proibida no right of way
passagem subterrânea underpass
passaporte *m* passport
passar to pass; to go by
pássaro *m* bird
passatempos *mpl* hobbies
passe *m* season ticket

passe go *(when crossing road)*; walk
passear to go for a walk
passeio *m* walk; pavement; trip
passeio de barco boat trip
passeio de carro *car ride*
pasta *f* paste
pasta dentífrica toothpaste
pastéis *mpl* pastries
pastéis de bacalhau small cod-cakes
pastel *m* pie; pastry *(cake)*
pastel folhado puff pastry
pastelaria *f* pastries; café; cake shop; coffee-shop
pastilha *f* pastille
pastilha elástica chewing gum
pastilhas para a garganta throat lozenges
pataniscas *fpl* salted cod fritters
patinagem *f* skating *(ice)*; roller-skating
patinar to skate
pátio *m* courtyard
pato *m* duck
pau *m* stick
pé *m* foot
a pé on foot
peão (peões) *m* pedestrian(s)
peça *f* part; play
peças e acessórios spares and accessories
peça... ask for...
pediatra *m/f* paediatrician
pedir to ask (for)
pedir alguma coisa to ask for something
pedir emprestado(a) to borrow
peito *m* breast; chest
peixaria *f* fishmonger's
peixe *m* fish
peixe congelado frozen fish
peixe-espada *m* scabbard fish
pele *f* fur; skin
pensão *f* guesthouse
meia pensão half board
pensão completa full board
pensão residencial boarding house
pensar to think
penso *m* sticking plaster
penso higiénico sanitary towel
pente *m* comb
peões *mpl* pedestrians
pepino *m* cucumber
pepino de conserva gherkin
pequeno(a) little; small
pequeno-almoço breakfast
pêra *f* pear
pêra abacate avocado pear
percebes *mpl* edible barnacles
percurso *m* route
perdão I beg your pardon; I'm sorry
perder to lose; to miss *(train, etc)*
perdido(a) lost
perdidos e achados lost and found; lost property
perdiz *f* partridge
pergunta *f* question
fazer uma pergunta to ask a question
perigo *m* danger
perigo de incêndio fire hazard
perigoso(a) dangerous
permitir to allow
perna *f* leg
pérola *f* pearl

pertencer: ***pertencer a*** to belong to
perto (de) near
peru *m* turkey
pesado(a) heavy
pêsames *mpl* condolences
pesar to weigh
pesca *f* fishing
pescada *f* hake
pescadinhas *fpl* whiting
pescar to fish
peso *m* weight
pesquisar to investigate; to search *(internet)*
pêssego *m* peach
pessoa *f* person
pessoal *adj* personal
pessoal *m* staff; personnel
petiscos *mpl* snacks; titbits
petróleo *m* oil
peúgas *fpl* socks
picada *f* sting
picado(a) chopped; minced
picante spicy
picar to sting
uma picada de mosquito a mosquito bite
pilha *f* pile; battery *(for torch)*
pílula *f* the pill
pimenta *f* pepper
pimento *m* pepper *(vegetable)*
PIN (pessoal) *m* PIN number
pintar to paint
pintura *f* painting
pior worse
piripiri *m* hot chilli dressing
pisca-pisca *m* indicator *(on car)*
piscina *f* swimming pool
piscina aberta outdoor swimming pool
piscina para crianças paddling pool
piso *m* floor; level; surface
piso escorregadio slippery surface
pista *f* track; runway
planta *f* plant; map
plataforma *f* platform
plateia *f* stalls *(in theatre)*
platinados *fpl* points *(in car)*
pneu *m* tyre
a pressão dos pneus tyre pressure
pó *m* dust; powder
pó de talco talcum powder
poço *m* well
poder to be able
polegar *m* thumb
polícia *f* police
polícia *m/f* policeman/woman
poluição *f* pollution
polvo *m* octopus
pomada *f* ointment
pomada para o calçado shoe polish
pomar *m* orchard
pombo *m* pigeon
ponte *f* bridge
ponto-morto *m* neutral *(car)*
população *f* population
por by *(through)*
por aqui/por ali this/that way
por hora per hour
por noite per night
por pessoa per person
pôr to put
porção *f* portion
porco *m* pig; pork
por favor please
pormenores *mpl* details
porque because
porquê? why?
porta *f* door
a porta No. ... gate number...
porta-bagagens *m* boot *(of car)*; luggage rack
porta-chaves *m* key ring
porta USB *f* USB port
portagem *f* motorway toll
portal *m* portal
porta-moedas *m* purse
portátil *m* laptop
porteiro *m* porter
porto *m* harbour
Porto: ***o Porto*** Oporto
o vinho do Porto Port wine
português *m* Portuguese *(language)*
português (portuguesa) Portuguese
posologia *f* dose *(medicine)*
postal *m* postcard

posto *m* post; job
posto clínico first aid post
posto de socorros first aid centre
pouco(a) little
pousada *f* historical/up-market hotel; inn
povo *m* people
povoação *f* small village
praça *f* square *(in town)*; market
praça de táxis taxi rank
praça de touros bullring
praga virtual *f* computer virus
praia *f* beach; seaside
prata *f* silver
prateleira *f* shelf
praticar to practise
prato *m* dish; plate; course of meal
prato da casa speciality of the house
prato do dia today's special
prazer *m* pleasure
prazer em conhecê-lo(a) pleased to meet you
precipício *m* cliff; precipice
precisar de to need

preciso(a): ***é preciso*** it is necessary
preço *m* price
preços de ocasião bargain prices
preços reduzidos reduced prices
preencher to fill in
preferir to prefer
prejuízo *m* damage
prémio *m* prize
prenda *f* gift
preocupado(a) worried
preparado(a) ready
presente *m* gift; present
preservativo *m* condom
pressão *f* pressure
pressão dos pneus tyre pressure
presunto *m* cured ham
preto(a) black
primavera *f* spring *(season)*
primeiro(a) first
primeiro andar first floor
de primeira classe first-class
primo(a) *m/f* cousin
princípio *m* beginning
prioridade *f* priority
prioridade à direita give way to the right
prisão *f* prison
ter prisão de ventre to be constipated
privado(a) *adj* private
procurar to look for
produto *m* product; proceeds
produtos alimentares foodstuffs
professor(a) *m/f* teacher
profissão *f* profession
profissão, idade, nome profession, age and name
profundidade *f* depth
profundo(a) deep
programa *m* programme
proibido(a) forbidden
proibida a entrada no entry
proibida a paragem no stopping
proibida a passagem no access
proibido estacionar no parking
proibido fumar no smoking
proibido pisar a relva do not walk on the grass
proibido tomar banho no bathing
promoção *f* special offer; promotion *(at work)*
pronto(a) ready
propriedade *f* estate *(property)*
proprietário(a) *m/f* owner
prospecto *m* pamphlet
prótese dentária *f* dental fittings
provar to taste; to try on
provisório(a) temporary
próximo(a) near; next
público *m* audience; public
pudim *m* pudding
pulmão *m* lung
pulseira *f* bracelet; wrist strap
pulso *m* wrist
pura lã *f* pure wool
purificador do ar *m* air freshener
puxar to pull
puxe pull *(sign)*

Q

quadro *m* picture; painting
qual which
qualidade *f* quality

quando when
quantidade *f* quantity
quanto(a) how much
quantos(as)? how many?
quanto tempo? how long? *(time)*
quarta-feira *f* Wednesday
quarto *m* room; bedroom
quarto de banho bathroom
quarto de casal double room
quarto com duas camas twin-bedded room
quarto individual single room
quarto *m* fourth; quarter
quatro-vezes-quatro (4x4) *m* 4x4; 4-wheel drive
um quarto de hora a quarter of an hour
que what
o que é? what is it?
quebra-mar *m* pier
quebrar to break
queda *f* fall
queijada *f* cheesecake
queijo *m* cheese
queimadura *f* burn
queimadura do sol sunburn *(painful)*
queixa *f* complaint
quero apresentar uma queixa I want to make a complaint
quem who
quente *adj* hot
querer to want; to wish
quilo(grama) (kg.) *m* kilo
quilómetro *m* kilometre
quinta *f* farm
quinta-feira *f* Thursday
quiosque *m* kiosk; newsstand
quotidiano(a) daily

R

R. *see* rua
rã *f* frog
rabanete *m* radish
rádio *m* radio
radiografia *f* X-ray
raia *f* skate *(fish)*
raiva *f* rabies
raíz *f* root
rapariga *f* girl
rapaz *m* boy
rápido *m* express *(train)*
rápido(a) fast
raposa *f* fox
raqueta *f* racquet; bat *(for table tennis)*
rasgar to tear
ratazana *f* rat
rato *m* mouse
R/C *see* rés-do-chão
real real; royal
reboques *mpl* breakdown service
rebuçado *m* boiled sweet
recado *m* message
dar um recado to give a message
receber to receive
receita *f* recipe
receita médica prescription
recepção *f* reception
recibo *m* receipt
reclamação *f* protest; official complaint
recolher to collect
recolha de bagagem *f* baggage reclaim
recomendar to recommend
recompensa *f* reward
reconhecer to recognize
recordação *f* souvenir
recordar-se to remember
rede *f* net
redução *f* reduction; discount
reembolsar to reimburse
refeição *f* meal
reformado(a) *m/f* senior citizen; retired
região *f* area *(region)*
região demarcada official wine-producing region
registar to register
regulamentos *mpl* regulations
Reino Unido *m* United Kingdom
relógio *m* watch; clock
relva *f* grass
não pisar a relva keep off the grass
remédio *m* medicine; remedy
remetente *m* sender
renda *f* lace; rent
rendas de bilros hand-woven lacework
reparação *f* repair

reparar to fix; to repair
repartição *f* state department
repetir to repeat
rés-do-chão (R/C) *m* ground floor
reserva de lugar *f* seat reservation
reservado(a) reserved
reservar to book; to reserve
residência *f* boarding house; residence
residir to live
respirar to breathe
responder to answer; to reply
resposta *f* answer
restaurante *m* restaurant
retalho *m* oddment
retrosaria *f* haberdashery
reunião *f* meeting
revelar to develop *(photos)*; to reveal
revisor(a) *m/f* ticket collector
revista *f* magazine
ribeiro *m* stream
rins *mpl* kidneys
rio *m* river
rissol *m* rissole

rochas *fpl* rocks
roda *f* wheel
rodovia *f* highway
rolha *f* cork
rolo *m* cartridge *(for camera)*; roll
rosé *adj* rosé *(wine)*
rosto *m* face
roteiro *m* guidebook
roubar to steal; to rob
roupa *f* clothes; clothing
roupa de cama bedding
roupa interior underwear
roxo(a) purple
rua (R.) *f* street
rubéola *f* German measles
ruído *m* noise
ruptura *f* break

S

S. *see* São
sábado *m* Saturday
sabão *m* soap
sabão em flocos soapflakes
sabão em pó soap powder
saber to know *(fact)*
sabonete *m* toilet soap
sabor *m* flavour; taste
saca-rolhas *m* corkscrew
saco *m* bag; handbag
saco cama sleeping bag
saco do lixo bin bag
safio *m* sea eel
saia *f* skirt
saída *f* exit; way out
saídas departures
sair to go out; to come out
sal *m* salt
sala *f* room
sala de chá tea room; café
sala de embarque airport lounge
sala de espera waiting room
sala de estar living room; lounge
sala de jantar dining room
salada *f* salad
salão *m* hall *(for concerts, etc)*
salário *m* wage; salary
saldo *m* sale
salgado(a) salty
salmão *m* salmon
salmão fumado smoked salmon
salmonete *m* red mullet
salpicão *m* spicy sausage
salsa *f* parsley
salsicha *f* sausage
salsicharia *f* delicatessen
salteado(a) sautéed
salvar to rescue; to save *(rescue)*
sandálias *fpl* sandals
sandes *f* sandwich
sandes de fiambre ham sandwich
sanduíche *f* sandwich
sangue *m* blood
sanitários *mpl* toilets
Santo(a) (Sto./Sta.) *m/f* Saint
santo(a) holy
santola *f* spider crab
São (S.) *m* Saint
sapataria *f* shoe shop
sapateira *f* type of crab
sapateiro *m* shoemaker; cobbler
sapato *m* shoe

saquinhos de chá *mpl* tea bags
sarampo *m* measles
sardinha *f* sardine
satisfeito(a) happy; satisfied
saudação *f* greeting
saudável healthy
saúde *f* health
saúde! cheers!
se if; whether
se faz favor (SFF) please
sé *f* cathedral
secador *m* dryer
secar to dry; to drain *(tank)*
secção *f* department
seco(a) dry
secretária *f* desk
secretário(a) *m/f* secretary
século *m* century
seda *f* silk
sede *f* thirst
ter sede to be thirsty
segredo *m* secret
seguinte following
seguir to follow
seguir pela direita keep to your right
seguir pela esquerda keep to your left
segunda-feira *f* Monday
segundo *m* second *(time)*
segundo(a) second
de segunda classe second-class
em segunda mão second-hand
segundo andar second floor
segurança *f* safety; security
segurar to hold
seguro *m* insurance
seguro contra terceiros third party insurance
seguro contra todos os riscos comprehensive insurance
seguro de viagem travel insurance
seguro(a) safe; reliable
seio *m* breast
selecção *f* selection
selo *m* stamp
selvagem wild
sem without
semáforos *mpl* traffic lights
semana *f* week
na semana passada last week
para a semana next week
por semana weekly *(rate, etc)*
semanal weekly
sempre always
senhor *m* sir; gentleman; you
Senhor Mr
senhora *f* lady; madam; you
Senhora Mrs, Ms
a casa de banho das Senhoras ladies' toilet
senhorio(a) *m/f* landlord/lady
sentar-se to sit (down)
sentido *m* sense; meaning
sentido único one-way street
sentir to feel
ser to be
serviço *m* service; cover charge
serviço de quartos room service
serviço (não) incluído service (not) included
serviço permanente 24-hour service
servidor *m* server
servir to serve
pode servir? can you serve?
sessão *f* session; performance
Setembro *m* September
(o) seu (a sua) his; her; your
sexta-feira *f* Friday
SFF *see* se faz favor
significar to mean
sim yes
simpático(a) nice; friendly
sinal *m* signal; deposit *(part payment)*
não há sinal there's no signal
sinal de impedido engaged tone
sinal de marcação dialling tone
sinal de trânsito road sign
sino *m* bell
site *m* website
sítio *m* place; spot
situado(a) situated
SMS *m* text message
só only; alone
sobre over; on top of; about
sobre o mar overlooking the sea

sobrecarga *f* excess load; surcharge
sobremesa *f* dessert
sobressalente spare
a roda sobressalente spare wheel
sobretudo *m* overcoat *(man's)*
sócio *m* member; partner
socorro *m* help; assistance
socorro 115 emergency service 999
socorros e sinistrados accidents and emergencies
sogro(a) *m/f* father-in-law/ mother-in-law
sol *m* sun
solteiro(a) single *(not married)*
solúvel soluble
som *m* sound
soma *f* amount *(sum)*
sombra *f* shadow *(in sun)*
sono *m* sleep
sopa *f* soup
sorte *f* luck; fortune
boa sorte good luck
sorvete *m* water ice; sorbet

sótão *m* attic
soutien *m* bra
squash *m* squash *(sport)*
sua *see* seu
subida *f* rise; ascent
subir to go up
sudeste *m* south-east
sudoeste *m* south-west
suficiente enough
sujo(a) dirty
sul *m* south
sumo *m* juice
suor *m* sweat
supermercado *m* supermarket
supositório *m* suppository
surdo(a) deaf
surf *m* surfing
suspensão *f* suspension *(car)*

T

tabacaria *f* tobacconist's; newsagent
tabaco *m* tobacco
tabela *f* list; table
taberna *f* wine bar
tabuleiro *m* tray
taça *f* cup *(trophy)*; goblet
tacão *m* heel
talão *m* voucher
talco *m* talc
talheres *mpl* cutlery
talho *m* butcher's
talvez perhaps
tamanho *m* size
também also; too
tamboril *m* monkfish
tampa *f* lid; cover; top; cap
tampões *mpl* tampons
tanto(a) so much
tão so
isto é tão bonito this is so beautiful
tapete *m* carpet; rug
tapetes e carpetes rugs and carpets
tarde *f* afternoon; early evening
boa tarde good afternoon; evening
tarde *adverb* late *(in the day)*
tarifa *f* charge; rate
tarifas de portagem toll charges
tarte *f* tart
tarte de amêndoa almond tart
tasca *f* tavern; cheap eating place
taxa *f* fee; rate
taxa de juro interest rate
taxa normal peak-time rate
taxa reduzida off-peak rate
teatro *m* theatre
tecido *m* fabric; tissue; cloth
teclado *m* keyboard
telecomandado(a) remote-controlled
teleférico *m* cable car
telefone *m* telephone
telefonista *f* operator
televisão *f* television
televisor *m* television set
telhado *m* roof
temperatura *f* temperature
tempero *m* dressing *(for salad)*; seasoning
tempestade *f* storm
tempo *m* weather; time *(duration)*
tempo inteiro full-time
tempo parcial part-time
temporada *f* season

temporário(a) temporary
tenda *f* tent
ténis *m* tennis
tenro(a) tender *(meat)*
tensão *f* tension
tensão arterial alta/baixa high/low blood pressure
tentar to try
ter to have
terça-feira *f* Tuesday
terceiro(a) third
terceiro andar third floor
para a terceira idade for the elderly
termas *fpl* spa
termo *m* (vacuum) flask
termómetro *m* thermometer
terra *f* earth; ground
terraço *m* veranda; balcony
terramoto *m* earthquake
terreno *m* ground; land
tesoura *f* scissors
tesouro *m* treasure
testemunha *f* witness
tímido(a) shy
tingir to dye
tinta *f* ink; paint
tinturaria *f* dry-cleaner's
tio(a) *m/f* uncle/aunt
tipo *m* sort; kind
tira-nódoas *m* stain remover
tirar to remove; to take out
tiro *m* shot
toalha *f* towel
toalhete de rosto *m* face cloth; flannel *(for washing)*
toalhetes refrescantes *mpl* baby wipes
tocar to touch; to ring; to play
tocar piano to play the piano
todo(a) all; the whole
em toda a parte everywhere
toda a gente everyone
todas as coisas everything
toldo *f* sunshade *(on beach)*
tomada *f* socket; power point
tomar to take; have drink/food
tomar antes de se deitar take before going to bed
tomar banho to bathe; to have a bath
tomar em jejum take on an empty stomach
tomar... vezes ao dia take... times a day
tomate *m* tomato
tonelada *f* ton
toranja *f* grapefruit
torcer to twist; to turn
torneio *m* tournament
torneira *f* tap
tornozelo *m* ankle
torrada *f* toast
torre *f* tower
torto(a) twisted
tosse *f* cough
tosta *f* toasted sandwich
totobola *m* football pools
totoloto *m* lottery
toucinho *m* bacon
tourada *f* bullfight
touro *m* bull
tóxico(a) poisonous; toxic
trabalhar to work *(person)*
trabalho *m* work
trabalhos na estrada roadworks
tradução *f* translation
traduzir to translate
tráfego *m* traffic
tranquilo(a) calm; quiet
transferir to transfer
trânsito *m* traffic
trânsito condicionado restricted traffic
trânsito proibido no entry
transpiração *f* perspiration; sweat
transportar to transport; to carry
transtorno *m* upset; inconvenience
trás: *para trás* backwards
a parte de trás the back
no banco de trás on the back seat *(car)*
tratamento *m* treatment
tratar de to treat; to deal with
travar to brake
travessa *f* lane *(in town)*; serving dish
travessia *f* crossing *(voyage)*
travão de mão *m* handbrake
travões *mpl* brakes
trazer to bring; to carry

triângulo *m* warning triangle
tribunal *m* court
trigo *m* wheat
triste sad
trocar to exchange; to change
troco *m* change *(money)*
trocos small change
trovoada *f* thunderstorm
truta *f* trout
tu you *(informal)*
tubo *m* exhaust pipe; tube; hose
tudo everything; all
turista *m/f* tourist

U

úlcera *f* ulcer
ultimamente lately; recently
último(a) last; latest
ultrapassar to overtake; to pass
um(a) a; an; one
unha *f* nail *(on finger, toe)*
único(a) single; unique; only
unidade *f* unit *(hi-fi, etc)*; unity

unir to join
universidade *f* university; college
urgência *f* urgency
urtiga *f* nettle
urze *f* heather
urso(a) *m/f* bear
usado(a) used *(car, etc)*
usar to use; to wear
uso *m* use
uso externo for external use
útil useful
utilização *f* use
utilizar to use
uva *f* grape

V

vaca *f* cow
vacina *f* vaccination
vagão *m* railway carriage; coach
vagão-restaurante *m* buffet car
vagar to be vacant
vagas *fpl* vacancies
vale *m* valley; coupon
valer to be worth
validação *f*: ***validação de bilhetes*** validate tickets
válido(a) valid
válido(a) até... valid until...
valor *m* value
válvula *f* valve; tap
vapor *m* steam
varanda *f* veranda; balcony
variado(a) varied
varicela *f* chickenpox
vários(as) several
vazio(a) empty
vegetal *m* vegetable
vegetais congelados frozen vegetables
vegetariano(a) vegetarian
veículo *m* vehicle
veículos pesados heavy goods vehicles
vela *f* sail; sailing
vela *f* spark plug; candle
velho(a) old
velocidade *f* gear; speed
velocidade limitada speed limit in force
velocímetro *m* speedometer
vencimento *m* wage; expiry date
venda *f* sale *(in general)*
venda proibida not for public sale
vendas e reparações sales and repairs
vender to sell
vende-se for sale
veneno *m* poison
vento *m* wind
ventoinha *f* fan *(electric)*
ver to see; to look at
verão *m* summer
verdade *f* truth
não é verdade? isn't it?
verdadeiro(a) true
verde green
vergas *fpl* wicker goods
verificar to check
vermelho(a) red
verniz *m* varnish
vertigem *f* dizziness; vertigo
vespa *f* wasp
véspera *f* the day before; the eve
vestiário *m* cloakroom; changing room
vestido *m* dress

vestir to dress; to wear
vestir-se to get dressed
vestuário *m* clothes
veterinário(a) *m/f* vet
vez *f* time; turn
às vezes occasionally; sometimes
uma vez once
duas vezes twice
muitas vezes often
é a sua vez it's your turn
via *f* lane
via via
via aérea by air mail
via nasal to be inhaled
via oral orally
viaduto *m* viaduct; flyover
viagem *f* trip; journey
viagem de negócios business trip
viajante *m/f* traveller
viajar to travel
vida *f* life
vidros *mpl* glassware
vila *f* small town
vinagre *m* vinegar
vindima *f* harvest *(of grapes)*
vinho *m* wine
vinho branco white wine
vinho da casa house wine
vinho de mesa table wine
vinho doce sweet wine
vinho espumante sparkling wine
vinho rosé rosé wine
vinho seco dry wine
vinho tinto red wine
vinho verde young wine
24-horas 24-hour
vir to come
virar to turn
vire à direita turn right
vire à esquerda turn left
vírgula *f* comma
vírus *m* computer virus
visitar to visit
vista *f* view
com linda vista with a beautiful view
visto *m* visa
vitela *f* veal
viúvo(a) *m/f* widower/widow
vivenda *f* chalet; villa
viver to live
vivo(a) alive
vizinho(a) *m/f* neighbour
você(s) you
volante *m* steering wheel
volta *f* turn
à volta (de) about
dar uma volta to go for a short walk/ride
em volta (de) around
voltagem *f* voltage
voltar to return *(go/come back)*
volto já I'll be back in a minute
volts *mpl* volts
vomitar to vomit
voo *m* flight
voo fretado charter flight
voo normal scheduled flight
vos you; to you
vós you
(o) vosso (a vossa) yours
voz *f* voice
vulcão *m* volcano

W

WC *f* toilet
wi-fi *m* wi-fi
wind-surf *m* windsurfing

X

xadrez *m* chess
xarope *m* syrup
xarope para a tosse cough syrup
xerez *m* sherry

Z

zero zero; nought
zona *f* zone
zona azul permitted parking zone
zona de banhos swimming area
zona interdita no thorough-fare